Transitions in

*American
Education*

Studies in the History of Education
Edward R. Beauchamp, *Series Editor*

Transitions in

American

Education

A Social History of Teaching

Donald H. Parkerson & Jo Ann Parkerson

RoutledgeFalmer
New York and London

Published in 2001 by
RoutledgeFalmer
29 West 35th Street
New York, NY 10001

Published in Great Britain in 2001 by
RoutledgeFalmer
11 New Fetter Lane
London EC4P 4EE

RoutledgeFalmer is an imprint of the Taylor & Francis Group

Printed in the United States of America on acid-free paper.
Design and typography: Jack Donner

10   9   8   7   6   5   4   3   2   1

Library of Congress Cataloging-in-Publication Data

Parkerson, Donald H. and Parkerson, Jo Ann
Transitions in American education : a social history of teaching / by Donald H. Parkerson
and Jo Ann Parkerson
Includes bibliographical references and index.
p. cm.
ISBN: 0-8153-3824-4 (hbk)   0-8153-3825-2 (pbk.)

To our mentors,
Richard, Craig, and Herb

Contents

Series Preface

RoutledgeFalmer Studies in the History of Education series includes not only volumes on the history of American and Western education, but also on the history of the development of education in non-Western societies. A major goal of this series is to provide new interpretations of educational history that are based on the best recent scholarship; each volume will provide an original analysis and interpretation of the topic under consideration. A wide variety of methodological approaches from the traditional to the innovative are used. In addition, this series especially welcomes studies that focus not only on schools but also on education as defined by Harvard historian Bernard Bailyn: "the transmission of culture across generations."

The major criteria for inclusion are (a) a manuscript of the highest quality, and (b) a topic of importance to understanding the field. The editor is open to readers' suggestions and looks forward to a long-term dialogue with them on the future direction of the series.

Edward R. Beauchamp

Preface

June is the saddest month for education. In the midst of celebration and excitement over graduation and promotion, thousands of teachers quietly resign their position after just a year or two in the classroom. Last year, Mary Cunningham was one of them.[1]

Mary had always wanted to be a teacher. As a child she often arranged her teddy bears and dolls on dining room chairs and pretended to teach them how to read. Later, as a baby-sitter, she made the young neighbor children sit quietly while she read to them for hours.

By the time she reached her early adult years, Mary was on the fast track to the classroom. In high school she joined the Future Teachers of America, and in college she was actively involved in the Student Education Association. Mary was a good student and had a successful student-teaching experience. At the age of twenty-one, full of idealism and enthusiasm, she confidently entered her own classroom.

But by the end of her first school year, she had resigned her position. What had happened? Why had her lifelong enthusiasm for teaching been crushed after just one year in the classroom? Indeed, why are thousands of other young teachers like her leaving the profession? Over the years, educators have desperately sought answers to these questions. And they have pointed to a number of good reasons for this rapid turnover among teachers.[2]

Among these is a growing alienation within the profession. Young men and women like Mary often leave teaching because they have become dangerously isolated from the experiences of other teachers both past and present. And, since they have little understanding of their own historical roots, teachers cannot understand why they often are ridiculed, challenged, and held responsible for many of the problems we face as a nation.

Mary adored her students and she loved teaching. But she also understood that she might have some disciplinary problems and she *certainly* knew that she would never get rich as a teacher. She was well prepared for each of these aspects of teaching. What eventually undermined her enthusiasm and led her to resign her position, however, came from several unexpected sources: parents, administrators, and even some of her fellow teachers.

Beginning with her first parent-teacher conference she sensed that something was very wrong. For example, several parents challenged the way she taught reading. Mary used a modified form of "whole language" instruction she had learned during her teacher training in college, but two different parents insisted that the "phonics method" was much superior and that she should change her approach immediately. Mary was puzzled. She had spent her whole life preparing to become a teacher. Now her methods were being ridiculed by people who had never the seen inside of a classroom as a teacher. One parent even threatened to "report her to the principal" and informed Mary that she had seen a commercial on television that "proved" that the phonics method "worked best." Apparently others in her state (especially members of the state legislature) also had seen that same commercial, the one where the first-grader "reads" the *Wall Street Journal* perfectly—but without a clue as to what the words mean. As a result, Mary was notified that the following fall, reading teachers would be required to use phonics as their *primary* method of reading instruction.

Mary was also frustrated by a lack of cooperation from both parents and administrators concerning a particularly difficult student. During the first few weeks of school she noticed that Todd was frequently angry and often became violent. One day as they were lining up for lunch, he pushed a classmate to the floor. When Mary corrected him, he threw a chair at her. Mary, of course, was deeply concerned with Todd's behavior. She tried in vain to contact his parents through notes and messages left on their answering machine, and she also discussed the matter with her principal. (There was no guidance counselor in her school.) The principal promised that Todd would be "tested" and assured her that once an evaluation had been made, he would either be removed from the classroom or she would receive assistance from the school district's "resource team." Mary completed the paperwork required for the battery of tests and then waited and waited.

In January of the school year, Todd was still disrupting the classroom and Mary found herself spending more and more time dealing with Todd's misbehavior. Increasingly frustrated with the situation, she again asked her principal for help. This time, however, he became defensive and insulting, noting that Todd's parents had refused to give permission for the psychological tests and had even suggested that it was Mary's fault that here was a problem in the first place. The principal then scolded her, barking that there was a long list of students waiting to be tested and that she had better learn how to deal with these kinds of problems if she wanted to remain in teaching. That May, Todd was still in the classroom; he had not been tested and his behavior had deteriorated even further. As a result, Mary's ability to teach as well as her general mental health had deteriorated.

Mary found little sympathy from her fellow teachers, many of whom appeared jaded and cynical or acted as if they couldn't care less. At the beginning of the school year Mary had looked forward to her planning periods, when she would be able to meet with and talk to other teachers in the school, but she soon found that her visits to the teacher's lounge were depressing and frustrating. On her first day, for example, one teacher asked her directly, "Mary, why in the world would you want to be a teacher in this day and age?" The teacher shook her head and said that if she had to do it over again, she would "*never* have chosen teaching as a career." Mary's idealistic response that she loved children and wanted to make a difference was met with derision and laughter. Later, when she sought advise about her disruptive student Todd, one teacher said simply, "Good luck, you'll need it!" Another told her to get used to it, as she had five similar problem students and they might likely be in Mary's class next year.

By the end of her first year in the classroom Mary had changed. She was no longer the idealistic young teacher who had entered the classroom the previous August. She was now confused, frustrated, and exhausted—physically and mentally. Mary had been criticized by parents who felt they knew best about reading instruction and assessments of her students' psychological problems. She had been alienated from her principal, who neither treated her as a professional nor supported her in the classroom. And finally, she felt isolated from her fellow teachers, who seemed unwilling to mentor her progress as a teacher or to embrace her as part of a community of teachers.

The ultimate source of Mary's problems, however, is American society's growing pessimism regarding the state of public education in this country. For some, the "golden age of education" is now just a distant memory. This romantic vision of the past, however, is misleading. If parents, administrators, teachers, and the general public understood the realities of American educational history they would recognize that public education is probably stronger today than at any time in our past, that teachers today are the best educated in history, and that if there ever was a "golden age of education," it is the present.

Of course, an understanding of the history of teaching will not eliminate the persistent problems of education, but parents, administrators, and teachers will be able to place those problems in a context that is broader than the current academic year. Moreover, by understanding the struggles of teachers in the past, educators will recognize their unique position in the history of this nation, as well as the important role that a strong community of teachers has played in sustaining public education for more than two centuries.

Transitions in American Education surveys American educational history but goes beyond the well-known story of great educators, philosophers, and reformers in the past. It demonstrates how changes in our society, politics, and economy have triggered two educational transitions, each occurring roughly at the dawn of a new century, and recounts how millions of teachers in the past have overcome persistent challenges and criticisms to develop a more comprehensive education for American children.

During America's first two educational transitions, teachers found themselves in an intellectual minefield. Their schools were criticized, their methods questioned and their effectiveness scrutinized. And today, as we enter our third educational transition, teachers find themselves in that same minefield. Clearly, this is a difficult time for educators. But by understanding the nature of educational change, teachers today will be able to deal more effectively with the persistent criticism of their profession. They also will be able to cut through the endless parade of curricular novelties, pseudo-reforms, and retro-reforms, and more effectively prepare for the future.

And yet, *Transitions in American Education* is more than a warning sign of trouble ahead. By understanding the cycles of change in education, teachers will be better prepared to face their challenges and embrace new opportunities. They will also be empowered as they recognize their direct lineage to millions of other teachers in the past who have similarly faced uncertain futures but somehow thrived. Parents and the concerned public will also benefit: by understanding this important but overlooked chapter of our history they will recognize the persistent challenges that individuals outside the educational community have routinely imposed on teachers and other educators. Moreover, they will be in a better position to appreciate their vital role in the support of teaching and the maintenance of "the greatest experiment in the history of man"— public education.

Acknowledgments

During the preparation of this manuscript, we received a great deal of encouragement and support. Don was awarded a sabbatical from the department of history at East Carolina University and was supported throughout by the department chair, Michael Palmer. Jo Ann also received support and encouragement from the chair of the department of education at Methodist College, Gillie Benstead.

We are especially indebted to our series editor, Edward Beauchamp, for the constructive criticism and insightful comments on this manuscript. Thanks also to Jeanne Shu, Seema Shah, and Karita Dos Santos of RoutledgeFalmer for their patience and professionalism. Don also appreciates the encouragement and support of his colleagues in the history department: Ken Wilburn, Carl Swanson, Charles Calhoun, Jan Stennette, and Mike Palmer. Jo Ann thanks her colleagues at Methodist College: Jaunita Heyward, Elizabeth Belford, Jerrie Bundy, Jim Foster, Jennifer Rohrer-Walsh, Maureen Molter, and Frank Beck for their interest in and support of her work. Also thanks to Maurice Eash, who provided inspiration at an early stage of this project.

We appreciate the assistance of the Joyner Library staff at East Carolina University, especially Pat Guyette of interlibrary loan, as well as Susan Pulsipher and the staff of Davis Memorial Library at Methodist College. Shirley Martin, of the East Carolina University history department office, provided assistance with printing chapters, and friends Cathy and Hans Fladung generously loaned their printer when ours finally died after long and faithful service.

Finally, we appreciate our mentors for their advice and encouragement over the years. Richard Jensen, professor emeritus of history, University of Illinois, Chicago, has encouraged, supported, and assisted Don in innumerable ways, including training in history and research methods. Craig Kridel, professor of education at the University of South Carolina carefully guided and advised Jo Ann through the doctoral program in curriculum and instruction. Without his early encouragement this book could never have been written. Herb Walberg, of the college of education at the University of Illinois, Chicago, provided Jo Ann with invaluable research experience, advice, and encouragement. This book is dedicated to Richard, Craig, and Herb, our mentors.

The Cycles
of Educational Change

1

The history of teaching in America is both an exhilarating and frustrating story. It is an inspiring account of how millions of idealistic men and women have dedicated their lives to the instruction of American children. But it is also a story of betrayal. Over the last two hundred years, teachers often have been unfairly criticized and even ridiculed. Their methods of instruction and selection of curricular materials have been challenged while their approaches to discipline and even their preparation and effectiveness in the classroom have routinely been second-guessed by politicans, educational reformers, and the public at large. The irony of this is that most Americans are satisfied that they themselves received a good primary education, and few complain about the education of their children. Nevertheless, a chorus of criticism about the state of teaching has echoed throughout our history. It is this paradox that has frustrated teachers for more than two centuries.

And yet, despite the cacophony of criticism there is a discernable pattern to it. In the last two hundred years, America has undergone two fundamental educational transitions. Each of these major shifts in educational policy has occurred at the dawn of a new century, and each was triggered by dramatic changes in the social, political, and economic conditions of the nation itself. In the difficult years preceding each of these educational transitions, teachers found themselves at the center of criticism. When popular reforms were put in place, however, this criticism gradually subsided and teachers regained their positions as respected members of society. We had reached a kind of educational equilibrium.

In the early nineteenth century, for example, the potpourri of colonial schools and their teachers were subjected to years of unrelenting criticism by reformers, statesmen, and working people across the land. The American Revolution (1776–1783) and the market revolution of the early to mid-1800s demanded new approaches to education and teaching. Eventually the common school emerged as the accepted model of education because it met the emerging social, political, and economic needs of the new republic. It provided a universal educational experience for all Americans (with some notable exceptions that we will discuss), and its teachers promoted the values of patriotic nationalism that helped unite the first thirteen colonies into a nation. Moreover, common-school teachers introduced students to the ideas of competition, ambition, and achievement that would help them prepare for the rigorous business world outside the classroom. In short, by the mid-1800s the common school had become widely accepted and its cadre of young schoolteachers were warmly embraced by a grateful nation. The first educational transition was complete.

By the end of the 1800s, however, Americans were poised for another transition as a result of the fundamental changes in our society and economy. This time the urban, corporate, and modern revolutions forced Americans to reconsider the gemstone of the early republic, the common school. As a result, teachers found themselves in the cross fire of educational change once again. Their preparation was questioned, their methods of instruction and selection of curriculum were seen as antiquated, and even the organization of their schools came under fire. American reformers eventually embraced a new educational form, the graded school, as the "one best system"and the corporate managerial model as the most appropriate administrative structure for these schools. The curriculum of the graded school was expanded and teachers were required to attend institutes or "normal schools" to be licenced. Once this new educational model was in place, criticisms of schools waned and the status of teachers improved dramatically. The second educational transition was complete. Once again we had reached a kind of educational equilibrium.

Today, in the wake of the demographic, governmental, and communications revolutions teachers find themselves on the precipice of yet another educational transition. And once again, educational reformers and the public at large have begun to question the validity of the graded school as well as the competency of our teachers. Significant educational reforms are under way and more lie ahead, but these should not cause despair. By understanding these educational transitions teachers will be better prepared to face the challenges of this millennium, and like generations of teachers in the past, they will survive.

THE FIRST EDUCATIONAL TRANSITION

America's first educational transition began in the early 1800s and was triggered by the forces of the democratic and market revolutions. In the decades preceding the American Revolution, however, the foundation of independence was cast by changes in both the intellectual and material life of the colonists. During these years there was a distinctive change in the colonists' attitudes toward religion that was reflected in a series of revivals (the Great Awakening) and the gradual secularization of society (the Enlightenment) during the 1700s. There also was a distinctive shift in the colonists' attitudes toward the prevailing economic system of mercantilism, and growing unrest over issues of land ownership, settlement, and taxation. Each of these changes would challenge and ultimately weaken the existing authority of colonial society and help prepare Americans for revolution.

Roots of the American Revolution

By the 1700s many established churches in the colonies appeared to be hopelessly out of touch with the people. Some ministers seemed to be "going through the motions" in their sermons while others stubbornly focused on the fine points of religious dogma rather than the real issues that concerned their congregations. Things began to change, however, when a series of evangelical revivals, known as the Great Awakening, swept through the colonies beginning in the 1720s. Led by emotional preachers such as Theodore Frelinghuysen of the Dutch Reformed Church, Gilbert Tennent, and Jonathan Edwards of the Presbyterian Church, and especially the charismatic Methodist George Whitfield, these revivals spread like wildfire throughout the northern colonies, in remote areas as well as cities like Boston.

In the South, the revivals were energized by the rise of the Baptists during the 1760s. These religious "radicals" rejected the finery and ostentatious display of wealth typical of the gentry class and directed their energies to "Christ's poor": back-country farmers, artisans, and the South's most oppressed class, African-American slaves. As a result, the Baptists helped to weaken traditional authority in colonies such as Virginia and North Carolina.

Although the evangelical fires had begun to subside by the eve of the Revolution, they had permanently changed the face of organized religion in the colonies. The clear message of the revivals was that salvation was a personal matter not dependent on traditional formal religion. As a result, ordinary people began to embrace religion not because of the training of the clergy but because of the persuasive power of the preachers themselves. This created an environment that was more tolerant of different religious denominations and also broke the monopoly of Congregationalism in the North and Anglicanism in the South. In short, the Great Awakening challenged the basis of both traditional religion and authority and helped to produce a colonial society that was more equal and accepting of diversity.

Paralleling the religious revivals of this era was a growing secularization of society known as the Enlightenment. The Enlightenment was a broad scientific and intellectual movement that challenged the inherited superstitions and traditions of the past and argued for a more rational approach to life. The movement was built on the scientific revolutions of the 1500s and 1600s in Western Europe, and had spread to the colonies during the mid-1700s. In colonial Philadelphia, for example, Benjamin Franklin had made practical use of these scientific advances by inventing the lightning rod, bifocal glasses, and the indoor heating and cooking stove. He also founded the first lending library in 1731, and helped to establish the American Philosophical Society in 1769. Through the work of Franklin and others like him, the scientific revolution took root and flourished in the colonies.[1]

Equally as important were the great European philosophers of this era: John Locke, Voltaire, Denis Diderot, and others. In his influential *Essay Concerning Human Understanding* (1689), for example, Locke had challenged the prevailing Calvinist (Congregationalist) doctrine of predestination by arguing that God had given humankind the capacity to learn and to improve. By extension, society also could be improved. Many of the important eighteenth-century intellectual leaders shared this basic notion and argued that by embracing science and rationality one could achieve "enlightenment." Voltaire developed these ideas in his *Philosophical Dictionary*, and later Diderot wrote extensively about issues of equality, liberty, and the rights of man in his *Encyclopedia*. These ideas eventually found their way to the colonies and were embraced by both intellectuals and political leaders on the eve of the Revolution.[2]

As might be expected, the ideas of the Enlightenment not only strengthened the colonists' notions of free will, equality, and liberty but also were important in advancing the cause of education. In fact, the colonies experienced a significant growth in the general literacy of both men and women during this period. This in turn helped to provide the colonists with a stronger sense of their own independence and a growing self-confidence to express these ideas. The colonists' new mind-set had strengthened the intellectual foundation of the American Revolution.

The intellectual revolution of the eighteenth century (the Great Awakening and the Enlightenment) helped the colonists overcome the vestiges of traditional religious authority, and introduced them to the ideas of equality, liberty, individual rights, and progress. Changes in their economic conditions, however, also helped to undermine traditional secular authority and further prepared them for revolution.

In the decades prior to 1763, England had been in a state of almost constant war with France. As a result England had, in effect, allowed the colonies to "rule themselves" politically and develop their own independent economy outside the confining system of British mercantilism. (See below for a discussion of mercantilism.) This period of "salutary neglect," as historians sometimes call it, fostered new feelings of economic and political independence.

When England's long war with France ended in 1763, however, there was an attempt to "turn back the clock" on the colonies and force them to abandon the political and economic liberties they had gained; but by that time, it was too late. During this period, the number of American merchants, artisans, and skilled workers had grown significantly, especially in cities. Armed with a new "commercial ethic," they had begun to challenge the authority of England and the crown. Many merchants, for example, resented mercantilism, arguing that this economic system was archaic and unfair. Under mercantilism, for example, merchants were allowed to trade *only* with England and colonies that were part of the British empire. Moreover, it was *illegal* for the colonists to engage in manufacturing because their exclusive role was to produce raw materials for England. As the number of middle-class American colonists increased, however, this economic dependency on England became more and more burdensome. The growing resentment of mercantilism would provide another cornerstone of the American revolution.

Things were also changing in the countryside during this period. Because of the great availability of inexpensive land throughout America, a new class of landholding yeoman farmers had grown over the years, with thousands migrating from the eastern seaboard well into the interior of the country. These yeomen were an independent lot and had a natural affinity to the idea of equality. As such they resented the arbitrary power of the gentry and were especially irritated by taxes on their land and issues of where they could settle. These issues provided yeomen with a strong incentive to heed the call for independence.

For example, in North Carolina, small-scale farmers from the interior of the state had been exploited by the royal governor's country court officials for many years. These farmers eventually created associations of "regulators" to challenge the authority of the governor and his allies. This challenge eventually would lead to armed engagements between the "regulators" and British troops in 1768 and in 1771 and clearly demonstrated the revolutionary unrest in the countryside.[3]

Similarly, in New York state, tenant farmers living along the Hudson River struggled against the "patroon system." Under this system, a throwback to the Middle Ages, large tracts of land were owned by a handful of wealthy families who then rented small plots to poor farm tenants. The enormous Van Rensselaer estate totaling over a million acres, for example, was a gift from the royal governor. By collecting rents from this land, the Van Rensselaers were able to live in unbelievable luxury. At the same time, they controlled the destinies of thousands of poor farmers. Violence finally erupted in 1766 when rents were raised in the region and hundreds of farmers were evicted or jailed because they could not pay their rent. In response, some New York farmers armed themselves and openly challenged the authority of the landholders while others resisted the court's action by breaking into jails to free their imprisoned neighbors. Although these "tenant wars," as they are sometimes called, would not be resolved until the next century, the problems in rural New York, like those in North Carolina, were symptomatic of a developing revolutionary spirit in the countryside.[4]

On the eve of the American Revolution, therefore, colonists had become more independent and self-confident and had begun to embrace the ideas of equality. The next step, armed rebellion, began in 1763 when England levied a series of burdensome taxes on the colonists to replenish the treasury, depleted during the long war with France. Beginning with the Sugar Act of 1763, through the infamous Stamp Act of 1765 and the Townsend Duties in 1767, the American colonists slowly began to recognize that they were being taxed without having direct representation in the English Parliament. Protest soon followed. Then, beginning in 1773, colonists protested Parliament's right to tax commodities like tea by staging the famous Boston Tea Party and other such "parties" up and down the Atlantic coast. This signaled the beginning of direct resistance. In response to this growing unrest, the colonists convened the first Continental Congress in Philadelphia during the fall of 1774. While moderation prevailed at this assembly, the delegates did form the Continental Association with the expressed purpose of boycotting British imports. The call for independence was now imminent. The following spring, events took a dramatic turn in a series of armed conflicts at Lexington, Concord, and Bunker Hill. The colonists were now on the threshold of revolution.

Within a year, two documents—Thomas Paine's *Common Sense* and Thomas Jefferson's *Declaration of Independence*—would help mobilize the American people by providing them with both a rationale and an inspiration for revolution. Paine exhorted everyday Americans in plain, direct language to throw off the yoke of monarchy and asked rhetorically, "Is it the interest of a man to be a boy all his life?" The answer for most Americans was a resounding no. Jefferson's more formal and inspirational document declared that "all men are created equal . . . endowed by their creator with certain inalienable rights." Then, borrowing ideas from the Enlightenment, he noted that "whenever any form of government becomes destructive of these ends, it is the right of the people to alter or to abolish it." The logic of rebellion was now clear.[5]

The war itself was a bloody affair, with American colonial troops struggling against a larger and professionally trained military force from England. Only after they secured an alliance with France were the colonists able to survive and eventually defeat the British at the Battle of Yorktown. The final Treaty of 1783 officially ended the war and opened the door to a new era in American history.

In the wake of these dramatic changes, Americans began to recognize that the diverse colonial educational experiments were not able to meet the challenges of the new Republic. These schools could not produce an educated electorate or an environment of equality; nor were they capable of forging a national identity. Gradually the "common school" was embraced as a solution that would, in theory at least, provide an education within the reach of all. Yet it would take more than a generation of vigorous debate for Americans to reach that consensus.[6]

Following the Revolution, many Americans envisioned some form of public education for the fledgling nation, but their visions of it differed considerably: some favored universal education to secure the fruits of individual liberty and equality hard won through our war of independence; others embraced public education to control what they saw as the selfish impulses of the individual and guarantee a measure of civic virtue among American children.

In December 1787, Thomas Jefferson articulated the first of these positions in a letter to James Madison. Writing from Paris, he noted, "Above all things I hope the education of the common people will be attended to; convinced that on this good sense we must rely with the most security for the preservation of a due degree of liberty." The benefits of education, he reasoned, would transcend the individual and provide a foundation upon which the republic could safely rest. In his "Notes on the State of Virginia," he even argued that "an amendment of our Constitution must here come in aid of the public education." For Jefferson, universal education was "necessary" in "rendering the people . . . guardians of their own liberty." To be sure, he saw universal primary education and the ultimate success of the new American republic as two sides of the same coin.[7]

While Jefferson feared the misuse of power by the few and saw public education as the only effective defense against tyranny, others were more concerned with the potential "anarchy and violence of the masses." For them, universal primary education was the only way to limit the "excesses" of democracy. Benjamin Rush, for example, called for the establishment of public schools to help control the innate selfishness of the individual. "Let our pupil be taught . . . that he does not belong to himself; but that he is public property." Public schools, he continued, "would produce one general uniform system of education [that would] tender the mass of people more homogeneous and thereby fit them more easily for uniform and peaceful government."[8]

Like others of his generation, Rush also felt that universal primary education would reduce crime noting that "the bachelor will in time save his tax . . . by being able to sleep with fewer bolts and locks on his doors. Fewer pillories and whipping posts and smaller jails, with their usual expenses and taxes will be necessary when our youth are properly educated."[9]

Thus, while their motivations may have differed, a consensus was beginning to emerge that recognized the importance of some form of universal primary education for the common man. This consensus was given concrete expression with the Congress of the Confederation's Land Ordinance of 1785 and the Northwest Ordinance of 1787. Under these plans, the federal government deeded land to the territories (later to become states) to be used for education. Clearly recognizing the importance of what they had done for education, the 1787 ordinance stated that "knowledge being necessary to good government and the happiness of mankind, schools and the means of education shall forever be encouraged."[10]

Following the ratification of the U.S. Constitution in 1789, however, federal support of public education became more abstract and symbolic. Then, with the adoption of the Tenth Amendment to the Constitution in 1793, the primary responsibility for schools shifted to the states. State support for primary public education, however, was less than enthusiastic during these years. Legislators often ignored pleas to establish primary schools and allowed less expensive forms of primary education such as the private elementary and religious schools to persist without much oversight.[11]

Nevertheless, things soon began to change. The extension of voting rights to white males of all classes, which had originated in the northeastern and mid-Atlantic states and then had spread slowly to other parts of the nation in the early 1800s, again brought the question of universal primary public education to the forefront of governmental policy. State political leaders were literally forced to consider the idea of offering free or inexpensive primary education to all of their citizens. While wealthy property-holding voters had been expected to provide an education for their own children, many new voters in the republic simply could not afford to pay the tuition of an expensive private school or hire a private tutor. As a result, the idea of free primary education slowly began to take shape.

In his report to the Pennsylvania House of Representatives in 1810, a young idealistic Nicholas Biddle reflected this new reform impulse. Public primary schools, he promised, would not only eliminate the "most odious of all distinctions ... the inequality between the educated and ignorant [but would provide] the brightest glory of a free nation and the firmest foundation of a free government."[12]

Noah Webster took a similar position in his famous essay, "On the Education of Youth in America." Drawing on the ideas of the Enlightenment, he insisted that "laws of education ought to be relative to the principles of government." In republican governments, like that of the United States, he wrote, "Education should ... be the first care of the legislature ... and the first article in the code of political regulations." He went on to explain that in several states of the union, fine colleges and academies had been established where "people of property" could send their children. However, there was "no provision ... for instructing the poorer ranks of people even in reading and writing. Yet in these same states every citizen who is worth a few shillings annually is entitled to vote for legislators."[13]

Governor DeWitt Clinton of New York echoed these sentiments in 1826, remarking, "The first duty of Government ... is the encouragement of education." The following year he stated, "The great bulwark of republican government is the cultivation of education; for the right of suffrage cannot be exercised ... without intelligence."[14]

The growing recognition of the importance of universal primary education was, of course, not restricted to the north. In the south, states like Virginia and North Carolina also were beginning to embrace the idea of public education. Unfortunately, several generations would pass before the entrenched power of the planter class could be broken and these ideas could take root. Similarly, as new states from the west were admitted to the union, they too declared their support for public education, at least in principle. The preamble to the Illinois Constitution of 1825 is a good example. It states "To enjoy our liberty and rights we must understand them ... it is a well established fact that no nation has ever continued long in the enjoyment of civil and political freedom [without] the improvement and cultivation of the intellectual energies of the whole."[15]

In short, political support for the common school often was based on the idea that the education of ordinary people was necessary for the success of the republic and the state. Of course, that support varied from state to state and often was at the center of heated political controversy. Nevertheless, there was a growing acceptance of the primary common school as a foundation for the new republic.

The Market Revolution

While the American Revolution helped shape the early political support for universal primary education in America, changes in the U.S. economy during the early 1800s convinced ordinary Americans of the necessity for educational reform. As the forces of the marketplace (the integrated cash economy rather than the system of barter and trade) transformed their social, political, and cultural life, many Americans demanded that a system of universal public education be established so that their sons and daughters could take advantage of these new opportunities.

In American cities, a dramatic economic transformation was taking place. As the economy of barter and exchange gradually gave way to one based on cash, the value of an individual's labor and social status also had begun to change. Traditional work had a specific "commodity value" and defined who one was as an individual. Work was a way of life and not just a job. Yet as Americans were drawn more fully into the market economy their labor assumed a "market value." Fine craftsmanship based on hours of hard work and years of apprenticeship meant little if there was no market for a product. Instead, the value of labor was now based on what the "market would bear." Because of this shift, primary education took on greater importance. If one's children's future depended on their understanding of changing market realities, then an appreciation of competition, hard work, determination, and achievement (not to mention the ability to read, cipher, and communicate) assumed greater value. These values and skills would allow them to survive and perhaps even thrive in the new market economy. The "silent compulsions of economic relations," therefore, encouraged broad support for the common school because it promised to be *both* an economic safety net and a vehicle of upward mobility.

Middle-class Americans were profoundly affected by the economic changes of the time. While the market economy provided many exciting opportunities for their advancement, the possibility of failure also was very real. Throughout this period there was widespread anxiety about *falling down* the occupational ladder and losing one's social and economic status. As a result, many middle-class Americans had begun to embrace the common school as a kind of economic safety net for their children. As one educational historian put it, "the anxiety of the middle classes about their children formed the driving force behind . . . public education."[16]

Many skilled artisans of the period found themselves in a similar situation. As the market economy transformed the way in which goods were produced, the skilled artisan's once secure social and economic position had begun to erode. Prior to the industrial revolution, these skilled craftsmen provided the vast majority of all products for market. Whether it was a pair of shoes, a suit of clothing, a piece of furniture, or a simple basket, the artisan made it all. With the advent of factory production, however, artisans saw little hope of a secure financial future. Factories could produce everything more cheaply. The inability of artisans to compete with factory production had doomed them as a class and, with their traditional avenues of individual mobility disappearing, they too embraced the common school as a means of occupational mobility for their children.[17]

Working people also began to accept the idea of the common school. They too recognized that only through education could their children make something of themselves. As early as the 1820s, some workingmen's organizations had already begun to fight for free primary public education in their communities. At a general meeting of mechanics and workingmen of New York City in 1829, for example, members resolved that the state of New York provide funds to "ensure the opportunity to every individual of obtaining a competent education before he shall have arrived at the age of maturity." Similarly, workingmen in Philadelphia urged members of the Pennsylvania state legislature to declare themselves in favor of "an equal and general system of education." Not satisfied with the results of this informal effort, they conducted their own investigation of education in the state and found it inadequate. They presented their findings to the legislature and demanded action.[18]

A few years later, in 1836, Seth Luther summarized many of these ideas in "An Address to the Workingmen of New England on the State of Education." In this small pamphlet he drew a connection between the maintenance of "a free government" and the availability of free education. Reflecting on the "suffering and privations" of Revolutionary War heroes and "the blood flowing like water from the hearts of freemen," he sounded "an alarm" against the "monopolized wealth" that had prevented working class children from receiving an education. Only through a system of universal education, he argued, could the "foundation of freedom and public safety . . . be secured: Children of the poor as well as the rich ought to be instructed both in letters and morals and NO STATE OR SOCIETY CAN EXCUSE THE NEGLECT OF IT." If society wished to avoid "excess, outrage and crime," he concluded, education must be made available to "every class of our citizens."[19]

Finally, while it is clear that some businessmen of this era were hostile to the idea of universal public education because it limited the pool of children able to work in their factories, more progressive entrepreneurs embraced the common school because it made good economic sense. As production moved from the task-oriented skilled work of the artisan to the time-oriented unskilled labor of the factory operative, businessmen had begun to demand new standards of discipline from their workers. Because this new discipline of hard work and punctuality was routinely stressed in the common school, many businessmen actively supported the movement toward universal education.[20]

In short, the hopes and anxieties of Americans living in cities, rooted in the harsh realities of the emerging market economy, helped transform their attitudes toward their children's future. They recognized that a haphazard or remedial education for them would no longer be acceptable. Now they had to receive the best "liberal" primary education available: one that would give them basic skills, nurture their competitive instincts, and help them recognize the importance of hard work and achievement. Moreover, the primary common school was seen as an ideal setting in which to mold American children into efficient workers and good citizens.

In America's sprawling countryside, farmers also were being changed by these powerful market forces. In fact, something remarkable was happening in rural America during the early to mid-1800s. Beginning slowly in the uncertain years following the Panic of 1837, during what contemporaries called the "hungry forties" through the 1850s and the Civil War, many American farmers were experiencing an unprecedented agricultural transition.[21]

Luther Tucker, the influential editor of *The Cultivator* understood this transition when he remarked in 1851 that "alongside the [rail]roads, whose iron bands unite our most distant cities, upon banks of rivers and canals, whose waters bear away the products of our soil, there have been springing up, intelligent thinking farmers."[22]

In fact, as Percy Bidwell and John Falconer noted in their pioneering *History of Agriculture in the Northern United States,* beginning in the 1840s, "the age of farming by extension of area had ceased and that by increased investment had well begun." Traditional methods of farming were being abandoned and scientific "book farming" was becoming more widespread.[23]

The transformation of the rural economy, however, was much more than the triumph of scientific book farming. Paralleling these new commercial production strategies was the emergence of a new class of farming people with specialized roles for men and women, and new attitudes toward their children's education.[24]

These commercial farmers began to see their children not simply as additional workers on the family farm but as part of the future generation of agriculturalists and leaders of their communities. Though certainly not universal, many commercial farmers had begun to recognize that a good common school education, rooted in the market values of competition, achievement, and discipline, would allow their children to succeed in this new world. In fact, their support of the common school was rooted in a kind of collective celebration of the great opportunities of the market economy.[25]

Commercial farm women of the nineteenth century were especially affected by these changes. The emerging market economy had promised them freedom, equality, and choice. In a more traditional, patriarchal world, a woman's social position had been defined by her family's status, transmitted through culture, and was manifested in a world of childbearing and domestic work. In the new world of the marketplace, however, a woman's status was defined, at least in theory, by *what she did* and not the traditional status of her father or husband. The marketplace had created a society based on merit where freedom, choice, and equality had become the ideal. Certainly for many commercial farm women of this era the choice to bear fewer children and then invest more time in their development and education was a reflection of these basic marketplace values. In fact most commercial farm women of this era had fewer children and they sent them to school much more often than their neighbors.[26]

Like their counterparts in the city, however, commercial farmers of the nineteenth century also understood that the great promise of the market revolution was not without its dangers. By entering the market economy they were offered the possibility of a bountiful material world; at the same time, however, the value of their labor, once fixed in the context of independent farming, now fluctuated with the prices of the market itself.

While an independent yeoman working outside the commercial market economy might have had a rather austere existence, even by the standards of the day, the value of his labor was fixed and he was usually able to meet his family's basic needs. The market might boom or bust, but the yeoman's humble but independent social status within the community was relatively constant. Of course, a serious injury, an early frost, a drought, or an infestation of insects could bring chaos to the yeoman farmer; but with a little help from friends, family, and community the yeoman would survive.

As yeomen farmers became more fully integrated in the market economy the situation changed dramatically: now the value of their labor reflected the fluctuations of market prices. Their ability to survive was now a function of the price their crops would bring. Their labor might yield a great bounty or then again it might bring them very little, depending on the market. Moreover, as they became more fully involved in the commercial market economy their social status became a function of how much money they earned, and not necessarily *what they did*. The farm, once the centerpiece of the yeoman's way of life, had gradually become little more than a vehicle to generate income. Clearly the market economy had transformed the value of the yeoman's labor, and with it, his entire life.

When farmers began to recognize the dangers associated with the market economy, it further strengthened these new attitudes toward their children's future. The anxieties associated with the marketplace reinforced the importance of their children's education. The education they might have received in the past was no longer sufficient for their children. Like their city cousins, commercial farmers had begun to understand that in order to succeed in this new world, their children must receive the very best primary education available, one that would provide them with basic skills, nurture their competitive instincts, and help them recognize the importance of hard work, determination, and achievement.

In short, the market economy helped to change Americans' attitudes toward their children's education. On the one hand it offered them the promise of a bountiful material world; on the other, it was a fickle master that required the "safety net" of education.

The American and market revolutions of the late 1700s and early 1800s transformed our system of primary education. By the eve of the American Civil War about 70 percent of children living in northern states were regularly attending school. Commercially oriented states like New York, Massachusetts, and Connecticut led the way. In the south, the attendance numbers were smaller but growing because of the work of a smaller core of progressive middle-class, artisans and commercial farmers.[27]

The common school had taken root in the new nation and flourished in both rural and urban communities. In one-room schoolhouses throughout the countryside and in the classrooms of American cities, common-school teachers taught American boys and girls such primary values of the marketplace as hard work, achievement, and competition, and they typically embraced a system of both rewards and humiliation (rather than corporal punishment) to discipline unruly students. The common school reflected the realities of the emerging democratic marketplace of the early republic, and its teachers were embraced by a grateful nation.

THE SECOND EDUCATIONAL TRANSITION

Our story, however, is far from complete. By the end of the 1800s America was once again being transformed, this time by the urban, corporate, and modern revolutions. And just as reformers in the early 1800s had been critical of colonial education experiments, American educators at the turn of the 1900s challenged the validity of the common school and criticized its youthful teachers. While the common school had worked well in the sparsely populated countryside and smaller cities of the early to mid-1800s, it struggled later in the century in the face of social and economic change. Once again, teachers found themselves in a firestorm of controversy and criticism. Their training was considered inadequate, their methods of instruction rejected as unscientific, and they themselves were even seen as incapable of administering their own schools. Moreover, the curriculum of the common school was seen as hopelessly outdated in the new modern era. American teachers had once again entered a period of protracted crisis but eventually would emerge better educated and more capable then ever.

The Urban Revolution

At the beginning of the 1800s, America was a rural nation. The vast majority of its population lived in the countryside with only about 5 percent of Americans living in cities that—by today's standards—were tiny. Yet as the migration from farms to cities and the pace of immigration from Europe quickened, urban centers grew dramatically as did the numbers of children attending school.

By the end of the nineteenth century, the United States was experiencing a profound shift of its population, from countryside to city. As agriculture became more mechanized, job opportunities for young men and women on farms began to disappear. It has been estimated that over a third of all rural Americans moved to these growing urban centers in the last three decades of the nineteenth century. Similarly, the number of immigrants from Europe increased significantly during these years. During the 1880s over 500,000 immigrants arrived in the U.S. each year and by the beginning of the 1900s, those numbers increased to more than one and a quarter million. And of course, the vast majority of immigrants moved directly to America's cities.

In addition to the rapid growth of immigration during the nineteenth century there also was a distinctive change in its character. America's first wave of immigration, which peaked after 1850, consisted chiefly of northern and western European people and included such groups as the Germans, English, Norwegians, and Irish. The second wave of immigration (1870–1920), called the "new migration" at the time, was dominated by southern and eastern Europeans and included Roman Catholic and Jewish immigrants from the countries of the Austro-Hungarian Empire, Belgium, Greece, Italy, and Poland. The inability of the common school to adapt to these new multicultural realities caused dramatic social and political conflict during this era, a conflict that brought two important results. First, it launched the modern parochial school movement, led by the Roman Catholic Irish; second, it helped to gradually shift the curriculum of the graded public school from its pan-Protestant focus to a more secular approach to both learning and moral education.

In addition to the problems associated with the growing diversity of American cities was the important question of race. Following America's bloody Civil War (1861–1865) slavery was forever abolished, but with the abolition of this insidious institution came a new set of problems.

More than four million former slaves, now called "freedmen," had to be fully integrated into American society. The difficulties associated with Reconstruction (1865–1877) and the growing racism in both the South and North during the so-called Jim Crow period of the late 1800s and early 1900s made that integration nearly impossible.

Throughout this difficult period, African Americans struggled for political, social, and economic justice as well as an adequate education for their children. Hundreds of thousands left their former plantations and moved to cities in both the South and North. However, Americans were often unwilling to accept their newest citizens: African Americans were systematically stripped of their civil and political rights and eventually separated from white Americans in public facilities and classrooms throughout the nation. The infamous *Plessy* v. *Ferguson* Supreme Court decision of 1896, for example, determined that public facilities throughout the nation could be "separate" as long as they were "equal." As a result, the new graded public school would be segregated on the basis of race for more than half a century. (The graded school will be discussed in more detail in the next few pages.)

The Corporate Revolution

In order to deal with the burgeoning numbers of new, culturally diverse students, educational reformers, especially in cities, sought a new organizational model. That model was the graded school, with an administrative structure based on the "new" American corporation. Of course, the corporation had always been a part of the American economy, but its use traditionally had been limited to banks and municipalities (such as incorporating towns). Most business concerns of the early 1800s were owned by individuals, single families, or partnerships, but as the size of companies expanded during the nineteenth century, businessmen sought other forms of organization.

The transition to the corporation began with the development of canals and railroads in the first half of the 1800s. These companies were often awarded corporate status because of the unique nature of their business activities that sometimes spanned hundreds of miles and employed thousands of workers. As a result, new administrative forms were needed to organize workers and new methods of raising money were required to finance them. Similarly, with such large-scale enterprises, there was a need to limit financial liability if they failed. The corporation seemed to be the logical organizational structure to solve each of these problems. Unlike a single owner (sole proprietorship) or group of owners (partnership), a corporation could sell shares of its stock on the open market and raise the necessary capital to construct the canal or railroad. And if the company failed or was sued, the liability burden would not fall on one or two individuals but would be spread across the general ownership of the company itself.[28]

Even more important for education was the changing organizational structure of these new corporations. Because of their enormous size, new ways of organizing men and women were needed. Once again, in the case of early canals and railroads, company operations often were spread over long distances, and direct supervision of workers by a single owner was impossible. As a result, these companies often hired "middle managers" to attend to construction, maintenance, routing, and personnel. Moreover, since there was such a diversity of operations and workers, these companies often divided their operations into distinct administrative divisions, each controlled by a middle manager who in turn was directly responsible to a central administrative office. Gradually the contours of the modern corporation were being defined by these nineteenth-century companies.[29]

The modern corporate model was enormously successful, and by the end of the 1800s it had become the preferred organizational structure for most companies. Soon corporate status was routinely being awarded to business concerns. So successful was this organizational form that for the next twenty years large American corporations went on a virtual "feeding frenzy" of other smaller, more vulnerable companies. Through mergers and takeovers hundreds of firms were absorbed each year by larger growing corporate giants. In fact it has been estimated that by the first decade of the 1900s 40 percent of all manufacturing assets in the United States were held by about 300 companies.[30]

Modernization

While the urban and corporate revolutions of the late 1800s physically transformed the United States, the revolution in modernity dramatically altered both the intellectual and philosophical basis of the nation. Modernism, as it came to be known during this era, can best be understood as an optimistic belief that all our problems (social, economic, political, medical, educational, etc.) could be solved through the coordinated efforts of science, technology, and government. Americans in the late 1800s gradually came to the conclusion that rapid progress was a natural part of our development; the future was bright indeed.

Some of our perplexing social problems could be solved through scientific analysis, for example. As a result, the field of sociology emerged as an important academic discipline at the end of the 1800s. Similarly, the field of modern economics emerged during this period to better understand the nature of the business cycle and demonstrate how we might deal more effectively with economic change. In fact, most of the professional academic disciplines today, such as political science and medicine were established in the last two decades of the 1800s as the wave of modernism spread to virtually every sector of society.

Political problems, the modernists argued, could also be eliminated if patronage (i.e., getting a job simply because you "knew someone") was removed from government and replaced with a system based on merit. One of the results of this at the national level was the creation of the Civil Service Commission in 1883 (the Pendleton Act). This agency established a system of merit examinations to select employees for work in the federal government. At the local level, many cities established the position of city manager to replace or help augment the duties of the elected mayor. Corrupt politics of the "smoke-filled room" presumably would be eliminated by the trained expert who understood budgets, administration, and finance.[31]

Federal and state governments also could be made to be more responsive to the growing needs of the American people. The introduction of new regulatory agencies like the Interstate Commerce Commission (ICC) and laws such as the Sherman Anti-Trust Act were seen as ways to deal with the problem of monopoly at the end of the 1800s. In the same way, many state governments adopted the reforms of "referendum" and "recall." *Referendum* allowed citizens to institute laws by placing important issues on the ballot rather than having to go through the lengthy legislative process to enact them. *Recall,* on the other hand, allowed citizens to remove corrupt politicians from office. Once government was fine tuned, the modernist argued, it could become a powerful tool to improve our world.[32]

Similarly, in the area of medicine and health, Americans became convinced that we could virtually eliminate disease through scientific medical research and the application of professional credentialing standards to the medical profession. The great breakthroughs in medicine during this period including the introduction of "germ theory," new vaccines, and improved surgical techniques served to reinforce these beliefs. Moreover, the creation of the American Medical Association, the establishment of eighty-six new medical schools in the United States between 1875 and 1900, and the establishment of rigorous standards of performance from medical students all testified to the growing professionalism of this field and the faith that the American people were investing in it. And as we shall see, educational reformers also would demand stricter licensing requirements for teachers during this period.[33]

Of course, not all Americans were convinced that the modern trinity of science, technology, and government could solve their problems, but growing numbers did. As a result, Americans entered the twentieth century with a collective sense of optimism in the future and a confidence that with the right application of professionalism, science, and governmental intervention, we could effectively deal with any contingency and solve any problem.

The urban, corporate, and modern revolutions triggered America's second educational transition and fundamentally transformed the schools of the nation. As the numbers of rural migrants and European immigrants flooded into American cities in the late 1800s, schools were overwhelmed. Educational reformers and politicians desperately searched for a new administrative structure for the schools to accommodate these children. The dramatic success of the modern corporation demonstrated to these reformers the great administrative possibilities for education. As schools restructured, state boards of education, school superintendents, and principals provided the various levels of management while teachers were forced to assume the role of hired employees with few proprietary rights. As we will see, teachers throughout the country responded to these changes through labor organization and protest that eventually led to the creation of the first national teachers union, the American Federation of Teachers, in 1916.

While the sheer numbers of new students attending schools at the turn of the twentieth century suggested the need for a new administrative structure for the schools, the presumptions of the modern revolution demanded both an expansion of the academic curriculum of the schools and a new graded system to meet these new curricular needs. The common school curriculum had focused on the "three R's" (reading, 'riting and, 'rithmetic) in the primary grades and the classical languages in the secondary "Latin schools." The expansion of science, technology, and the growing international position of the United States, however, demanded that new academic subjects be taught. As a result, science courses like biology, physics, and chemistry were gradually added to the curriculum. Similarly, modern foreign language instruction also became part of the new curriculum of schools in the early 1900s. And finally, while patriotism had always been part of the common school curriculum, now specific new courses in American history, geography, civics, and government were established.

As the school curriculum gradually expanded, however, it became more and more difficult for one teacher to address all subjects, as she had done in the one-room schoolhouse. Moreover, educational research had clearly shown that as children aged, they progressed through distinctive developmental stages with specific kinds of curricular materials appropriate for each stage (see chapter 6). The ungraded common school no longer seemed to make sense. As a result, schools gradually were divided into smaller graded classrooms each with its own teacher. In fact, by the second half of the 1800s, a variety of graded school experiments had begun to emerge throughout the country. In addition, a number of high schools were established in some of the more progressive urban centers. Eventually, graded elementary schools were matched with high schools in communities to provide the classic graded pattern or "educational ladder." The high school curriculum, moreover, was standardized by the adoption of the "Carnegie unit," a course consisting of five class periods each week during the academic year. This system of curricular bookkeeping became the standard by the early 1900s and continues to define the public school today.[34]

Of course, this system did not emerge overnight, and its ultimate form varied from community to community. In smaller cities the common school remained the dominant educational format until the 1870s while in many rural areas it persisted well into the twentieth century. Yet by the first decades of this century, the ideal school was the graded elementary school (K–8), linked in a comprehensive system to the public high school.

The final component of change was teacher preparation. Throughout most of the 1800s the common school curriculum was basic and as a result most schoolteachers were not required to have much in the way of formal education or teacher training. In fact, as we will see, school boards were more concerned with a teacher's "morals" than her educational credentials. A common-school teacher in the countryside might have completed a primary education before she began teaching although many taught a winter or even a summer term while they were still attending school themselves; others had only a rudimentary common-school education. Most, however, had virtually no formal training as teachers. In larger cities, requirements tended to be a bit more rigorous. (Their pay was also considerably higher: male teachers in cities earned about three times as much as their rural counterparts while female city teachers earned more than twice that of rural women teachers. See chapter 3 for other pay comparisons.) City teachers were often required to complete their studies at an academy or seminary where they might receive some teacher training. And by the last quarter of the century, a handful of teachers had attended normal schools where they received formal teacher training.

With the expanding curriculum and body of knowledge taught in the classroom, however, there was a growing demand for more rigorous teacher training. By the late 1800s and early 1900s school districts began to require that teachers attend more school and receive more rigorous teacher training. The cities led the way in this regard: many urban school districts, reorganized on the corporate model, mandated that teachers receive a normal school education, often two years of post-secondary education.

Gradually this became the standard and eventually these requirements made their way into the countryside as well. This trend in credentialing would continue, and by the 1950s teachers typically were required to receive a four-year college degree from an accredited department or school of education in either the college or university setting. Today, virtually all public school teachers have a college degree in education and the majority of teachers have master's degrees.[35]

In short, the modern comprehensive system of the graded school and high school with its hierarchial administrative structure and professionally trained teachers emerged from the turmoil of the late 1800s and early 1900s and gradually was refined over the next several decades. The second educational transition was complete.

Fig. 1.1 Transitions in American Education

	I American Revolution/ Market Revolution 1776–1825	II Urban/Corporate/ Modern Revolutions 1877–1925	III Demographic/ Communications/ Governmental Revolutions 1975–present
Structure	"Democratic" Common School	Graded School/ High School	One Diversified System
Control	Local	State/Municipal	Federal (through credentials; states move to advocacy)
Discipline	Corporal/ Psychological	Psychological/ Industrial	Behavioral/ Democratic/ Self-Esteem
Moral Education	Religious/ Pan-Protestant/ Virtue-Centered	Moral Codes	Cognitive Moral Development/ Constitutional Literacy
Instructional Focus	Memorization/ Recitation/ Religion	Understanding/ Memorization/ Patriotism	Comprehension/ Application/ Competency
Attendance	White Males (70%) Females (50%) African Americans (10%)	White Males & Females (75%) African Americans (35%) Immigrants (30–60%)	Black/White Male/Female (90%) New Immigrants (60%)

THE STRUCTURE OF THIS BOOK

As we shall see, the modern graded school model has been in place for much of this century but is now being challenged by a host of new political and educational reformers. While each of the following chapters will deal in part with this contemporary upheaval in education, in chapter 10 we will return to America's third educational transition and discuss what teachers might expect from it.

In the meantime, however, the next eight chapters will revisit our first two educational transitions and focus on how they have fundamentally changed the nature of education and teaching. In chapters 2 and 3 we turn our attention to America's multicultural, multiracial heritage and how it has continued to provide challenges and opportunities for teachers. Then, in chapters 4 and 5 we will discuss how women, ethnic minorities, and people of color have overcome tremendous opposition from both the educational community and the nation as a whole to enter the teaching profession.

In chapters 6–9 we describe the fundamental changes both inside and outside the classroom and examine the gradual shift from local to state and finally to *virtual* federal control of education through national academic standards. In chapter 6 we turn our attention to the changes in instructional methods and pedagogy from memorization and recitation to comprehension and understanding. Chapter 7 focuses on the issue of moral education in America from religious indoctrination to civic morality, values clarification, cognitive moral development, and character education. In chapter 8 we turn our attention to the dramatic changes in classroom discipline, from the whipping post and dunce cap of the colonial and early national periods to more modern methods based on classroom psychology and the development of self-esteem. Finally, in chapter 9 we shift our attention to the struggle of teachers over the last three centuries to achieve autonomy and control in the classroom and professional respect from the community at large.

In short, each of these chapters tells the story of men and women struggling to teach in the face of overwhelming obstacles but who somehow, some way found the strength and courage to change the lives of children.

2

Our Diverse
Cultural History

Our white, Anglo-Saxon Protestant history is a myth. Over the years however, some have denied our diverse heritage and instead have demanded a conformity from all its people based on the culture of a small group of Americans. During the common school era, this narrow vision led to the development of a "pan-Protestant" curriculum that eventually spawned decades of social and cultural conflict. This conflict also led to a major schism within the public schools that launched America's first parochial school movement and resulted in millions of children leaving the public schools as the Roman Catholic Church established its own system of private schools.

Today, many Americans continue to assume that our nation was once ethnically homogeneous and that it only recently has become diversified. As a result, they associate the problems of contemporary society with the growing plurality of our nation and often resent the current shift toward a multicultural curriculum in the public schools.

As we shall see however, America has *always* been a diverse nation. From its earliest settlements in the 1600s to the present day, ethnic diversity has been the rule and not the exception in American society. Yet the lesson of diversity is a difficult one for some to understand and continues to cause social, political, and cultural conflicts concerning the direction of public education.

CULTURAL DIVERSITY IN COLONIAL AMERICA

The diverse types of schools in the American colonies reflected our rich ethnic and cultural heritage. In New England, for example, devout Calvinists (Puritans) created a system of public primary and secondary education with the purpose of reinforcing their religious values. The diversity of the middle colonies such as New York, New Jersey, and Pennsylvania, on the other hand, made it more difficult to establish a unified system of schooling in that region. As a result, these settlers looked to their churches to provide a basic education for their children. Finally, in the South, strong cultural links to England led to the adoption of that country's "laissez faire" approach to education. This system included home tutoring and private schools for the wealthy and occasionally charity or monitorial schools for the poor.

New England

The Puritan settlement of New England is an important chapter in the history of teaching in America because it was here that the first "public" schools in the colonies were established. In order to understand the Puritans and their role in education however, we must return to the late 1550s. At the beginning of Elizabeth I's reign as queen (1558–1603) England officially became a Protestant nation and established the Church of England. Yet the ongoing struggles associated with the Protestant reformation and counter reformation still raging in Europe frightened many Englishmen. They feared that the ideas and values of Roman Catholicism might resurface in their nation. In addition to these deep concerns was the perception of a "moral decline" of English society. The signs of this decline seemed to be everywhere. The expansion of the commercial economy, rapid urbanization, the growing wealth gap between the rich and the poor, the development of a permanently poor underclass, and the growth of unchecked individualism all pointed to what they saw as a deterioration of "traditional values."[1]

The followers of John Calvin, the most vocal critics of these changes, were at the center of the growing reform movement within the Church of England. These "Puritans," as they were called, wanted to purify the church of its "papal" influences and to establish a moral basis for English society. During Elizabeth I's long reign (1558–1603), the Puritans grew in numbers and gained considerable power. By then they had placed ministers in hundreds of local churches throughout the nation, secured many seats in parliament, and had even gained control of several colleges at Oxford.

When James I ascended to the throne of England following the death of Elizabeth, however, things began to change. James saw the Puritans as a threat to his power and over the next two decades his relationship with them deteriorated. James's successor, Charles I, carried on this tradition. He "declared war" on the Puritans and referred to them as the "most dangerous enemy of the state." This situation led to the "Great Migration" of Puritans from England during the 1630s. The Puritans' goal was to established a visionary colony in the New World. Within a decade nearly 20,000 English Puritans had settled in New England.[2]

While their migration and settlement in the New World was quite successful, Puritan leaders soon recognized that children were not receiving from their parents the kind of religious training and education they felt was necessary. As a result they quickly attended to the educational needs of their children. The system they eventually created would be emulated by other colonies and states for the next two centuries.

The Puritans had a strong work ethic that was derived from their concept of a religious "calling." Work was seen as the central means of serving God and as such they saw all work as equally worthwhile. As a result, the souls of all men were also equal. At the same time however, the Puritans were highly authoritarian. In order to maintain their strict moral commitments, they gave their spiritual leaders enormous power. That power was translated into a potent secular authority when they settled in the New World. The result was a community based on the idea of equality but subject to the central authority of the church. Their commitment to equality created the need to educate *all the children* in religious values, while the powerful authority of church leaders assured that towns in the colonies would support public education.[3]

In 1642, the leaders of the colony enacted the first education law in America. This law directed town leaders to determine whether Puritan children were receiving an adequate education at home, especially if they were being taught "to read and understand the principles of religion." It soon became clear that Puritan children were not, and that some form of compulsory schooling was necessary. A Massachusetts law of 1647 was enacted to achieve that goal. In the preamble to this important statute, Puritan leaders made clear its primary religious intention, saying, "One chief point of the old deluder, Satan, [is] to keep men from knowledge of the scriptures, by keeping them in an unknown tongue." The law required that towns "having 50 householders . . . appoint teachers . . . and provide for his wages. . . ." It is also mandated that towns of 100 householders "provide a [Latin] grammar school to fit youths for the university."[4]

Thus by the mid-1600s the Puritans had established a model of public education that gradually would be adopted in other New England colonies over the next century. So powerful was this educational system that it spread west as New Englanders migrated to New York and the upper Midwest in the next two centuries. It also endured as New England gradually became more heterogenous and abandoned its theocratic basis of government.

The Middle Colonies

While New England would gradually became more diversified later in the colonial period, in the middle colonies of New York, New Jersey, and Pennsylvania distinct ethnic communities were a prominent feature of early settlement. And since there was no broad and unified culture in these colonies, settlers often looked to their churches to provide an education for their children. As a result, on the eve of the American Revolution, church-controlled schools and private academies were the norm in this region.

Throughout much of its early history, New York enjoyed a rich diversity of ethnic people. During the early 1600s, for example, New Amsterdam (later called New York, when the British seized the colony from Holland) was an amalgam of ethnic people. As one contemporary observer noted, at least eighteen different languages were spoken in and near New York City. The Dutch established a large settlement in the central region of the city that eventually extended north into the Hudson River Valley. On Long Island English settlers predominated, but scattered throughout the colony were Norwegians, Danes, Jews, Irish, Scots Irish, and Germans.[5]

The religious diversity of New York was even more striking. As a result of the open immigration policies of the Dutch in the 1600s, many oppressed groups such as the French-speaking Walloons (Protestant exiles from the lower Netherlands), French Huguenots, Baptists, Quakers, Presbyterians, Lutherans, and Mennonites made their way to the colony. During the 1700s the colony became even more diverse with the arrival of French Calvinists, French Lutherans, Sabbatarians, Anti-Sabbatarians, Anabaptists, Independents, and even Dunkers. Each of these groups found a measure of religious freedom in New York State.[6]

New Jersey was originally part of the colony of New Amsterdam and it too had a rich ethnic and religious heritage, though not as diverse as New York's or Pennsylvania's. During the 1600s, the western part of the colony was settled by Quakers, with Dutch and Swedish settlers in the East. Then, as migration from New York and New England began in the 1700s, thousands of Scots, Scots Irish, Germans and displaced New Englanders flooded into the colony.[7]

Pennsylvania, however, was the most heterogeneous of all the middle colonies. Since its founding by William Penn in the early 1600s, Pennsylvania had become a refuge for people who had been persecuted for their religious beliefs. Penn had originally envisioned the colony as a haven for Quakers (Friends). These religious "radicals" rejected much of the ceremony and ecclesiastical hierarchies of the established churches in Western Europe. They also insisted that all ranks, classes, and privileges within society should be leveled and stubbornly refused to defer to their political "superiors." For example, they would not remove their hats in the presence of nobility, and they would address political leaders with the informal "thou" rather than the more polite "you." As a result, Quakers were seen as dangerous by the leaders of most Protestant nations and often were persecuted by established governments.[8]

Penn's "Holy Experiment" was founded on the principle of religious freedom and was guaranteed by the "Great Law," enacted by the Colonial Assembly in the 1680s. Pennsylvania's reputation as a place of religious freedom spread rapidly throughout the colonies by word of mouth and in Europe as a result of William Penn's own aggressive promotion. His famous account of the colony written in 1681 was translated into several European languages. It welcomed everyone to the colony including poor laborers, farmers, artisans, and those who were "shut out from . . . great nations under settled customs." He then sent agents to Holland, France and the German communities along the Rhine River to encourage settlement in this special place.[9]

The results were dramatic. Thousands of colonial "dissenters" from Connecticut and other parts of New England settled in Pennsylvania's rich Wyoming Valley. Similarly, many Europeans, who had been persecuted because of their religious beliefs or who had been displaced because of economic change, also sought asylum in Pennsylvania. For example, thousands of Germans who had suffered through a century of religious war as well as a depressed agricultural economy were the first to make their way to the colony. Typically the Germans who settled in Pennsylvania were either Lutherans or Calvinists, but other persecuted groups from the region came as well. These included the Amish, the Seventh-Day Adventists, the Schwenfelders, the New Borns, the Inspired, the Separatists, the River Brethren, the Moravians, and many others. By the time of the American Revolution, it was estimated that at least thirty different German religious groups were living in Lancaster County, Pennsylvania, alone.[10]

In addition to these German-speaking people, thousands of Scots Irish settled in Pennsylvania. Originally these Scottish people had migrated to Northern Ireland with the help of the British in the 1600s—they were encouraged to settle in Ireland to help "civilize" the "wild Irish"—but by the 1700s they too were experiencing economic difficulties and religious persecution. As a result of trade restrictions on their exports and a series of financial disasters during these years, the once proud Scottish settlers in Ireland had been reduced to poverty. Then, beginning in the early 1700s, the Church of Ireland (an offshoot of the Church of England) demanded that they convert and support the established church. They refused. As the level of religious persecution increased, thousands of Scotsmen migrated to Pennsylvania and settled in the foothills of the northern Appalachian Mountains.[11]

The schools that developed in the middle colonies reflected this rich ethnic and religious diversity. In New York, members of the Dutch

Reformed Church were active in providing education for their children. The famous New Amsterdam Petition of 1649, for example, noted the pitiful state of schools in the colony and demanded that the church take a more aggressive position on education. Peter Stuyvesant responded and helped establish a number of primary schools in the city. Later, as the Dutch settled in Albany and Kingston, New York, the Dutch Reformed Church established schools in those cities as well. The curriculum of these schools centered on memorizing the catechism, but sometimes it was supplemented by the "ABC book," the collected Gospels and Epistles, and a few books on basic arithmetic. These schools, moreover, were taught in the Dutch language until the eve of the American Revolution in 1772. Finally, in addition to these primary institutions, the Dutch Reformed Church established a handful of "secondary" schools using the "Latin school" model.[12]

The German Lutheran parish elementary school was one of the most recognizable of these early religious schools and provided a basic model for many German-speaking groups in Pennsylvania. These schools followed the lead of the Dutch Reformed Church and focused on religious training, learning the catechism and memorizing its rules of religious and moral behavior. School was often taught by the local pastor or by a schoolteacher who had close connections to the church. These teachers typically had no formal teacher training but were well-meaning, educated members of the congregation who loved children.[13]

The Quakers also had a long tradition of education in Europe and brought these ideas with them to America. As we shall see in future chapters, the Quakers were among the first to accept both women and African Americans as students. They also pioneered new instructional techniques in the context of religious education.

In Roman Catholic settlements like those in Pennsylvania and New York, a private elementary school tradition slowly developed. Typically organized and controlled by the parish priest with the help of local community members, Catholic schools came about during the 1700s. Like their Lutheran counterparts, these schools were oriented toward religious education. They used a catechism as the basis of instruction, and had the goal of preparing younger students for their first communion.[14]

Finally, in more self-contained religious settlements, such as those of the Moravians in Pennsylvania, the primary school was an important part of the community. School attendance was required in these settlements, and teachers within the faith instructed young boys and girls in basic reading, arithmetic, and religious instruction.[15]

In short, the rich ethnic and religious diversity of the middle colonies was reflected in a wide range of educational experiments, each of which centered on religious and moral education. The quality of these schools varied dramatically from community to community, and they often appeared and then disappeared as a result of individual and community interest. In some towns they thrived for generations. Other communities provided virtually no formal primary schooling for children, preferring that families provide them with a basic education of reading and writing.

The South

Like the middle colonies, the South had a rich ethnic mixture. From Virginia to the South Carolina border, English and Welsh Anglicans had settled in the early 1600s and predominated throughout much of the colonial period. And yet there were numerous pockets of other ethnic groups in the region. In the southern piedmont and coastal plain of North Carolina, for example, there were large settlements of Scots Highlanders and Scots Irish who had migrated to the colony during the 1700s. These independent-minded Scotsmen provided the fertile ground for the Baptist revivals of this period (see chapter 1). In fact, on the eve of the American Revolution nearly half of all North Carolina churches were Baptist. The Scots Irish, on the other hand, settled in the foothills of the southern Appalachians from Virginia through the Carolinas. There also were numerous isolated settlements of German and Swiss farmers in the foothills of the Carolinas extending south through Georgia. In Maryland, a diverse group of Roman Catholics who had escaped the ravages of religious wars in the 1600s settled in coastal communities in and around Baltimore. Finally, African-American slaves became the dominant ethnic group in the tobacco growing regions of Virginia and in the fertile agricultural areas along the Carolina and Georgia Coasts.[16]

While settlers in the middle colonies embraced a variety of primary educational experiments, usually centering on religion, the South, with its strong cultural links to the Church of England (Anglicanism), adopted a laissez-faire approach to education that was typical of the mother country. In fact, until the Great Awakening in the mid-1700s, nearly two-thirds of all Southern churches were Anglican, representing about 60 percent of all that denomination's churches in the colonies. In Virginia, for example, over three-quarters of all churches were Anglican as late as 1750. In these communities private schools and in-home tutoring for the wealthy planter class was the norm with a few charity schools for the very poor. Moreover, the continued growth of slavery allowed this segregated, private-school system to persist until the late 1800s.[17]

In-home tutoring was commonplace among the wealthy planter class throughout the South. Isolated plantations often were self-sufficient operations, and in that tradition planters often hired a teacher/tutor to attend to the educational needs of the children in the household; tutors either lived with the family in the plantation mansion or in an adjacent dwelling. During the 1600s, only the wealthiest families were able to hire tutors, who often were recruited from England or Scotland. By the 1700s, however, male seminary students from Harvard or Yale colleges might be commissioned to teach for a season or two and often provided the planter's children with a primary and sometimes even a secondary education. Once again, however, only the very wealthy were able to take advantage of this private, individualized form of education.[18]

There were other avenues to education in the colonial South (and elsewhere). These included apprenticeship and privately endowed charity schools. For example, in 1672 Virginia enacted a law that compelled artisan masters to provide their orphaned servants with apprenticeship in a trade. By the early 1700s, masters also were required to teach orphans to read and write. In 1748 the law was expanded and required that indigent children be bound over to a master for the purpose of apprenticeship.[19]

Beyond apprenticeship and minimal reading education, however, there were few opportunities for poor children. There had been early attempts to provide a basic education for Indian children in the Virginia colony but that experiment was short lived. Similarly, there were plans for a free school in Virginia (the East India School) that collapsed before they had much of an impact. Both of these experiments ended in 1622 with the great Indian massacre. Nevertheless by the middle of the 1600s, a handful of endowed free schools had been established. These included the Symms and Eaton free schools and a number of smaller institutions including those established by Richard Russell in Norfolk, Henry Peasley in Gloucester County, and Francis Pritchard in Lancaster County. These schools typically were administered by the county court or the local vestry and were designed for poor and orphaned children.[20]

For African Americans, free or enslaved, on the other hand, formal education was extremely rare. Prior to the 1800s a few charity schools had been established to provide education for black slaves, with religious groups taking the lead. For example, Thomas Bacon started an Episcopal charity school in St. Peter's Parish, Virginia, in 1750 and a few years earlier the Society for the Propagation of the Gospel in Foreign Parts, an Anglican missionary concern, established a school for young black children modeled after its successful school in Philadelphia. This school employed black teachers and for over two decades it provided a primary education for about sixty children per year. A few other charity schools were established in the South but they were pathetically few in number.[21]

In some areas of the South, religious groups like the Quakers were persistent in their support of black education during the nineteenth century. The North Carolina Manumission Society, for example, established a Sunday school to teach black children to read and write. However, that school was closed within a few years when it was discovered that the Quakers were teaching more than just Bible study.[22]

A good-hearted slaveholder might allow the plantation tutor to teach the sons and daughters of house slaves to read. And occasionally a precocious black slave might be instructed by a member of the plantation household. Frederick Douglass, the great black abolitionist, for example, was taught to read by his owner's wife. Some slaves were self-taught and passed on those skills to their children, but typically, the education of slaves was viewed as dangerous and was forbidden by law and custom. Slaves, of course, had a thriving oral culture complete with their own morality tales and a rich folklore and music handed down from generation to generation. And many slaves learned trades that were useful to the plantation owner. These included masonry, blacksmithing, carpentry, cooking, and even bookkeeping. Later these skills would provide the economic basis for the free black communities throughout the South. But formal schooling would have to wait until after the American Civil War.[23]

Throughout the colonial period, then, the South embraced a two-tiered approach to education. Sons and daughters of wealthy planters often had home tutoring available to them. For the very poor, orphaned, or occasionally, the black slave, on the other hand, there was the possibility of apprenticeship, and a few were able to attend a privately endowed charity school. The vast majority of Southern children, however, had few educational options other than the occasional community school or private instruction from family or friends.

THE COMMON SCHOOL IN THE EARLY REPUBLIC

In short, the ethnic and religious diversity of colonial America was reflected in its schools. From the shores of Massachusetts to the coast of Georgia, virtually every type of school and educational experiment had been implemented over the years. From New England's ambitious system of "public" primary and secondary schools to the middle colonies religious and private schools to the South's tradition of home tutors and charity schools, the colonies had tried it all.

Yet something was wrong. As we have seen, these diverse educational experiments seemed to make sense in the colonies. But following the American Revolution and the market revolution of the late 1700s and early 1800s these schools were seen as inadequate in a number of ways. Americans began to realize that their sons and daughters needed an education that would inform them of their civic responsibilities in the new republic and provide them with the skills and values necessary to successfully compete in the emerging market economy. Moreover, the new nation needed a school system that would be "within the reach of all," not just the lucky few, who by virtue of their birth had access to education.

The "common school" of the nineteenth century was a monumental compromise, designed to meet the needs of young America by providing *symbolic* national support for education, with states and local communities maintaining control. In order for this political compromise to work, however, the common-school curriculum was based loosely on the culture of the nation's ruling elite who generally were rural, "native born" Protestants. Eventually this would cause major problems for education.

Although most children in the colonies received some education, it varied dramatically by class, race, religion, and as we have seen, region. Typically, wealthy colonists in each of the regions were able to attend to the educational needs of their children by hiring tutors or sending their children to private schools. Armed with the basics of reading and writing, the young sons of the gentry or merchant classes were able to attend a Latin school that could prepare them for a college education either in England or later, in the 1700s, at Harvard, Yale, William and Mary, Kings College, or a host of others.

Children of colonial artisans, tradesmen, clerks, and farmers, on the other hand, were not as fortunate, and often were unable to receive a formal education during this period. Sometimes the sons and daughters of these working people had access to a "community school" or "religious school," but more often than not they might spend a few months in a "dame school" or learn to read and "cipher" from a literate parent or relative. Beyond the basics, however, their education typically took a more practical turn with emphasis on apprenticeship in a trade or agriculture. Learning the skills of a carpenter, mason, wheelwright, or farmer often took years and was accomplished at their father's or grandfather's workbench or plow. Young artisan or farm girls, on the other hand, learned their domestic skills in the crowded cabin or kitchen garden, watching and imitating mother, aunt, and grandmother. For these children, the family was the center of their educational experience.

Poor children, however, typically had little formal education with the exception of the few who attended charity schools scattered throughout the colonies. The public schools in the Massachusetts Bay Colony were an exception but even here educational opportunities varied dramatically between Puritan communities. In other parts of the colonies, however, opportunities for indigent children were uneven. In the middle colonies, some local churches did their part, providing a basic religious education for the poor. And in parts of the South, like Virginia, apprenticeship laws mandated that young servants be trained in a trade while they worked off their indenture. The effectiveness of these laws, of course, ultimately depended on the goodwill of the artisan master. Finally, while some slaves managed to learn to read and occasionally were able to pass along these skills to a son or daughter, most were deprived of any formal schooling.

In short, access to formal education during the colonial period varied by one's economic class, gender, religious denomination, race, and region. It represented both the best intentions and greatest neglect, and it reflected the rich ethnic and religious diversity of the emerging nation.

Good intentions were not enough, however, and neglect was even worse. From the time of the American Revolution, responsible patriots understood the central role of education in the development of the nation. And as these former colonists attempted to create a republic, it became clear that the diverse forms of education available to their children during the colonial period were at best inadequate for the new nation. Children needed a common set of cultural and social experiences in order to appreciate the concepts of nationhood and civic responsibility. While the decentralized religious and ethnic approaches to education seemed to work during the colonial period, those experiments were simply too uneven and too narrowly centered on religious training.

As we have seen, following the Revolution statesmen throughout the former colonies began to call for some form of "common school" experience. Benjamin Rush, for example, argued that public common schools would help to "fit [young Americans] more easily for uniform peaceful government." In fact, for statesmen like Rush, the common school was the only avenue to a unified republic.[24]

Thomas Jefferson, on the other hand, also recognized the importance of a "common school" as "essentially necessary" to provide a defense against power-hungry politicians. As a wealthy planter from Virginia, Jefferson had seen how the inequities of education in his colony had created a rigid class system and a powerful aristocracy that he felt was antithetical to the new democratic republic. As a result, he fought passionately for some form of universal education throughout his life.[25]

Other leaders like Noah Webster pointed out that an educated citizenry was central to the success of the republic. People needed to make responsible decisions about their elected leaders and the issues that faced them. While citizens "worth a few shillings" were allowed to vote, he wrote, there were no "provisions made for instructing their children even in reading and writing."[26]

In chapter 1 we saw that the symbolic national support for public education and a "common" school approach was manifested in the Land Ordinance of 1785 and the Northwest Ordinance of 1787. These provisions gave new states substantial land grants earmarked for educational use and energized the common school movement of the early 1800s.

While it would take over a generation to realize the educational dreams of reformers like Rush, Jefferson, Webster and many others, the common-school movement had taken root and begun to grow in the first half of the 1800s. Many of these "common schools" were little more than converted sheds, barns, or abandoned cabins, though the romantic image of the "little red schoolhouse" continues to this day. Nevertheless, countless common-school teachers during this period quietly pursued the vision of the founding fathers and embraced a curriculum that would nurture a passionate patriotism among their young charges.

For young Americans of diverse ethnic and religious backgrounds, the road to nationalism and patriotism began with the development of the idea of "civic virtue," what Webster called a student's "moral and social duties." By first developing the idea that there was something greater and more important in the world than your own desires and parochial community interests, teachers were then able to instruct young children as to the importance of the nation. And when primary reading books such as William McGuffey's *Eclectic Readers* series became available in the late 1830s, lessons on patriotism and civic virtue became the mainstay of reading instruction.[27]

Market Values in the Curriculum

Providing a common political culture for the emerging nation was one important pillar of the common-school movement in the early republic; the other was the preparation of students for the market economy of the early 1800s. Not only did the new republic demand a sense of patriotism from its citizens, but changes in the economy called for a new economic culture as well. The emerging market economy fundamentally changed Americans of all religions and ethnic backgrounds. It gave them and their families a taste of the new consumer culture, it improved their material lifestyles, and it provided them with a common vision of a rational, merit-based society that promised both national and individual growth. In short, the market revolution transformed American industry, agriculture, transportation, and social relations, and also provided a model upon which the common-school pedagogy was based.[28]

In his *Twelfth Annual Report of 1848*, famed educator Horace Mann summarized the relationship between the market revolution and education. He wrote that the common school was a good training ground for commercial and industrial occupations and would also help farmers become more successful in the marketplace by seeing "the wisdom of scientific agriculture." Teachers understood this idea very well: in order to succeed in this new business-oriented world, students would have to develop values of hard work, determination, and a keen sense of competition.[29]

The Examination

As a result, testing gradually developed as an instrument to not only stimulate competitive instincts but also to measure student achievement in relation to others in the classroom or schoolhouse. At first the "exam" was oral, little more than memorized verses or poems recited before the schoolmaster. Later, spelling and ciphering "bees" became important measures of success as well as a form of community entertainment. By the mid-1800s, however, the written examination had become an important tool with which to measure student achievement, and the "report card" detailed a student's success and failure to his parents. As the "stakes" of achievement become clearer and more emphasis was placed on the examination, students realized that only through hard work and determination could they compete successfully in spelling, arithmetic, or reading.[30]

Slowly and quietly through the early years of the 1800s, American teachers promoted a new political and economic culture. On the one hand, their reading instruction helped nurture a fervent patriotism and a civic virtue among students. On the other hand, their methods of instruction stimulated competitive instincts and a desire to achieve through hard work and determination. These values helped unite diverse religious and ethnic peoples into a common worldview.

The Pan-Protestant Curriculum

While the common school sought to encourage patriotism and develop the values of the marketplace among diverse Americans, its curriculum was firmly rooted in the values and culture of Protestantism. This would eventually cause the school problems. Fearing that the growing number of Roman Catholic immigrants to this country would misdirect young, impressionable (Protestant) boys and girls, educators and members of district school boards of the 1800s panicked. As Protestant Calvin Cotton preached in 1839, "Christian morality and piety in connextion [sic] with the intelligence of the common people are the *last hope* of the American Republic."[31]

Yet while educators of this period wanted to include Protestant values in the curriculum, most recommended that they be free of their sectarian, denominational content. D. P. Page, the great pedagogue, was very clear on this point. We are "dependent," he argued, "on life-giving truths" of Protestant Christianity. However, "when I say religious training I do not mean sectarianism." For Page "there is a common ground we can occupy." This common ground was "pan-Protestantism."[32]

Pan-Protestantism was clearly evident in most of the common-school readers of this period, including the important McGuffey series. McGuffey's *Eclectic First Reader,* for example, placed great emphasis on religion. Of the forty-five lessons in the *First Reader*, ten directly mentioned God while two others referred to the Protestant Bible. This *Reader* informed young students that God gave us food, clothes, the sun and the rain. In the lesson called "Thick Shade," for example, students were told that God not only made the shade but also created the rich man and the poor, the dark man and the fair, the wise man and the fool. What is more, God saw everything, both the good and the bad deeds of little children. In "The Little Chimney Sweep," students were told that to lie was to sin against God. In "Good Advice," students were told that sins must be confessed to God before they can be forgiven. Finally, little children were encouraged to pray to God at bedtime and were told that the Bible instructed them never to use profanity or drink alcohol.[33]

A good example of how the McGuffey readers reinforced the emerging Protestant value of temperance was presented in the story plainly titled "Don't Take Strong Drink." Why? Because the Bible said so. Clearly, while temperance was a secular value, embraced by middle-class Protestants, it was often given the legitimacy of biblical Scripture. Other selections warned students of the dire consequences of drinking. In one lesson, "The Whiskey Boy," little John "got tipsy every day," and by the age of eight he had become a drunkard. Eventually, he was found drunk in the street and was brought to a poorhouse. John had now become a burden to society, and perhaps as punishment for his actions, he died within two weeks. The lesson ended with the rhetorical question: "How do you think his father felt now?"[34]

By including pan-Protestant moral lessons that bridged the gap between the biblical and the secular, the stories' general appeal to impressionable young Americans was strengthened significantly. The problem, as we shall see however, was that not all American children were Protestant. And while this moral orientation appeared to be logical and appealed to many Americans, it would eventually cause a major schism within the common-school movement.

3

The Struggle
for Diversity

The common school of the nineteenth century was successful in many ways. It helped to unite the independent states of the new republic into something of a coherent nation, and it provided a common political culture for America's youngest citizens. It offered a primary education for American children in rural areas and developing cities, and it introduced them to the values and skills necessary to compete successfully in the new market economy.

But the common school was flawed. As we have seen, its curriculum was based, in part, on a system of religious and cultural values we have called pan-Protestantism. And while this orientation appealed to broad segments of native, rural America, it failed to embrace America's newest citizens, ethnic children from Europe and African Americans. This flaw caused religious and cultural conflicts that eventually would create a major schism in the common-school movement.

RELIGIOUS AND CULTURAL CONFLICT

As Irish, German, and then southern and eastern Europeans flooded American cities in two powerful waves of immigration in the 1800s, the Protestant-oriented common-school curriculum became a growing source of alienation. Although most new immigrants enthusiastically supported their new adopted country and often were the most fervent patriots, many objected to what they saw as public schools' interference with their religion and values.

Many Roman Catholics, for example, opposed the Protestant orientation of the primary school curriculum. And there was good reason. Since their early settlement in this nation, Roman Catholics had been treated with contempt by Protestant America. During the mid-1800s, anti-Catholic riots were common in towns and cities across the country. In Philadelphia, for example, a conflict over the use of the "Roman Catholic" Bible for instruction spawned a series of "Bible riots" that left thirteen dead and local Catholic churches in ruins. There was even a major political party formed (the Know-Nothings) that proposed sending immigrants, especially Irish Catholics, back to Europe.[1]

For many Protestants, Roman Catholicism seemed incompatible with democracy and the new republic. Its connection to a "foreign pope" appeared to be un-American, its religious ceremony (mass) was presented in a strange language (Latin), and it even appeared to some that Roman Catholics worshiped "craven images" because of the religious statuary present in many Catholic churches.[2]

These attitudes were not just among the uninformed and uneducated in society; many notables of the era also were prejudiced. Lyman Beecher, the renowned American religious leader, educator, reformer, and father of Harriet Beecher Stowe (*Uncle Tom's Cabin*), for example, campaigned throughout his life against the spread of "popery" in schools. Preaching in Boston's Hanover Street Church, he routinely proclaimed his hostility toward Catholics, and many historians hold him responsible for instigating a series of anti-Catholic riots that led to the sacking of the Convent of Ursulene in Charlestown. Later, when Beecher moved west to Cincinnati, he urged the migration of more Protestant ministers to the region because, as he wrote, the "Catholics and infidels have got the start on us." Finally, in his popular publication *A Plea for the West*, he wrote that the coming battle over public education would be a clear choice between the "dark forces of superstition or evangelical light; despotism or liberty."[3]

Even without this violence and blatant anti-Catholic rhetoric, however, the "Protestant curriculum" of many public schools alienated Roman Catholic newcomers. During the middle decades of the 1800s, for example, many Catholics in New York City objected to the routine use of the King James version of the Bible in schools as well as textbooks that ridiculed Roman Catholicism. For example, when a plan to include religious (Protestant) teachings in the public schools was introduced, Roman Catholics petitioned the board of aldermen of New York City for a separate share of the common-school fund for use in Catholic schools. They argued that the proposed curriculum was insulting to them. To prove their point, they presented to the aldermen the following passage from an approved textbook: "Huss, John, [was] a zealous reformer from Popery. He was bold and persevering but at length, trusting himself to the deceitful Catholics, he was by them brought to trial, condemned as a heretic and burnt at the stake."[4]

The furor over this issue further inflamed the hatred of Catholics and led directly to the New York City anti-Catholic riots of 1842. This violent controversy ended when the state allowed certain "Roman Catholic" wards to define their own curriculum. But the compromise was short-lived, and Roman Catholics eventually were forced to create their own separate school system. In a series of plenary councils beginning in 1852, the modern Catholic school system gradually emerged. The first plenary council encouraged parents to establish schools "based on religious principles, accompanied by religious practices . . . and always subordinate to religious influences." Eventually the Third Plenary Council of 1884 formalized a system of Catholic schools and mandated that every parish establish a Catholic school and that Catholic parents send their children to that school.[5]

While the debate over the content of curriculum was central to the Roman Catholic/Protestant school controversies of the 1800s, there were other important cultural battlegrounds between the public schools and new immigrants during this period. Europeans from many countries, for example, rejected the values of temperance and prohibition that had become an important component of the public school curriculum. For these new Americans, this moral focus conflicted with their cultural beliefs.

Temperance

As we have seen, most primary readers of this era, including the influential McGuffey series, emphasized the "evils of drink." While this may have appealed to white, middle-class, Protestant Americans, it was at direct odds with both Roman Catholic and Jewish immigrants, who routinely used alcohol in their religious ceremonies and sometimes drank wine with the evening meal. When young sons and daughters came home from school after reading stories like "The Whiskey Boy" or "Don't Take Strong Drink" they may have been ashamed when they saw their fathers and mothers sipping wine or drinking beer.[6]

Social Mobility

Similarly, while many European immigrants to this country embraced the ideal of education as a vehicle of social and occupational mobility for their children, sending children to school often seemed a luxury when there were bills to pay and brothers and sisters to feed. As a result, while most European immigrants sent their children to school, their rates of attendance sometimes declined in the upper primary grades and certainly in high school. While dropping out of school to work in order to help support the family was seen as an important value for many immigrants (as well as some poor white Americans), educators routinely criticized that decision as backward or selfish. In other words, the cultural clash over the question of family values versus individual success was often a source of irritation between ethnic families and the common school during this period. This problem persists today with some new Asian and Hispanic immigrants.

English-Only Instruction

Finally, since virtually all instruction at the primary and secondary level was given in English, many immigrants suffered. German-, Polish-, Russian-, and Italian-speaking immigrants, for example, resented English-only instruction that often branded their children as deficient and even ignorant because they had difficulty with the language. Immigrant families often placed a premium on maintaining at least a measure of their culture and spoke their native language in the home. Immigrant children, on the other hand, typically were made to feel ashamed of their "foreign ways," both inside and outside the school, and as a result often attempted to assimilate quickly into the dominant American culture. This caused tension within the immigrant family and fueled resentment of the public schools. Again, this is a problem that we continue to see today among many immigrant groups.

AFRICAN AMERICANS

While the cultural conflict between the dominant Protestant population and other Christian and non-Christian people would continue to rage in the common schools throughout the 1800s, the question of race would ultimately have a deeper and more lasting impact on public education in this country.

As the common school blossomed during the 1800s and provided an education for hundreds of thousands of white children, African Americans, enslaved or free, often did without. In the colonial South, as we have seen, slave children had very few opportunities for education other than the goodwill of a slave owner or the occasional charity school. By the early 1800s things had gotten even worse. Following the Denmark Vesey slave rebellion of 1822 and the Nat Turner uprising a few years later, many Southern states passed laws that made the education of slaves illegal. North Carolina, for example, prohibited teaching slaves to read or write, "the use of figures excepted." The penalty for a white person violating the law was a fine of $100 to $200 or imprisonment, while a free black caught teaching slaves to read could receive twenty to thirty-nine lashes. A slave violating the law would receive "39 lashes on his or her bare back." Similar laws were passed throughout the South.[7]

In the North, educational opportunities for free black children existed during the 1800s but were limited. A few communities allowed integrated schools, though most would remain segregated throughout this period. A New York law passed in 1823, for example, established a number of schools exclusively for the "colored race." This law would remain in effect until 1900. On the other hand, some religious groups like the Quakers continued their support of black education. They often provided schooling for free blacks, typically held in black churches. The crowning achievement of the Quakers in this area however, was the African Free School. This institution provided education for hundreds of black children during the early 1800s. And until it merged with the New York public schools in 1835, the African Free School produced a number of distinguished graduates. These included Ira Aldridge, the great Shakespearean actor known as "the Negro Tragedian"; James McCune Smith, America's first black pharmacist and director of the Colored Orphan Asylum of New York City; John Russwurm, editor of the first African-American newspaper, *Freedman's Journal*, and later superintendent of schools in Liberia; and Martin Delaney, graduate of Harvard Medical School, noted scholar, and medical officer in the Union Army.[8]

More often than not, however, free blacks themselves played the greatest role in the primary education of their own children during this period. Black preachers often doubled as teachers following their Sunday sermons and through their own churches they created many schools in northern and "border states." The African Methodist Episcopal Church and the Baptists, for example, were responsible for establishing hundreds of black schools throughout this period. Similarly, a group of black Roman Catholic nuns established the Saint Francis Academy in Baltimore in 1829 for the secondary education of black children.[9]

The Great Anomaly of the Common School: African-American Education

The turning point for African-American education however, was the Civil War. Even before the conflict ended, a number of abolitionist organizations had begun to attend to the educational needs of former slaves (freedmen). As early as 1862, for example, the New England Freedmen's Association and the Boston Education Commission sent several hundred white teachers to Hilton Head, South Carolina, to establish schools in this sea island community. (The sea islands were captured by Union forces in early 1862.) This experiment was quite successful and led to a number of similar educational efforts by such organizations as the Philadelphia Freedmen's Relief Association, which chartered the Port Royal Relief Committee. By the end of the war, this organization had established schools in North and South Carolina, Maryland, Virginia, the District of Columbia, Alabama, Mississippi, and Tennessee. The Friends Association for the

Aid and Elevation of the Freemen also was active, sponsoring fourteen schools in Virginia and South Carolina. Additionally, the free black African Civilization Society had employed 129 teachers and instructed over eight thousand students by the end of the war.[10]

When slavery officially ended in 1865, a new era of educational reform swept the South. Building on the pioneering work of these and other organizations, the Freedmen's Bureau was established by the federal government to attend to the educational needs of former slaves. This created what Booker T. Washington once called "a veritable fever" for education. Thousands of idealistic young men and women from the North came south to teach in schools established by the Freedmen's Bureau. At its peak in 1869, there were over nine thousand teachers in Freedmen's Bureau schools. Their impact was dramatic. In addition, the Freedmen's Bureau, with the help of Northern churches, helped establish a number of colleges to train black teachers. In the late 1860s, for example, Fisk, Atlanta, Tugaloo, and other universities were formed for this purpose; these early teachers colleges promised to fuel an educational revolution in the South.[11]

The Backlash during Reconstruction

The Freedmen's Bureau school experiment was quite successful. But as a central part of the plan of Reconstruction, it was opposed and resented by many white Southerners. In fact, throughout the entire period of Reconstruction (1865–1877) states in the South fought desperately to bring back their conservative governments, destroy the Freedmen's Bureau, and generally return things to the way they were prior to the war. In North Carolina, for example, white Democrats waged a campaign of intimidation and terror on Freedmen's Bureau representatives, Republicans, and former slaves. A white Republican had his throat cut and a black organizer was hanged in a courthouse square with a sign pinned to his shirt reading "Bewar, ye guilty, both black and white." Moreover, countless African Americans were whipped and tortured, and their homes burned. Even white Southerners who showed any sympathy for the freedmen were often fired from their jobs or harassed until they left their communities. Local officials typically turned a deaf ear to the madness, often blaming blacks and white "radicals" for the violence.[12]

In Mississippi, white Democrats used similar tactics, and also formed armed militia groups that would march defiantly into black communities, intimidate residents, and break up political meetings and social gatherings. Mississippi also passed a series of laws that systematically disenfranchised black voters on the basis of property or literacy requirements. Blacks were required to pay a poll tax before voting and also to prove to election officals that they were "literate" by successfully reading a passage from the U.S. Constitution or some other document. Poor whites, on the other hand, often were exempted from these restrictions by legal loopholes such as the "understanding clause" or the "good character" clause. Under these provisions, a white man (women could not vote) who could prove that he "understood the meaning" of a passage or could demonstrate that he was a "respected" member of the community, through a letter of recommendation, was allowed to vote even if he could not pay the poll tax or was totally illiterate. The effect of these laws virtually disenfranchised blacks for nearly a hundred years until the Voting Rights Act of 1965. The Mississippi Plan, as it was called at the time, was seen as a solution to the "Negro problem" and was eagerly adopted by a number of other states in the South. Without political power, the progress of freedmen education was all but doomed.[13]

The tactics of intimidation were successful and when Reconstruction ended in 1877 each of the former Confederate states returned political power and social control to the "old guard" planting class under newly rewritten state constitutions. While white Southerners called this "victory" a redemption, for freedmen and their fragile experiment in education it seemed like revenge.[14]

Even before this "redemption," however, there had been a growing hostility toward the education of blacks. At first, most Southerners either ignored the Freedmen's Bureau schools or made them the butt of cruel jokes. Yet as they found out that "Yankee schoolmarms" were teaching young black children that they were *equal* to whites or that the Republican Party was their friend, things began to change. Even the most tolerant Southern whites were stunned when they heard little black children singing "John Brown" or "Marching Through Georgia" during class sessions. As a result, some Freedmen Bureau schools were burned and a number of male teachers tarred and feathered or beaten. More often, Yankee teachers were denied hotel rooms or accommodations in boarding houses and they were routinely harassed by members of the community. Sarah Jane Foster, for example, was a teacher from New England who went south to teach freedmen following the war. Foster endured constant humiliation and had difficulty finding accommodations. In 1866 she noted in her diary that she had been "slandered by the mob" and accused of walking "arm and arm with colored men" night after night. As a result, she was forced out of her boarding house, but eventually moved in with a Mrs. Bayles, who was "not afraid much of public scorn, having once taught the blacks here herself."[15]

Education after Reconstruction

Following Reconstruction, most Southerners recognized the pressing need for public education. States like North Carolina adopted a system of segregated schools, with limited state funding based on a per capita basis awarded to individual counties. This system, typical of many Southern states, was pushed through the legislature by former planters who championed self-serving revenue provisions in their new state constitutions that forbade local taxation for public schools. As a result of this system, counties with large numbers of black children (typically former slave plantation areas) received the "lions share" of public funding, much of which was then siphoned off to pay for white schools in the county. On the other hand, "back country" counties that had few plantations and former slaves received little of the meager school funds from the state. The result of this system was that wealthier counties of the state received the vast majority of state monies for public education and most of that money went to white schools.[16]

By the 1880s the conflict between "back country" yeomen and wealthy planters reached a climax with the emergence of the Southern Farmers Alliance, the grange, and populist movements. Populist farmers, such as Georgia's Tom Watson, sought to ally themselves with poor blacks against the entrenched power of the planters. In a rousing speech on the eve of the 1892 congressional election, for example, Watson declared that "the colored tenant is in the same boat as the white tenant, the colored laborer with the white laborer." This of course, frightened the old-guard planters and their Democratic Party allies. As a result, they systematically attacked Watson, as well as others associated with the Southern Farmers Alliance and used fraud and intimidation to destroy this "fusionist" (the fusion of poor blacks and whites) interracial political movement. Tom Watson lost his bid for a congressional seat, but later it was discovered that he had been the victim of widespread voting fraud. In Richmond County, Georgia, for example, the number of votes cast against him were twice the actual population of the county.[17]

Beyond voting fraud however, the old-guard planter class used racism to secure their elections throughout the South. By pitting poor whites against their political allies in the Southern Farmers Alliance, they were able to regain their political and social power and end forever the threat of the fusionists. In North Carolina, for example, old-guard Democrats organized a white supremacy lecture series, led by politicians such as Charles Aycock. These lectures warned whites in the state of the dangers of "Negro rule." States also employed "paramilitary units" like the Red Shirts and Rough Riders to terrorize populists, Republicans, and African

Americans. Their tactics were effective, and by the end of the century the fusionist movement had all but collapsed.[18]

With the fear of Alliance men, fusionists, and Republicans now gone, the newly reconstructed Democratic Party throughout the South typically embarked on a policy of "progressive" reforms including education. In Virginia and North Carolina, for example, the old-guard wealthy planters submitted to the demands of yeomen farmers and allowed local taxation for public education. Now firmly in control, white supremists expanded public education with segregated facilities. For example, Aycock (who had built his reputation as a race baiter) became governor of North Carolina in 1900 and initiated a new era of public education with racial segregation as its dark capstone. In just thirty-five years, the educational experiment of the Freedmen's Bureau schools had been effectively subverted. The glaring failure of the common school to embrace all children was now exposed.[19]

Despite the promise of the Thirteenth, Fourteenth, and Fifteenth, Amendments to the U.S. Constitution (the Thirteenth freed the slaves; the Fourteenth provided for the civil rights of the freedmen, and the Fifteenth gave black men the right to vote), the social and economic position of former slaves clearly deteriorated after 1877. This period is sometimes called the era of Jim Crow segregation. As we have seen, when Reconstruction ended in 1877 political power returned to the former Southern planters. Southern states, resentful of the political and social rights that former slaves now "enjoyed" under the U.S. Constitution, passed state legislation to put blacks "back in their place." Many states stripped blacks of their right to vote by mandating that they pass a literacy test before being allowed to vote. Others instituted "black codes" that placed curfews on former slaves and declared that unemployed African Americans were "vagrants," and thus subject to arrest. Those who were jailed under these provisions could be released only if they returned to their former masters and worked for them in some kind of sharecropping arrangement. Further, many states made it illegal for blacks to carry weapons, to congregate, to testify against whites in courts, or even to ride in the same rail car. Eventually this kind of legalized segregation found support in the U.S. Supreme Court *Plessy v. Ferguson* decision of 1896, which declared segregation legal as long as facilities were "equal." This "separate but equal" doctrine was the dark cornerstone of racial segregation for the next half century.[20]

In addition to these legal burdens, many blacks were subjected to intimidation and humiliation by a hostile white community. Of course, not all whites can be held responsible for this kind of behavior, but thousands of local mobs, "black cavalry," and "Negro shooters" regularly harassed blacks, and Ku Klux Klansmen systematically intimidated and hanged thousands of others. By the end of the century, lynchings in the South had reached epidemic proportions, peaking at over two hundred per year in the late 1890s and early 1900s.[21]

The Migration North

Because of these conditions, many blacks were fed up and ready to leave the South, to make a new life for themselves and provide an education for their children. All they needed was opportunity; that opportunity came as a result of the Great War in Europe. When World War I began in 1914, European immigration to the United States slowed to a trickle. And since over four million American men eventually would be sent to Europe to fight, there was a serious shortage of industrial workers. As a result, American manufacturers in the North actively recruited African-American workers through factory labor agents and provided relatively good-paying jobs for thousands. Moreover, African-American newspapers like Chicago's *Daily Defender* enthusiastically recruited Southern blacks to come north for good-paying jobs. In Chicago, for example, the number of blacks in industrial occupations grew from about 3,000 in 1916 to over 50,000 by the end of the war. By 1920 over 300,000 African Americans had made the move to Chicago's South Side, and to other Midwestern cities like Cleveland and Detroit. New York's Harlem also became a Mecca for blacks during the decade with over 87,000 settling in that one neighborhood. African Americans not only brought their labor to the North but their jazz, blues, literature, and art as well. Their culture would transform Northern society.[22]

As immigration restriction laws were passed during the 1920s dramatically limiting the numbers of Europeans who were allowed in this country, the migration of blacks continued unabated. Thousands moved to Detroit and secured high-paying jobs in the emerging auto industry. Ford Motor Company, for example, employed only fifty blacks in 1916 but by 1926 over ten thousand African Americans were working for Ford. Others found work in the growing meat packing industries in East St. Louis, Kansas City, and of course, Chicago's great South Side stockyards. Fueled by these and other jobs, Chicago's black population grew from about 44,000 in 1910 to nearly a quarter million (234,000) in 1930. Other Northern cities experienced similar growth during this period.[23]

The Great Depression of the 1930s slowed the migration of blacks to the North as jobs in industrial cities disappeared. Beginning in the early 1940s, however, through the years of World War II and into the 1950s, blacks once again left the South in record numbers for opportunities in the North. This phase of the migration was even greater than the first because black families had established connections in many Northern cities, making the settlement process much easier. During the booming 1950s, for example, Detroit's black population nearly doubled, from 16 percent of the population to 29 percent. In Chicago the percentage of blacks in the city grew from 14 percent to 23 percent, increasing by as many as 2300 people per week in the middle of the decade.[24]

The effect of the black migration was dramatic. All told, over a half million African Americans permanently left the South and settled in Midwestern and Eastern cities. The population of both regions had been altered and so had opportunities for blacks to receive a decent education.

This is not to say that African-American people had an easy time of it in the North; far from it. Many discovered that while wages might have been higher in the north, discrimination and racial predjudice existed in those cities as well. During the summer of 1919, for example, Chicago was rocked by four days of race riots that destroyed much of the black community and killed over thirty-five people, with hundreds injured. This and other race riots in places such as St. Louis demonstrated that the promise of opportunity and freedom in the North might not easily be fulfilled.[25]

African-American Education in the North

Clearly, when African Americans began to migrate to the urban North, they discovered that racism was their constant traveling companion. Prior to their arrival, most schools in the North were either integrated with a handful of black children or were segregated on the basis of traditional residential patterns. But as the numbers of blacks in urban centers increased, communities often responded with new "concerns" over the integration of schools. The situation in Indianapolis during the 1920s is a good example of this change in attitude and policy. As Emma Lou Thornbrough has shown in her "Segregation in Indiana during the Klan Era of the 1920s," Indianapolis had adopted a policy of tacit integration during the first decades of the twentieth century, but during the 1920s most schools in that city became segregated on the basis of color.

Following the adoption of the Fourteenth Amendment, Indiana had abandoned most of the "black codes" that abridged the rights of African Americans. Nevertheless, two remnants of this antiblack legislation remained. The first was a strict prohibition against interracial marriages, and the second was a law that allowed local school districts the option of maintaining segregated schools. In addition, there was a great deal of de facto segregation in the state—separation of the races based on the patterns of residence or the traditions of a community. Washington County, for example, noted in its 1916 history that if had "for several decades boasted that no colored man or woman lived within her borders."[26]

When blacks began to move into Indiana communities in large numbers during the 1920s, the white population responded with restrictive policies. Politicians made a number of arguments for segregation. The first was that the presence of blacks in white schools posed a "health threat" to white children, the second was that blacks would get a better education in segregated all-black schools, and a third was economic. The Federation of Civic Clubs of Indianapolis, for example, argued that since tuberculosis was widespread among blacks in the city, the presence of black children in white schools was a danger to the children of the community. The Indianapolis Chamber of Commerce, on the other hand, avoided the "health problem argument" but called for separate facilities that were "modern and completely equipped." Finally, the Mapleton Civic Association argued against racial integration because it would depreciate "property values fifty percent or more." Of course, not all white residents of Indianapolis were race-baiting segregationists. Groups like the Better Indianapolis Civic League, for example, opposed racial segregation of schools, arguing that such action was "unjust, un-American, and against the spirit of democratic ideals. . . ." But despite this well-reasoned argument, the Indianapolis Board of School Commissioners caved in to the demands of the segregationists and established a system of segregated schools in the city. Their 1922 report declared that it was in the best interest of black children to have their own schools that would provide them with "maximum educational opportunity." By 1929, Indianapolis schools were completely segregated.[27]

Not all Northern communities had the same experiences as Indianapolis. Some cities, like Chicago, avoided legal segregation but since the city had a history of residential segregation, the schools were de facto segregated. Other smaller Northern communities had no history of black settlement; as a result, the schools remained all white for much of the twentieth century.

The Struggle for Schools

Throughout this period, however, there was a growing effort on the part of hundreds of African-American and liberal white groups to fight segregation and racial injustice in both their communities and schools. Although there was a tradition of local protest that had been a part of the black culture since the time of slavery, the emergence of Jim Crow laws in the South and North following Reconstruction spawned a number of vigorous national groups. For example, Booker T. Washington formed the National Negro Business League in 1900 with the purpose of promoting economic opportunities and equal justice in the courts; later, the National Urban League was formed to help provide opportunities for the black migrants to Northern cities. Then in 1905, W. E. B. DuBois and a group of twenty-nine black intellectuals launched the famed Niagara Movement. In their persuasive manifesto they called for racial justice and an end to segregation. Out of this organization came the NAACP (National Association for the Advancement of Colored People) in 1909, formed in part to use the legal system to fight racial injustice and segregation. Hundreds of other groups also fought for racial justice. The important point to remember, however, was that during this time, what some historians refer to as the "forgotten years" of the black revolution, the movement toward racial justice continued to grow in strength and in numbers.[28]

World War II was a turning point, however. Over a half a million black soldiers served during the war, with about 80,000 going overseas. As before, blacks were sent to segregated units and most endured continued prejudice in army towns throughout the war. And yet, many African Americans acquired an education or marketable skills during their training that helped them get jobs when the war ended. Many illiterate blacks, especially from the South, also received a basic education unavailable to them prior to their military service. Following the war, black veterans, like their white counterparts, were eligible for the GI Bill of Rights, which provided them with low-cost home mortgages and grants for higher education. Finally, African Americans who served in the armed forces returned with a renewed sense of their own identity, confident that their participation in the war would initiate the shift toward racial justice in the United States.[29]

While change was not immediate, it was imminent. In 1946 President Harry Truman appointed a civil rights committee to investigate racial injustice. The following year the committee painted a bleak picture, reporting that black Americans were discriminated against throughout the country. In response, Truman sent a ten-point civil rights program to Congress (the first since Reconstruction) and then issued an executive order to eliminate discrimination in federal facilities. As part of this order, the military eventually was integrated. These breakthroughs were highlighted even further in 1947 when Jackie Robinson "broke the color line" in major league baseball and began his brilliant professional athletic career. Now even the national pastime was integrated. Change was in the air.[30]

Simple Justice

More important for education, however, was that a quiet revolution in race relations was taking place. In response to the new policy initiatives of President Truman, the Justice Department began to file legal briefs on behalf of the NAACP, challenging the constitutionality of racial discrimination in housing, interstate transportation, and education. Within just a few years, working with both the Justice Department and the NAACP, Oliver Brown sued the board of education of Topeka, Kansas, to allow his eight-year-old daughter, Linda Brown, to attend an all-white school. Three years later, in the landmark decision *Brown v. Board of Education of Topeka* (May 17, 1954) the United States Supreme Court declared that the *Plessy v. Ferguson* "separate but equal" ruling was wrong, noting that "separate facilities are inherently unequal." By 1955 the Court began implementing the decision and ordered local school boards to integrate "with all deliberate speed."[31]

Within weeks, President Dwight D. Eisenhower reluctantly ordered the integration of schools in Washington, D.C. as a national model. Yet the process of "desegregation" was a slow and difficult one, especially in the South. In one school district after another desegregation was opposed, sometimes violently, by white parents and members of the white community. That violence came to national attention in Little Rock, Arkansas, in 1957. As part of the plan to desegregate Little Rock's Central High School that year, nine black students were scheduled to be admitted. The governor of the state, Orval Faubus, however, had different plans. He activated the National Guard and with fixed bayonets, they turned the black students away. This nationally televised scene outraged many Americans and energized the civil rights struggle. Within three weeks, National Guard troops were ordered to leave and once again, the black students tried to enter Central High. This time, they were harassed by angry white mobs with chants of "Two-four-six-eight, we ain't gonna integrate." Once again the American people were outraged, and President Eisenhower was forced to take drastic action. He mobilized paratroopers from the 101st Airborne and nationalized the state militia of Arkansas to protect the rights of these young black Americans. The black students entered the school, and a new era of school desegregation officially began.[32]

Over the next decade, the civil rights movement made dramatic gains in desegregating public facilities through the Civil Rights Act of 1964, providing job opportunities through affirmative action programs and gaining legal rights through the Voting Rights Act of 1965. From the onset of the black migration in the 1920s to the early 1970s, when the Supreme Court declared that school busing to achieve racial desegregation was constitutional, American society had made slow progress toward the goal of racial justice. Of course, not all black people were of "one mind" regarding the presumed benefits of "desegregation." While most activists had fought for better schools and funding through integration, some perceived the dangers of this new social experiment. In Hyde County, North Carolina, for example, African-American residents fought to retain their all-black school because that institution had been a source of inspiration to the community for decades. Their struggle to keep their small school ran counter to the mainstream civil rights movement and the conventional wisdom of the day.[33]

This movement demonstrated, moreover, that many African Americans had a keen sense of the potential problems of school integration and a clear understanding of the importance of community-based education. As with so many social experiments in American history, school desegregation has had both positive and negative effects for black children. On the one hand, it certainly promised better facilities and equal funding for blacks and whites; on the other, many African-American children had difficulty adjusting to integrated schools and were often shunted into special classes or declared learning disabled because of these difficulties. The demand on the part of some blacks today for all-black charter schools may seem strange to liberal-minded Americans who traditionally have embraced desegregation as a solution to our racial problems. What these demands demonstrate, however, is that there are no social panaceas for racial equality in education.

THE CHANGING FACE OF IMMIGRATION

The 1960s brought many changes to this nation, including a new policy on immigration as part of the Great Society programs. By shifting our immigration quotas from those based on national origin to those based on economic need or ideology, the face of immigration and migration was changed. Gone were the millions of European immigrants streaming through Ellis Island and other ports of entry. Gone, too, were the train-loads of African Americans from the rural South searching and struggling for opportunities in the North. Now Asian and Hispanic people formed the centerpiece of America's immigrant population.

In the early 1960s relatively few immigrants came from countries in Asia, Mexico, and other Latin American and Carribbean nations, but by the early 1970s nearly 40 percent of all immigrants were Asian, while about half came from countries to the south of the United States. Today, Hispanic and Asian people represent the largest immigrant groups in this country; still, both groups have a long history of migration to this country, especially to the West.

Chinese and Japanese

Chinese migration to the United States began in the early 1850s, when news of California's gold rush spread across the Pacific. Lured to what was called the "Land of Golden Mountains," thousands of immigrants from southern China made their way to this country. Rather than discovering gold, however, most found only hard work in mining, service industries, and railroad construction. By the time California passed its restrictive immigration legislation against further Asian immigration in the 1880s, over a quarter of a million Chinese had settled in the West.

As Chinese immigration slowed dramatically, Japanese people began to settle in both Hawaii and California. Although there had been a number of early Japanese settlements in both of these locations, not until the 1890s did their numbers increase significantly. Between 1890 and 1900, for example, the number of Japanese in California grew tenfold, from about 2,000 settlers to over 24,000. In Hawaii, however, the number of Japanese immigrants grew from about 6,000 to over 60,000.[34]

The rapid growth in the number of Japanese settlers in Hawaii transformed the political and social life of the islands. By 1900, Japanese represented about 40 percent of the entire population of Hawaii. This allowed the Japanese to assimilate rapidly into the host society and to have a significant impact on the political life of the islands. Some native Hawaiians embraced Japanese traditions (such as leaving one's shoes at the door before entering a home) while others incorporated Japanese foods such as sushi, sashimi, and tempura into their diets. There was also a great deal of intermarriage between Japanese and island people.

The large numbers of settlers, the more open attitudes of the island people toward people of different cultures, and Japanese intermarriage with native Hawaiians allowed the Japanese to avoid the excessive nativist legislation and prejudice that would soon become common on the mainland.

Indeed, the Japanese in California had a much more difficult time, politically, socially, and economically. By the early 1900s, California nativists, alarmed by what they saw as the growing "Asian horde," began to lobby the legislature, claiming that the state was being overrun by Japanese people. As a result of their actions, the state passed the Webb-Heney Act in 1913. This law denied Japanese people U.S. citizenship and made it illegal for them to own agricultural land or lease it for more than three consecutive years. This legislation was followed by the infamous California Alien Land Act of 1920 that made it illegal for Japanese who had held title to lands before 1913 to transfer ownership to others in their family. As a result of this legislation, many Japanese were forced off the land and moved into California's growing urban centers, where they often took jobs as busboys, gardeners, and common laborers. Despite these problems, the Japanese continued to settle in communities throughout the Golden State, and their numbers reached nearly 140,000 just prior to World War II. And yet, they never represented more than 1 percent of the entire population of the state and only slightly more than 2 percent in the city of Los Angeles.[35]

While Japanese settlers endured considerable political, economic, and social discrimination in the first decades of the century, during World War II that discrimination became even more vicious and racist. The Japanese attack on Pearl Harbor in December of 1941 not only brought the U.S. into World War II, it also made life for Issei (foreign-born Japanese Americans) and Nisei (American-born Japanese Americans) unbearable. Energized by the tragic events in Hawaii, politicians through the states (especially on the West Coast) demanded a solution to the "Japanese Problem." Eventually they convinced President Franklin D. Roosevelt that this was a serious issue, and on February 19, 1942, he reluctantly signed Executive Order no. 9066 to move "dangerous persons" (notably Japanese) to "relocation camps." By August of that year, more than 110,000 Japanese (64 percent of whom were American citizens) were forced from their homes and placed in remote camps located in California, Arizona, Colorado, Wyoming, Utah, and Arkansas. Life in these camps was monotonous at best; at worst, it was dehumanizing. Of course, these camps cannot be compared to the death camps established by Nazi Germany during the war, in which millions of Jews, Poles, Russians, and other "Non-Aryan" people were exterminated in gas chambers and ovens. Nevertheless, they represent a pathetic chapter in American civil rights history. In 1944 the Supreme Court decision *Endo v. United States* declared that the camps were unconstitutional and soon most of them were closed. But the damage to thousands of Japanese people— men, women, and children—had been done. Many had lost everything as a result of their forced internment, while others bore permanent psychological scars.[36]

As might be expected, many Japanese refused to return to their former homes, and thousands chose to establish communities in Midwestern cities like Chicago, Cleveland, and Minneapolis. In fact, over ten thousand Japanese settled into Chicago's Little Tokyo in the immediate postwar period. Others made their way to the East Coast and established communities in New York City and New Jersey. Those who did return to California slowly rebuilt their lives, and in the decades that followed they fought against the injustices that they had been subjected to during the war. In 1946 the Alien Land Act was virtually dismantled, and by 1952 it was declared unconstitutional by the California Supreme Court. Moreover, as the sting of war gradually began to wane during the late 1950s and 1960s, a new generation of Californians became more open to the Japanese and gradually accepted them as part of their growing multicultural society.[37]

Today the Japanese are often respected members of our society and have had an important impact on our political, cultural, and social life. The acceptance of Japanese-manufactured products and methods, our fascination with their culture, and our (gradual) embrace of their food all testify to the great strides that we have made as a people.

In Hawaii, where Japanese people avoided the overt racism of relocation during the war, relations are even better. As we have seen, the Japanese have had a profound impact on multicultural Hawaii, which now boasts a mixture of Polynesian, Asian, and Euro-American cultural forms. Although there are problems on the islands, in many ways, Hawaii has become the American model of racial toleration and balance. Perhaps as we search for a solution to our ongoing multicultural debate we should look no further than the fiftieth state.[38]

The New Asian Immigration

Depite our racist policies toward many Asian people over the years, by the mid-1960s things began to change. As a result of our fundamental shift in immigration policy, the number of Asian immigrants to this country slowly began to rise. And by the 1980s, the number of "new Asian" immigrants to the United States had increased dramatically. Thousands of Samoans, Koreans, Taiwanese, Filipinos, Cambodians, and Vietnamese people joined Japanese Americans and settled in southern California and other parts of the state. Typically, south Asian Indians and Filipinos as well as Chinese and Koreans were middle class when they arrived in this country, and as a result, their assimilation has been much smoother than was that of other groups. Their enrollment in elementary, secondary, and postsecondary educational institutions is among the highest in the country, and they also have higher levels of business ownership than most immigrants. Like the Japanese before them, these new Asian immigrants embraced a set of middle-class values that not only helped them succeed in the American economy but helped their children to achieve in school. As part of this middle-class ethic (as well as their native culture) they were brought up to work hard, conform to the standards of the host community, and respect authority. While maintenance of their own culture also was important to these people, assimilation to U.S. norms was encouraged. Young Japanese, Asian, Indians, Filipinos, Chinese, and Koreans are enthusiastic about learning English and often embrace the powerful material culture of America. This "will to assimilate" has helped many "new Asians" do well in school and achieve a measure of success later in life.[39]

On the other hand, the experiences of Southeastern Asian people, such as Cambodians and Vietnamese, have been much more difficult. Like millions of immigrants before them, these agriculturally based people often lack the urban skills necessary to compete successfully for jobs, and many suffered a kind of psychic trauma as a result of their exile from repressive political regimes and war-torn nations. As a result of these experiences, many of these immigrants have been slower to learn English and have often preferred to settle in insular ethnic comunities. While this has provided them with a refuge from a sometimes hostile American society, it has also slowed their assimilation into society and their success in school.[40]

Mexicans and Puerto Ricans

Like the Chinese, Mexican people have also had a long history of immigration and settlement in the United States. For centuries, Mexican people had lived in the old Southwest and in southern California. Their rich heritage can still be found everywhere in the West. Prior to the War of 1846, Mexico controlled much of what is now the western part of the United States. The Treaty of Guadalupe Hidalgo ended the Mexican War and provided that the United States take possession of over 520,000 square miles of land (including all of California) and assume political control over the region's 75,000 Spanish-speaking inhabitants.

Although relations would remain strained with the Mexican government for years to come, thousands of poor Mexican people crossed the Rio Grande or the desert of southern California seeking a new life in this country. Like other immigrant groups, the reception to their arrival was mixed. On the one hand, they were discriminated against by a growing white population; on the other, many were able to find a degree of success in this new land.

During the 1920s, many Mexican people took advantage of America's new restrictive immigration policies aimed at southern and eastern European people. In the wake of this legislation, Mexicans had a "window of opportunity" to come to this country for jobs and a new life. Many Mexicans made their way to the fertile agricultural regions of southern California, where they found employment as agricultural workers. Often living in primitive camps with little sanitation and virtually no rights, Mexican laborers persisted and eventually were able to establish permanent settlements in the region. By the end of the 1920s, Mexicans constituted one of the largest immigrant groups in the country with nearly

500,000 residents. In Los Angeles alone, Mexican immigrants represented about one-fifth of the entire population.

In addition to America's growing Mexican population in the West, thousands of Puerto Ricans immigrated to this country beginning in the 1920s. As the harvesting of Puerto Rico's principal crop, sugar cane, became more mechanized, nearly 40 percent of the poor laborers on that island were literally forced off the land. One key destination for these people was New York City's East Harlem, often called Spanish Harlem or El Barrio.

Yet as the hard times of the 1930s descended on the country, the number of Mexican and Puerto Rican immigrants declined sharply. Jobs were no longer plentiful, and the few that remained were often reserved for "native" white Americans. A familiar pattern of prejudice, typical during periods of economic slowdown, had once again emerged. Signs reading "No Niggers, Mexicans, and Dogs" often greeted America's newest citizens. In California, thousands of Mexican farmworkers were rounded up and sent back to Mexico in open rail cars. More than a quarter of a million were forcibly returned during the dark years of the Depression.[41]

With the onset of World War II, however, Mexican Americans were once again encouraged to return to the United States as farmworkers. These *braceros* (helping hands) were desperately needed as the number of white American workers dwindled. Yet despite their important economic role, Mexican Americans were subjected to relentless hostility during this period. The famous "zoot suit" riot in Los Angeles during the war was just one example of the persistent nativism that Mexican people would have to endure.[42]

Following the war, the U.S. government formalized the bracero program with Mexico in the Migratory Labor Agreement of 1948. Under this arrangement, Mexican farmworkers were encouraged to come to this country during the harvest but were expected to return when their seasonal work was complete. Although life for the braceros was plagued by low wages, discrimination, and lack of opportunities, many remained illegally in this country, accepting low-paying jobs as dishwashers, busboys, and laborers with the hope of "making it." In times of economic slowdown however, many were rounded up and again forcibly sent back to Mexico. During the recession of 1953, for example, over a million Mexicans (mostly illegal) were deported as part of Operation Wetback. Incredibly, the following year, 1954, as the economy rebounded and the need for agricultural workers resumed, about 450,000 braceros were again invited to return to this country. This love-hate relationship with Mexican people continues to this day and has left a deep scar on our relations with them.[43]

Cubans

By the end of the 1950s and early 1960s Hispanic immigrants from Mexico and Puerto Rico were joined by thousands of Cuban refugees. Following the Cuban socialist revolution in 1959, many supporters of the Batista regime, as well as a host of business owners and professionals fearful of the new government under Fidel Castro, left the island and settled in the South Miami, Florida, area that would become Little Havana. Between 1959 and 1962 over 150,000 Cubans migrated to this country. Immigration slowed in the next few years as relations between the United States and Cuba became strained and flights between the two countries were prohibited. However when President Lyndon Johnson signed a "memorandum of understanding" with Cuba in late 1965, flights resumed and immigration grew dramatically, with over 257,000 arriving by 1972, when the airlift was again suspended. Since then, immigration from the island has slowed considerably, except for the thousands of Cuban "boat people" who were released by Castro in the early 1980s.[44]

While the Cuban immigrants who fled the country in the late 1950s and early 1960s were generally wealthier and better educated than most Hispanics in this country, it is certainly not true that all Cubans who settled in South Miami were former governmental officials or millionaires. Moreover, Cuban immigrants who arrived during the late 1970s and 1980s were much poorer than the so-called golden exiles that fled Castro immediately following the revolution.

Nevertheless, Cuban Americans today are different from other Hispanic Americans and Cubans still living on the island in three important ways. First, Cuban Americans are predominantly white. Because class and race were inexorably tied together in prerevolutionary Cuba, the first wave of exiles fleeing the socialist revolution were wealthier white immigrants. Once these original exile communities were established, they remained white. In fact, over 90 percent of the Cuban population in Miami is white while that number is closer to 70 percent in Cuba.[45]

Second, the Cuban American population is much older than the general population of other Hispanic Americans or native Cubans. Because many middle-aged Cubans fled the island in or soon after 1959, the proportion of older Cuban Americans today is more then three times greater than the Cuban population at large, or other Hispanic groups in the United States. Of course, this places a considerable strain on the Cuban population, and also reinforces traditional political attitudes within the Cuban-American community.[46]

In fact, this political conservatism represents the third major difference between Cuban Americans and other Hispanic groups in this country. The anti-Castro political posture of the postrevolutionary Cuban refugee population has colored the politics of the entire Cuban community. Unlike Hispanic people throughout the United States who general have supported liberal Democratic politics over the years, Cubans in south Miami are much more conservative and have traditionally supported Republican political candidates. Moreover, the recent political upheavals in Little Havana over the custody of Elián Gonzalez demonstrate the ongoing conservativism of the Cuban-American community.[47]

In short, the refugee experiences of postrevolutionary Cuban immigrants have created a unique community, quite different from the general Hispanic population of this country and certainly distinct from the Cuban population on the island. Partly because of this uniqueness, however, Cuban Americans are better educated than other Hispanic groups. For example, the majority of Cuban Americans over the age of twenty-five have graduated from high school, and one in six has a college degree. From the very first, middle-class Cubans in the South Miami area established their own private elementary and secondary schools under the auspices of the Roman Catholic Church and encouraged their children to attend regularly. Many were concerned with the social upheaval in public schools during the 1960s, and most were determined to maintain their culture and language in the United States. In recent years, many private secular schools have been established by members of the community. Classes in these schools, like their Catholic counterparts, are taught in Spanish, and the curriculum places special emphasis on their version of Cuban history, especially its repudiation of Castro and the revolution of 1959.[48]

Native Americans

In addition to this nation's growing Hispanic population, thousands of Native American people began to migrate to Northern cities during these years. Native Americans, of course, were not newcomers to this country but traditionally had lived outside of American society, first in scattered tribes throughout the country and then beginning in the 1800s on federally imposed Indian reservations. As Indian people were exposed to the booming material economy and culture of American society through radio and television, however, many became disenchanted with the "old ways" and their simple, austere lives. Like other groups, they too wanted a share of the "good life," and began migrating north in the 1960s; Like others before them, Indian people often found prejudice, racism, and hatred instead. Today, isolated Indian communities from Texas to Illinois are among the poorest in the nation. Indian children, like poor immigrants, have had a great deal of difficulty adjusting to public schools. And while estimates vary, it appears that only one in four Indian children will graduate from high school. The cycle of poverty is repeated among America's first residents.[49]

THE IMMIGRATION ACT OF 1965 AND BEYOND

By the mid-1960s, our "on again, off again" relationship with Mexican immigrants and our total restriction of Asian immigrants began to change. In addition, with the return of good economic times, the number of Puerto Ricans moving to El Barrio in New York grew dramatically. As a result of the Immigration Act of 1965, pushed through Congress as part of the liberal Great Society programs, the United States opened the doors of immigration to people whose labor and skills were needed here. By the late 1970s and early 1980s the effect of this new immigration policy was being felt throughout the country. In addition to Mexican, Puerto Rican, and Cuban people, other Hispanic immigrants from El Salvador, Guatemala, Nicaragua, and Honduras made their way to this country. Along with their important skills and labor they also brought with them a rich diversity of culture.

Yet as the vigorous U.S. economy slowed in the early 1980s, it appeared, once again, that all was not well. In 1983, for example, Attorney General William French Smith alarmed the American people by declaring that we had "lost control of our borders." With the impression that millions of illegal immigrants were flooding the country from the south and taking jobs away from "real" Americans, Congress passed the Immigration Reform and Control Act of 1986. This law, amended in 1990, attempted to curb illegal immigration and offered immigrant amnesty to those were already in this country illegally. Despite this legislation, with the resumption of growth of the U.S. economy, the numbers of new immigrants exploded. In just two years between 1988 and 1990, for example, the numbers of immigrants who arrived in this country more than doubled from about 600,000 to more than 1,500,000. Millions more have entered this country since then.[50]

Problems of Immigrant Education Today

Of course, many of these new arrivals were school-age children. Although figures vary for different groups, approximately one-third were under the age of eighteen. Many of these children had limited English proficiency, with only about 15 percent of new immigrant families speaking any English in the home. Once again, schools were confronted with crucial decisions regarding the assessment and placement of immigrant children. This included their grade-level assignment, whether they were placed in regular classrooms or provided with special education, and whether they needed English language instruction. Formal assessment measures including standardized tests were especially problematic for these immigrant children who were neither fluent in English nor familiar with American schooling and culture. Moreover, educational decisions such as promotion or graduation were often made on the basis of a single test score, placing many immigrant children at a great disadvantage. Informal assessment measures were also flawed. For example, when a Vietnamese family migrated to a Chicago suburb in the early 1980s, the principal simply eyed the three children and said, "Hmm . . . looks like kindergarten, first, and third grades." His placement decision, like that of thousands of others before and after, was based exclusively on the *size* of the children.[51]

Bilingual Education

Today more than 2.6 million students are classified as having Limited English Proficiency, or LEP. These students can be found in nearly every district of the country, with one in six American teachers charged with the responsibility of teaching at least one LEP student. Prior to the 1960s, schools typically used "submersion" (sink or swim!) as the primary method of instruction for immigrant children. If a child could not speak the English language, he was simply left behind. Most dropped out. During the 1960s however, these policies began to change. As part of the new liberal environment of this era and as a result of pressure from the Hispanic community, Congress passed the Bilingual Education Act of 1968. This law mandated that schools provide some form of language assistance to students whose primary language was not English. A few years later, the Supreme Court ruled in *Lau v. Nichols* that schools must do something to help non-English-speaking students learn. This decision put an end to the practice of submersion, at least for the time being.

Since *Lau v. Nichols,* three models of bilingual education have emerged in this country. In the first model, *structured immersion*, instruction is provided by a teacher who is bilingual but the teacher speaks entirely in English and encourages her students to use English. However, the lack of bilingual teachers, especially teachers who are fluent in the wide variety of Asian languages and/or other regional dialects, limits the effectiveness of this approach. The second model is *transitional bilingual education*. Here, teachers instruct students in their native language in a few subjects in conjunction with classes in English as a Second Language (ESL). Yet again, because there are few qualified teachers proficient in several languages this method is less successful than it might be. The final model, *bilingual/ bicultural maintenance*, attempts to develop proficiency in English as well as a student's native language by providing course work in both. Using this approach, the curriculum also includes courses in the student's ethnic culture.[52]

While each of these approaches has had some success in helping immigrant children learn to read and assimilate into American society, there has also been a powerful conservative backlash against any form of bilingualism. Typically, conservative political action groups like U.S. English and English First have relentlessly pressured state legislatures to pass English-only laws that forbid any form of bilingual education. Convinced that the new immigrants are a threat to American society and culture, these groups have been quite successful in their campaigns. Beginning with California in the 1980s, more than twenty states have now passed English-only laws, declaring to our diverse society that English is the only acceptable language. More recently (and shockingly), California voters passed the infamous Proposition 187 in 1994 that required teachers and health care professionals to deny education or assistance to children of "illegal aliens," and even to report them to the police! While these measures may seem reasonable to some white Americans, they have had a chilling effect on the immigrant community and have placed teachers in very difficult positions.

If history is our guide, we will see further political pressure for "Americanization" and more English-only legislation at the state and local levels. Similarly, while ethnic assimilation will continue, as it always has, the future will also see a growing demand for alternative schools. As the federal government assumes greater virtual control over education (through national standards) and the states become a force of advocacy rather than direct power, we will gradually move to a more pluralistic conception of society that matches the diversity of our classrooms, nation, and international community. In chapter 10 we will return to these important issues.

Women Enter Teaching

The ongoing struggle of European, Asian, Hispanic, and African-American people to assimilate into this country and to partake of its educational opportunities has been matched by American teachers themselves. For over two centuries, women, ethnic, and black teachers have also sought to attain positions in the field and to be accepted as professionals. Today there are more women and people of color in teaching than at any time in our nation's history, but this achievement in diversity did not come without a struggle. Their story reflects the history of our nation and is a testimony to the tenacity and courageousness of generations of teachers in the past.

During the colonial era America's schoolteachers were men, and throughout much of our nation's early history men dominated the profession. Men were preferred as teachers for a number of reasons. First, they were better educated and were presumed to have superior intellects. Except for Puritan girls, who received a primary education in public schools, a few young women in religious schools and a handful of girls from wealthy families, colonial women seldom had access to formal education. As a result, on the eve of the American Revolution, while some women could read, few were able to write and many could neither read nor write. Second, during the colonial period, men were considered better able to handle children in the classroom because discipline meant physically overpowering young students. The primary instrument of discipline from the earliest settlement well into the 1800s was the ferule (ruler), the whipping post, the rattan, or simply the back of the hand. Young boys were routinely whipped, slapped, or punched for such "offenses" as whispering or not knowing their assigned lessons. It would be another century before these forms of corporal punishment would begin to disappear from the schoolhouse. Until then, however, the stronger, larger, male schoolmaster was seen as indispensable in maintaining order in the classroom. Its no surprise then that men dominated the teaching profession for well over a century and a half of our nation's history.

COLONIAL SCHOOLTEACHERS

There were four general types of schoolteachers during America's colonial period. The first were schoolmasters of colonial New England. The second were the church officials who often presided over religious schools in the middle colonies and elsewhere. The third were the private tutors who taught generations of children in plantation houses in the South and in merchant homes in Northern cities. And the fourth were a small number of women who taught young children in community or neighborhood schools, sometimes called "dame" schools, or who instructed a few children informally in their homes.

New England's Schoolmasters

Perhaps the best known of the colonial teachers were the New England schoolmasters. These sometimes stern masters have been immortalized in the literature and were responsible for educating generations of New England boys in classical grammar schools. Collectively they presided over New England's grand experiment in public education.

New England schoolmasters typically were hired by the leaders (selectmen) of towns. Records from Northampton, Massachusetts, for example, indicate that they hired a Mr. Cornish as their first teacher in 1664. He was to teach for a period of six months that year and was expected to supplement his meager income with farming. Similar arrangements were made with other schoolmasters throughout this period. Farmer Cornish, as he was known, was a fine teacher with considerable talent but he had the bad habit of using profanity in the classroom. Eventually he was fined twenty shillings by the court for cursing.[1]

Although Farmer Cornish's tenure as a teacher was rather short, lasting only about two years, other New England schoolmasters spent most of their lives in the classroom. Among the most famous of these longtime teachers was Mr. Ezekiel Cheever. Cheever taught in New England schools continuously for over seventy years. In fact, until his death in 1708 he was still teaching.[2]

Ezekiel Cheever's legacy to American public education was immense. He began his career in his early twenties in 1638, teaching Latin in his New Haven, Connecticut, home. Within a few years he was officially hired as a schoolmaster, and he spent the next decade in that position perfecting his techniques of instruction. It was during this period (in 1645) that Cheever published his classic introduction to Latin: *A Short Introduction to the Latin Tongue*. This book, affectionately known as "Cheevers Accidence," was the mainstay of the grammar-school curriculum throughout the colonial period and was republished as late as 1838, nearly two hundred years after it was written.[3]

Following his success in New Haven, Cheever taught for eleven years in Ipswich, Massachusetts, and then in Charlestown, where he taught for another nine years. It was in Charlestown in 1670 that the Boston selectmen took note of his remarkable achievements and hired him as the schoolmaster of the Boston Grammar School. Cheever spent the next thirty-two years of his life teaching the mysteries of classical languages to the young boys of Boston. During that time he developed a reputation as a patient master who preferred encouraging his students to whipping them into submission.[4]

Many of the early New England schoolmasters, like Cheever, received their education in England. Others had only informal training before they entered the classroom. By the 1700s, however, more and more schoolmasters had graduated from Yale or Harvard College and were studying for the ministry. During their ministerial training, many earned an income by teaching school. Others taught a semester or two while they waited for a pulpit to become available. In fact there was an old New England saying that went "scratch a teacher and find a preacher." The system worked well for both the community in search of a good teacher and the prospective minister in search of additional income. The selectmen of Lynn, Massachusetts, for example, hired the Reverend Mr. Shepherd in 1700 as their schoolmaster. Shepherd was educated in the colonies and served as teacher for at least thirteen years before entering the ministry. Similarly, in 1698 Josiah Cotton was hired as schoolmaster of Marblehead, Massachusetts. Cotton was a recent graduate of Harvard College and also was studying for the ministry. After teaching for several terms he left to take a position in a nearby church. Later when he returned to visit Marblehead he discovered that the town leaders had been unable to hire another schoolmaster, and he agreed to teach another term. Such was the bond that often developed between the town and their schoolmasters.[5]

Teachers in Religious Schools

While New England schoolmasters typically were pious Calvinists or young ministerial students, church officials in the middle colonies often served as schoolteachers in addition to their spiritual responsibilities. These included pastors, ministers, priests, and lay church leaders. These men taught in Dutch Reformed, German Lutheran, Quaker, Roman Catholic, Mennonite, and hundreds of other types of religious schools that dotted the landscape of colonial America. Each of these religious schools taught its own specific interpretation of the Scriptures, usually in its own language and with its own catechism.

Tutors

In addition to the New England schoolmasters and church officials in religious schools there was another group of male teachers during the colonial period that worked with individuals or small groups of children. These were the private tutors. Although tutors could be found in all the colonies, primarily among the wealthy, most taught on Southern plantations and in the households of wealthy merchants in America's growing cities.

During the early colonial period, there were few individuals qualified to teach, and most tutors were either recruited from England or were drawn from the ranks of indentured servants. These "servants" were ordinary men who had agreed to work for a "master" for five to seven years to "work off" the cost of their voyage to this country. Although most indentured servants were either children or young men with few skills, occasionally a man with education seeking a new life for himself would agree to tutor the children of his "master" as part of his indenture.

Such was the case of George Washington's tutor, "Hobby," who taught the future father of the nation to read and write. Hobby lived a long life and was proud of his famous pupil. He often boasted that "between his knees he had laid the foundation of Washington's greatness." Although Hobby was a capable tutor, not all were. Another of George's early teachers, Mr. Williams, has been described as knowing "as little as Balaam's Ass!"[6]

Later in the colonial period, the quality of tutors improved, and most were graduates of colonial colleges. In fact, in the period immediately preceding the American Revolution a number of colleges were formed and joined the ranks of Harvard, Yale, and William and Mary. These included the College of Philadelphia in 1755, the College of New Jersey (later Princeton) in 1746, Kings College (later Columbia) in 1754, the College of Rhode Island (later Brown) in 1764, and Queens College (later Rutgers) in 1766.

Gradually, the nature of tutoring became more formalized, with written contracts specifying responsibilities and pay. This was especially true in the South, where tutors often had to travel hundreds of miles to remote plantations. Depending on the commission contract, the tutor might receive room and board and a small stipend. Sometimes the contract stipulated that the tutor would have free access to a plot of land to grow vegetables. And sometimes he was allowed to set up a small school in one of the buildings of the plantation to help educate other children in the community. By charging a small tuition, the ambitious tutor might even turn a small profit. Although the quality of home tutoring varied considerably, many young Southern gentlemen received a fine education and went on to Oxford or Cambridge Universities, or later in the colonial era, to a Northern college to complete their educations.

Women Teachers in Dame Schools

Clearly, the teaching profession was dominated by men from the early colonial period to the early years of the new republic. In relative obscurity, however, some women did teach in what have been called "dame schools." These early primary schools served to teach young neighborhood children their ABC's and provide them with some instruction in how to read and write.

The dame schools arose out of necessity. Although primary education and apprenticeship training typically were provided by a mother, father, or grandparent, many families simply did not have the skills or the time to instruct their children. As we have seen, most women had little access to formal education and, depending on their class and region, many men also were illiterate during the colonial period. Those women who could read and write were often called upon by members of the community to assume the important role of teacher. Some dame schools were private, and some received partial funding from the town, some survived on small student tuitions, while others received full financial support from the community. In many ways, these dame schools were the precursor to the "common" primary school of the 1800s. Moreover, they represented the first opportunity for women to teach.

There are few direct references to women teaching during the early colonial era, but New England colonial records indicate that women taught in dame schools as early as the 1600s. One town, for example, recorded that they "paid Widow Walker ten shillings for schooling small children," while another noted that they "paid for boarding schooldame, at three shillings per week." Records from Deerfield, Massachusetts, note, in passing, that Hannah Beaman's class was interrupted by an Indian attack in the summer of 1694. She and all her children ran for their lives, and reached the fort safely.[7]

By the end of the 1600s and beginning of the 1700s dame schools had become more common and we see more references to their contractual arrangements and duties. The records of Northfield, Massachusetts, for example, note that in 1721 the wife of the local blacksmith was hired as their first schooldame. Mrs. Field taught a class of young students in her home for seven months of the year during the late spring, the summer, and early fall. Her pupils paid a modest tuition of four pence per week.

In addition to her teaching duties, Mrs. Field also made shirts that she sold to the Indians and sewed britches for her brother-in-law for six pence per pair. Another schooldame of note was Rebecca Moffitt, who taught in Windham, Massachusetts, in 1691, and supported herself by charging her students a penny a day for their instruction! Similarly the town records of Springfield, Massachusetts recorded that in 1682 the selectmen "encourage[d] (Goodwife Mirick) in the good work of training up of children and teaching children to read, that she should have three pence a week for every child, that she takes to perform this good work for."[8]

Women not only taught in New England but also in Quaker schools throughout the colonies. The Friends School in Philadelphia, for example, pioneered in the employment of women as teachers. The minutes of the Philadelphia Monthly Meeting of 1699 noted that money was allocated "to pay the schoolmasters and the mistresses salaries." A few years later, in 1702, these same records mention Olive Songhurt's salary as a teacher. Similarly, Quaker records note that Rebekah Burchall taught poor children at the Friends school from 1755 to 1761. Her duties also included the supervision of young girls during "Meetings."[9]

THE GROWING ACCEPTANCE OF WOMEN AS TEACHERS

Yet while there were a handful of women teachers in colonial America, there was still strong opposition to their employment. And only by the end of the 1700s and the beginning of the 1800s did these attitudes begin to change. As noted in chapter 1, the American Revolution and market revolution of this period had begun to fundamentally transform our ideas about the nature of teaching and the role of women in the profession.

The Education of Women

The most important factor that helped change these entrenched ideas and propel women into the teaching profession was their growing education and literacy. This achievement, however, took years of struggle. Centuries of conventional wisdom had maintained that only men should receive an education, and only gradually did this idea begin to change. As we have seen, some young New England girls received a basic primary education though even in these colonies their level of literacy reached only about half that of boys two decades after the American Revolution.[10]

As noted in chapter 1, Massachusetts Bay Colony's early education law (the Old Deluder Law of 1647) required that every town of fifty households appoint a teacher to instruct all children to write and read; but there were different interpretations of what constituted "all children." Throughout the 1600s and well into the 1700s many towns like Farmington,

Connecticut, simply refused to allow girls into their schools. At a town meeting in 1687, for example, the people of Farmington declared in a resolution that "all children is to be understood as only male children that are through their horn book."Many other towns would continue that tradition.[11]

There were a few exceptions. One of the first towns in New England to admit girls to school was Hampton, New Hampshire, in 1649. The agreement with schoolmaster John Legot stated that he "teach the children of or belonging to the town, both male and female [who] are capable of learning to write and read and cast accounts." The following year, residents of Waterton, Massachusettts, instructed schoolmaster Richard Norcross that he should accommodate "any maiden [having] the desire to learn to write."[12]

For the most part however, girls routinely were prohibited from attending New England schools until the end of the 1700s. In Boston, for example, girls were not allowed to go to school until 1789, when town officials established reading and writing schools in three different sections of the city. While each of these schools instructed both boys and girls, they attended on a rotating basis at different times of the day. Yet even with this innovation, girls were not allowed to attend school year round until 1828. Medford followed this example and a schoolmaster was contracted to teach girls for two hours a day but only after the boys were dismissed. Thus, while the Massachusetts Bay Colony had the most "progressive" educational laws in the colonies, girls typically did not participate fully in this great educational experiment. Only by the end of the colonial period was it generally seen as "acceptable" for girls to attend school.[13]

While New England struggled with the idea of allowing girls in schools (especially to learn to write), the Quakers, as we have seen, often included girls in their schools from the earliest settlement. In 1685 Thomas Budd laid out an educational plan for Pennsylvania and New Jersey that included the education of both boys and girls, taught separately, with slightly different curriculums: boys learned to read, write, and cipher while girls learned to read, write, and sew! This emphasis on the more "practical" aspects of female education would continue throughout colonial times.[14]

Because of widespread cultural opposition to the education of women, female literacy was low throughout the colonial period. And even when young girls did receive an education, it was usually limited to the basics. Susan B. Anthony for example, recalled that when her father, Daniel Anthony, sent her and two sisters to the district school in New York, the schoolmaster refused to teach them long division! He stubbornly argued that this was an unnecessary skill for women, who would be better served by learning how to cook, sew, and clean house.[15]

Notwithstanding Susan B. Anthony's conservative schoolmaster, by the time of the American Revolution a distinctive change was in the air. Women as well as men had been transformed by the spirit of Enlightenment and the excitement of liberty, freedom, and democracy. As these ideas permeated colonial American society in the mid 1700s, the level of female literacy gradually began to increase. As the revolutionary fervor spread throughout the colonies during the late 1770s, women and men were drawn headlong into the exciting events of the day. Now more than ever it seemed natural for women to be able to read and write in order to assume responsible "republican motherhood" and to help nurture those revolutionary ideas in their sons. Gradually the prohibition against the education of women waned and at the same time women became more assertive in demanding equal educational opportunities.[16]

In the years following the Revolution through the early 1800s, six "female academies" were established to provide a viable secondary education for women. One of the most important of these was the Young Ladies Academy of Philadelphia, founded in 1787. This academy was the first publicly incorporated institution in the nation and was established to teach "Young Ladies in Reading, Writing, Arithmetic, English Grammar, Composition, Rhetoric and Geography." Their progress was monitored by a board of "gentlemen Visitors" who examined the "Ladies" and awarded prizes based on their achievement. The academy drew students from all over the new nation and soon demonstrated that women were as capable as men even in a rigorous academic environment.[17]

Teacher Education for Women

While the Young Ladies Academy was important in establishing the idea of rigorous education for women, two other institutions, established in the early 1800s, would begin a tradition of teacher training for women. These two institutions were Emma Willard's Troy Female Seminary and Mary Lyons' Mt. Holyoke Female Seminary. The Troy Female seminary, established in 1821, not only provided women with an academic education but also was the first to offer comprehensive instruction in teaching. In fact, the Troy Seminary was turning out well-trained teachers decades before the first "normal school" was opened in Lexington, Massachusetts, in July of 1839. By 1863 it has been estimated that the seminary had trained and "sent out to teach" nearly six hundred teachers.[18]

Mary Lyons opened her Mt. Holyoke Seminary in 1837 and admitted eighty female students. Among her more innovative ideas was to create an institution comparable to men's colleges. This was achieved through rigorous entrance examinations, minimum-age entrance requirements, and a curriculum that required seven courses in science and mathematics for graduation. Lyons also used written compositions and lectures as the basis of instruction. Many of her graduates became common-schoolteachers and she also encouraged her graduates to enter the sciences and become college teachers and researchers, to "go where no one else will go and do what no one else will do." Her innovations were unheard of at any other female instititon at the time but within a generation, hers would become the model of women's education throughout the country.[19]

By the middle of the 1800s, the pioneering work of Emma Willard, Mary Lyons, and hundreds of other educators throughout the country was having a positive effect on the acceptance of female education. By then, most communities in the North had opened their schoolhouse doors to girls, and nearly two hundred private schools for women and female academies had been established. In fact, by the beginning of the American Civil War, between 60 and 70 percent of young children attended some school and with some exceptions, girls attended at about the same rate as boys. Thus, while primary education was far from universal during these years, the majority of young white girls in Northern states were receiving some formal education in common schools. This of course had a dramatic effect on women entering the teaching profession because it provided school districts with increasing numbers of educated, ambitious, and clearly underemployed young women who could teach.[20]

Wages of Women Teachers

Beyond the growing numbers of women available to teach, perhaps the most important reason that educational reformers supported their employment was money. As states like New York, Pennsylvania, and Massachusetts embraced some form of "universal" common schooling, the costs of this idealistic experiment soon became apparent. Unfortunately most local school districts were unwilling to pay for good teachers (some things never seem to change). Moreover, as wages rose slowly from the 1840s through the end of the Civil War in 1865 and as new occupational opportunities for men expanded the problem became more acute. It was more and more difficult to contract male schoolteachers, much less keep them for more than a term (if they lasted that long) at what amounted to subsistence wages.

Alanzo Potter, the great pedagogue, certainly recognized this problem. In his *The School and the School Master*, he bristled at the pathetic parsimony of local school districts regarding teacher pay. He noted that they wanted the best teachers available "provided . . . they are the cheapest."

These attitudes, he felt, were largely responsible for the rapid turnover of male schoolmasters and a growing difficulty in securing qualified teachers. In his *The District School as It Was*, for example, Warren Burton noted that during the 1820s and 1830s, he had a different schoolmaster each year, some of whom did not even complete the term. Each of his schoolmasters had a completely different teaching style, used different books, and initiated a different curriculum. And of course, the quality of their teaching varied dramatically.[21]

The lack of consistency of curriculum and continuity among teachers was recognized as a critical problem by many educational reformers of the day. For Potter and others the ideal solution to this predicament was to have schools "taught by a female" year round, which would "give scholars the advantage of having the same instructress throughout . . . the year." Moreover, as Potter noted (perhaps quietly gritting his teeth) the use of female teachers "would be a cheap system." With these five magic words, he struck a chord that would resonate throughout American society and help women enter the classrooms of the nation.[22]

By examining the salary figures compiled by educational reformer Randolph Burgess, we can see that women teachers clearly were a "cheap system." During this period, rural women teachers earned 35 to 40 percent less than male teachers, while women teachers in cities earned about 63 to 67 less than male counterparts. Not only were women teachers' wages lower than those of men, but they were at the subsistence level. In the countryside, for example, women teachers were paid about $2.50 per week in the early 1840s while a common laborer earned about $4.80 per week—a wage roughly half that of the wages of the lowest-paid male worker. By the end of the Civil War, rural women teachers were earning more money per week but still 40 percent less than unskilled common laborers did. On the other hand, "highly paid" women teachers in cities still made 31 cents less per week than unskilled laborers. Even when we consider the fact that some women teachers had the "privilege" of boarding in the community usually at a reduced rate, their wages were absurdly low.[23]

Discipline

One final argument against the use of female teachers remained: discipline. How could "timid and delicate women . . . retain charge . . . in a school [where] large and rude boys are congregated?" The ultimate answer to that question was rooted in the profound changes in discipline that had been transforming child rearing for more than a hundred years (see chapter 8 for a more comprehensive discussion of discipline in the classroom).

In the century and a half since John Locke first introduced his revolutionary ideas concerning child rearing in *Some Thoughts Concerning Education*, British and American parents had slowly begun to "spare the rod" and embrace a more rational, psychological approach to discipline. As Locke noted, physical discipline was the "lazy and short way of government [and] the most unfit of any to be used in education." Rather, Locke recommended early vigorous training of children and the development of rational attitudes. He favored a disciplinary regime that included praise for achievement and good behavior coupled with shame and humiliation for failure and poor deportment.[24]

These new ideas gradually were incorporated into "childrens" literature during the mid-1700s. John Newbery's popular *Little Pretty Pocket Book*, for example, demonstrated to children that hard work and achievement were rewarded with success in business while "slovency" often resulted in humiliation. By the early 1800s, Joseph Lancaster had shown quite effectively that the Lockean approach to discipline worked well. In his famous Borough School in England, and later in a number of monitorial schools in this country, Lancaster (with the help of his youthful monitors) taught as many as 350 pupils in one enormous classroom. Lancaster rejected the use of the whipping post and rod in favor of incentives of praise (and prizes) as well as humiliation (like having your hands washed by a girl in front of the class) as powerful methods of both instruction and discipline."[25]

Thus, by the early 1800s, these new ideas were gradually being accepted by middle-class families in both urban and rural communities throughout the United States. Older, traditional attitudes toward discipline that had seen children conceived in original sin, and sometimes requiring physical punishment to be saved, were being abandoned. More and more Americans agreed with Locke that the child's mind was innocent and malleable, like "[f]ountains of some rivers . . . where the gentle application of the hand turns the flexible water in channels that make them take quite contrary courses."[26]

Most educational reformers of this period clearly understood this important shift in disciplinary attitudes and often used it as an argument to support female teachers. Alanzo Potter for example, was convinced that a female teacher could effectively handle a classroom of young and unruly boys. For him, the days of the rod and whipping post as the primary means of discipline were at an end. He argued that "in the government of schools moral influence should be substituted as far as possible, in place of mere coercion [and] women are in most respects, preeminently qualified to administer such discipline."[27]

Urbanization

Finally, the growth of cities during the 1800s helped women enter the classrooms of the nation. Although women teachers were becoming more common in *commercial* agricultural regions throughout the country, women provided the core of teachers in city schools. By the late 1800s, for example, about one-third of all teachers in the countryside were female, but 90 percent of all teachers in cities were women. Educational historians Myra Strober and David Tyack have noted that the dramatic rise of women in teaching was associated with urbanization because in rural areas women had higher economic utility and "a daughter's domestic service [was] more highly valued. . . ." Similarly, Strober and Langford have noted that in less developed areas of the country, economic development had been slower and as a result, women were more likely to remain in their domestic sphere. "Rural and southern women were likely to be involved in home production and less available for many types of work outside the home, including teaching, than their urban and northern sisters."[28]

As we can recall from chapter 1, by the end of the 1800s cities had begun to adopt graded schools, longer school years, and larger, more bureaucratized administrative systems. Each of these factors helped women enter the teaching field. In graded schools, women teachers could avoid extreme disciplinary problems by sending unruly students to a male principal. Women teachers, moreover, were seen as ideally suited to the more formalized structured curriculum of the urban school. As Strober and Langford have noted, "Officials believed that women teachers would be much more compliant in carrying out centralized direction."[29]

Similarly, as the curriculum and administration of the urban common school became more centralized, men began to leave the profession. As schools adopted the bureaucratic form of organization, certification requirements were often directed by the state or municipality rather than the local districts (much less the trustee). School years often were extended, and many men were not willing to teach year round because they could not supplement their low salaries with seasonal occupations like farming. In fact, for many men, this had been the appeal of teaching in the first place.

In Iowa, for example, when reformers mandated longer school terms and compulsory attendance at summer teacher institutes, men abandoned teaching. In 1874 Iowa passed a school law designed to improve public education in the state. The law mandated that counties offer summer training institutes for teachers and required "educators to attend these sessions at their own expense." These institutes could last as long as four weeks and would interfere with alternative employment opportunities. As a result, from 1874 to 1890 the number of new male teachers declined by about 14 percent while the number of new female teachers more than doubled. In short, as the graded school took hold in American cities, the number of women teachers increased significantly.[30]

THE MARKET REVOLUTION AND WOMEN TEACHERS

Women entered the teaching profession not just because demand for them to teach had increased; something much more fundamental was at work here. In addition to these important factors, the market revolution of the late 1700s and 1800s helped to transform women's lives, changing the way they perceived themselves and, in turn, how others perceived them. This fundamental transformation encouraged women to improve themselves, to embrace social and occupational mobility; and for many, it helped them to shatter the traditional patriarchal bonds that had rooted them in the domestic sphere.

In other words, beyond the powerful forces that *pulled* women into teaching were those factors that were *pushing* women into this new, modern profession. Women succeeded in dominating the teaching profession not simply because men decided it was no longer worthwhile for them to "keep school." Women fought for their jobs. They struggled for their positions and eventually they won them. Clearly the growing demand for women teachers would have had little impact on the entrance of women into the profession if most had wanted to remain at home and maintain their traditional place within the household.

Similarly, if these women had refused to make the personal sacrifices of loneliness and separation from loved ones and family through migration, as well as suffer the daily indignities of teaching difficult children, dealing with capricious parents and school boards, cleaning and maintaining rundown schools, and boarding in what often was a very hostile environment, schoolteaching might have remained the domain of men. Yet hundreds of thousands of young women made these difficult decisions and eagerly entered the teaching profession.

Just how did the market revolution trigger these changes? There are at least two answers to this question. First, women who grew up in the early 1800s were profoundly changed by the consumer revolution and the rise of materialism during these years. Second, the intellectual foundations of the market revolution unleashed the latent promise of personal freedom, equality, and choice based on the presumptions of the meritocratic society. In short, the emerging marketplace provided both the material and intellectual basis of social equality and mobility for women.

Consumerism and Materialism

Women in cities were the first to be affected by these dramatic changes. As older forms of economic production were replaced by the factory system, and as hundreds of new industries grew in size and structure, a new middle class with disposable income began to emerge in America. There had always been a small number of Americans who were able to purchase consumer goods but as a result of the industrial revolution, that number soared. By the 1830s this new middle class joined merchants, proprietors, and professionals to create a large consumer class demanding more and more products from farm and factory. These were not wealthy people but their spending had a dramatic impact in creating the urban consumer society of the 1800s.

This economic expansion was not limited to American cities, however. America's enormous countryside was also growing economically and experiencing its own consumer revolution. During the middle decades of the 1800s many northern rural communities experienced the first "Golden Age of Agriculture." In the years preceding the Civil War, the prices of agricultural commodities rose significantly. The dramatic growth of cities (especially inland industrial cities) during these years increased the demand, and therefore the prices, of farm products. As canals and railroads reached well into the agricultural hinterland, farmers were able to transport their products to coastal areas for export abroad, to new settlements in the West, and to the specialized plantations in the South. These were exciting times.[31]

Meanwhile, as profits increased, many Northern farmers were able to purchase the vast array of consumer products that had become available. During the 1850s and 1860s, for example, the number of manufacturing establishments and industrial workers in the United States more than doubled while the value added through manufacturing tripled. This helped to flood the market with thousands of new, cheap consumer products from cotton cloth, shoes, pins and needles, and matches to grandfather clocks, cotton mattresses, paint, varnish, and sewing machines. As the great agricultural historians Percy Bidwell and John Falconer noted, "The wants of the farm family were expanding rapidly . . . the farmer's daughters wanted better clothes and pianos like those of their city cousins." The consumer age had dawned![32]

This growing consumerism among American men and women was a central component of the emerging market revolution. As demand for manufactured consumer products soared and prices tumbled, thousands were drawn into the consumer society. Even the venerable Alexis de Tocqueville (author of *Democracy in America*) recognized the unique power of the consumer society, noting that as men and women tasted the fruits of their labor they became "eager to increase the means of satisfying these tastes more completely."[33]

Many a young woman in the North had begun to recognize that in order to obtain a new dress, a hat, some books, or any of a thousand other cheap material goods, she must have cash. And many saw teaching as one of the few ways to acquire that cash. This is not to suggest that women teachers in the mid-1800s were "born to shop," but simply that their growing consumerism was drawing them headlong into the market revolution.

When Sarah Ann Gue completed her teaching responsibilities for the winter term in April of 1848, she went with her brother Benjamin to collect her pay. In just two hours hence she had managed to spend virtually everything she had earned! Her brother recorded Sara Ann's shopping spree of Friday April 21, 1848 in his diary. He wrote that it was "warm and pleasant" and about noon he took his mother and Sarah Ann to "Palmyra on a trading expedition." They arrived about one o'clock and during the next two hours Sarah Ann "bought a new dress, a carpet, a looking glass, a bureau and a setee, the whole of which cost $18½, [and] after buying a lot of trumpery [they] went home."[34]

Sarah Ann had taught an entire term to earn her first pay as a teacher and in a whirlwind "trading expedition" she spent it all. While this may not have been the experience of all mid-1800 schoolteachers, the ritualistic "shopping spree" following payday certainly was not uncommon then—nor is it now.

By embracing the simple material logic of the market revolution, women began to change. They began to recognize that through their own hard work and determination they could make something of themselves, purchase a few things, and at the same time elevate their social position. Thus, while women schoolteachers of this era typically had a strong, idealistic (sometimes evangelical) commitment to nurturing and teaching young children, they also were upwardly mobile and ambitious.

Intellectual Foundations of the Market Revolution

The critical link between growing consumerism and upward mobility was a powerful one, and provides us with one explanation of why thousands of young women assertively sought teaching jobs in the 1800s. Yet beyond the material basis of the market economy was a set of intellectual assumptions that also appealed to many women and helped them enter teaching. These included the promise of individual freedom, equality, and choice. The basis of these assumptions was the meritocratic society.

The market revolution that transformed America during these years meant much more than being able to buy "a lot of trumpery," as Benjamin

Gue called it. It meant a fundamental restructuring of the norms of society itself. In an earlier time, the basis of power and authority was rooted in family position and gender and reinforced through a time-honored system of deference (accepting the idea that some individuals had permanently higher status than your own). In the absence of clear avenues of social and occupational mobility, a young man's position within society was usually derived from his family. Similarly, a young women's place in society, in most cases, was a function of her father's status and, after marriage, of her husband's. Of course, there were cases of upward (and downward) mobility in traditional society but these were relatively rare—that is, until the market revolution.

The market revolution changed the basis of social position from *who one was* to *what one did*. While one's family's position continued to help define social and occupational status, the possibility of upward mobility as a product of individual action had become a reality as well; for women that *possibility* was important, and very exciting. If a woman's social status was no longer completely dependent on the social position of others, namely her father or her husband, then women, like men, were free to choose and free to achieve as individuals.[35]

Of course, most women recognized that they still lacked the political freedom that guaranteed these basic, individual rights. Moreover, most women would maintain some degree of deference within the traditional patriarchal order and continue to derive much of their social status from their fathers and husbands. But the doors had been opened, if only slightly, and the view on the other side was exciting indeed.

Race and Ethnicity in the Teaching Profession

People of color and those of ethnic origins faced different problems than women, but in many ways they, too, were able to enter the teaching profession because of a growing demand for their services and fundamental changes in society's attitudes toward them. From the colonial period through the 1800s African Americans and ethnic minorities often were barred from teaching because of widespread cultural and legal prohibitions. However, in segregated schools and in private and parochial institutions, these men and women taught in obscurity. Only in recent years have they begun to enter the public schools in significant numbers. This achievement has not come easily, and has required decades of struggle against prejudice and misunderstanding. This is the story of that struggle.

AFRICAN-AMERICAN TEACHERS

As we have seen in chapter 2, the education of African-American children during the colonial period was sporadic at best and as might be expected, only a handful of blacks taught. While some African Americans did receive an education in "public" institutions during this period, most of these "experiments" were initiated by religious institutions. The Church of England (Anglicans), for example, established the Society for the Propagation of the Gospel in Foreign Parts in 1696 to help "Christianize" slaves in the colonies. In that year they dispatched Thomas Bray to Maryland to establish a school for the children of black slaves. About the same time, the Reverend Samuel Thomas of Goose Creek, South Carolina, established a school for black children and adults. And later, in 1755, Hugh Bryan, a progressive Presbyterian, established a school for slaves in Virginia.[1]

While these schools had an impact on the education of black slaves, the most successful of these colonial educational experiments, in terms of sheer numbers, was a school for African Americans established in 1704 in New York City. In that year Elias Neau, a French immigrant, began teaching slaves in his home. By 1708 he had moved the school to New York's Trinity Church as the enrollment reached 200 slaves. Neau died in 1722 but the Trinity Church school continued its mission for nearly fifty years, until 1770.[2]

The Quakers, however, were the most aggressive in providing for the education of African-American slaves and free blacks during the colonial period. The famous teacher Anthony Benezet, a Quaker, for example, opened a successful Negro school in Philadelphia in 1772. The following year Quakers in Rhode Island established a reading and writing school for "colored" children, and in 1798 the Boston Friends established another "colored" school supervised by Elisher Sylvester. Finally, as discussed in chapter 3, the African Free School was established by Quakers in New York City in 1787. In addition to these segregated schools the Quakers were the first to allow black and white children to attend school together. This tradition began in Pennsylvania and New Jersey after the Revolution and quickly spread to most of the Northern states by the early 1800s.[3]

Racial prejudice against African Americans, however, was the ever-present counterpoint to most educational experiments in the North and South. Some black schools were closed by law, while others had to endure mob violence and harassment from the white community. Such was the case at Prudence Crandall's private school in Canterbury, Connecticut. In 1831 Crandall established a private school for girls, and shortly thereafter she admitted a black girl. The reaction of the community to this move was swift and violent. First, her neighbors threatened her and the school, and when that failed, to move Crandall white parents withdrew their daughters from the school. Although Crandall was forced to close that school, a few years later she established an institution for girls of "color." When her enrollment of "colored girls" reached fifteen, however, the community once again reacted with threats of violence and at a public meeting they threatened to close the school. Although these threats did not work, within a few months Connecticut passed a "black law" that made illegal "the establish[ment] of any school for the education of non-resident blacks" or "teach[ing] in any such school." Crandall resisted the law, was arrested and jailed, and her house was mysteriously destroyed by fire. When she was released, Crandall left town and abandoned her dream of a school for black children. While not all black schools and teachers of black students were subjected to this kind of intimidation, violence, and legal maneuvering, Prudence Crandall's experiences were not uncommon in the antebellum North. We must remember that not all Northerners had abolitionist sympathies, and despite the relatively small numbers of blacks living north of the Mason-Dixon line there was widespread prejudice against African Americans throughout this period.[4]

Considering the importance of slavery to the southern plantation system, it's no wonder that attitudes toward black education in the South were even less tolerant. As we have seen, while many planters encouraged their slaves to learn a trade or develop a skill that would be useful to the plantation economy, there was a widespread belief in the intellectual inferiority of African Americans. (These attitudes were also prevalent in the North.) Even those who advocated equal access to education often argued that it was not in the best interest of the slaves to receive an "academic" education. Many others simply felt it was dangerous to educate blacks for fear of a slave insurrection. That fear seemed to be realized in the bloody Denmark Vesey and Nat Turner rebellions beginning in the early 1820s. In the wake of these rebellions most Southern states passed restrictive laws that denied blacks access to any form of education.[5]

"Clandestine" Schools

While the education of black slaves often was prohibited by state laws, there were "clandestine" schools throughout the South that brought the rudiments of education to slaves. Moreover, these schools typically were taught by African Americans themselves. One of the first historians to chronicle this sort of teaching among slaves was Carter Woodson. By examining scattered plantation records and oral histories, he documented numerous cases of black slaves who taught in obscurity prior to the Civil War. Julian Froumountaine, for example, taught in a slave school beginning in 1819. When legal prohibitions against the education of slaves were passed in 1830, the school simply went "underground" and operated secretly. Woodson also documented that in the early 1800s a Miss DeaVeaux taught children and adults to read. She continued these secret activities for more than twenty-five years, unbeknownst to her master and the white community. Milla Granson was another example of a black slave who went on to teach other slaves in the early 1800s. Granson was taught to read and write by her master's children and later was granted permission to teach other slaves on the plantation. When she was sold to a Mississippi plantation owner, she taught "midnight" classes off a back alley in Natchez, Mississippi, and later established a "Sabbath school." As a result of these efforts, hundreds of slaves were educated.[6]

Through the work of Julian Froumontaine, Miss DeaVeaux, Milla Granson, and countless other African-American teachers, thousands of slaves received the rudiments of education. Teaching in secrecy, they not only brought literacy to an enslaved people but forced open the doors of schoolhouses, if only slightly, to allow black teachers into the nation's classrooms.

A Veritable Fever: Education during Reconstruction

The turning point for African-American education and teaching began during the Civil War and then picked up momentum with the establishment of the Freedmen's Bureau schools during Reconstruction. As we have seen in chapter 2, these efforts provided a primary education for many black children and adults, as thousands of schools for the education of former African-American slaves were opened. By the end of Reconstruction, the literacy rate among African Americans had increased significantly.

Although the foundation of primary education was being laid in the South, most reformers recognized that only through the establishment of black teacher-training institutes could the goal of equality for African-American schools be achieved. In response to this critical need, Freedmen's Bureau schools, philanthropists, missionary groups, black self-help groups, and other organizations established numerous African-American "normal training schools" during this period. These schools not only provided African Americans with their first real chance of entering the classroom as professional teachers, but also assured the continued growth of black education when Reconstruction ended in 1877.

Immediately following the war, for example, the Freedmen's Bureau, working in conjunction with Northern churches, established teacher training schools such as Fisk, Tugaloo, and Atlanta Universities. Within a few years philanthropist George Peabody established a fund of $1 million to be used for education in the South, especially for the training of black teachers. Other groups like the American Missionary Association and the Philadelphia Freedmen's Relief Association would also have a major impact on black teacher training. The American Missionary Association, for example, established twenty-one normal teacher-training schools in the South in the late 1860s and 1870s, while the Philadelphia group established an important normal and industrial school for the training of black teachers in Washington, D.C.[7]

At the same time, a number of African-American self-help groups also were formed to aid in the training of black teachers. Among the first of these was the African Civilization Society, which through its own fund raising and the aid of the Freedmen's Bureau, established schools in a number of Southern states and helped train 129 black teachers over the next decade.[8]

Prejudice in the Freedmen's Bureau School

While the great promise of teaching was held out to African Americans, the struggle for equal opportunity and respect as professionals was elusive. Freedmen's Bureau schools and other charitable institutions of this era did hire black teachers, but white teachers often were chosen over blacks to teach in these schools. This was because of the lack of teacher-training institutions for blacks in the North as well as generalized racial prejudice, even among the most ardent abolitionists.

As we have seen, during the antebellum period (1800–1861) African Americans typically were denied even the rudiments of education, much less a normal school or college education. As late as 1861, for example, Oberlin College in Ohio was one of the few institutions that admitted blacks (and women). Racial prejudice also acted as a barrier to blacks who wanted to teach in Freedmen's Bureau schools. The applications of many educated African Americans were routinely denied by both bureau offi-cials and groups like the American Missionary Association, who sent thou-sands of teachers south during Reconstruction.

Some African-American teaching applications were rejected because they had little or no teacher training, but it is also clear that many well-qualified applicants were rejected as well. Charlotte Forten, for example, had an extensive formal education including a course of study at the Salem State Normal School in Massachusetts, where she also taught. Charlotte got the runaround before her request was formally denied by the Boston chapter of the American Missionary Association. She then applied in her hometown of Philadelphia with a recommendation from the noted author John Greenleaf Whittier, and was finally accepted.[9]

When African-American teachers reached their assigned schools in the South however, they also experienced prejudice from their administra-tors and white teachers. Sara Stanley and Edmonice Highgate, for exam-ple, wrote several letters to officials in the American Missionary Association complaining that many qualified black teachers were being sent to what they saw as "undesirable locations" such as small, rural, pri-mary schools. Prime assignments in urban schools typically were reserved for white teachers. And even when qualified black teachers were assigned to city schools, they often became assistants under the direction of white teachers. Thus, while Freedmen's Bureau schools provided blacks with their first real teaching opportunities in "public schools," black teachers still had to fight to achieve equality in the classroom.[10]

Private Black Schools

The solution for some black teachers was to establish their own private schools, but here too they faced many difficulties. The lives of Lucy Laney and Mary McLeod Bethune illustrate these problems but also demonstrate how persistence can sometimes lead to success. Laney was born into slavery in 1854 in Macon, Georgia. She was taught to read by the sister of a plan-tation owner and later she received her primary and secondary education in Freedmen's Bureau schools. She then enrolled in Atlanta University, where she graduated first in her class. She began her teaching career in Savannah, Georgia, and later, through her persistent efforts, she was sponsored by the Presbyterian Mission Board to open her own school. She then garnered financial support from her white benefactor, F. H. Haines, and named the school in her honor. The school opened in 1886 and soon enrolled over two hundred black children. By 1915 Laney had educated hundreds of black children in both elementary and secondary grades and employed twenty-two black teachers.[11]

Mary McLeod Bethune, another pioneer in African-American education, was born Mary McLeod in 1875 in Mayesville, South Carolina, the daughter of former slaves. At the age of seven she enrolled in the Trinity Christian Mission School and daily walked five miles each way to receive her education. By the time she was ten, McLeod had graduated and was awarded a tuition scholarship to attend what later would become Barber-Scotia College. To earn her room and board, she cleaned the school and did laundry. Following her course of study, she traveled to Chicago, where she attended Moody Bible Institute.[12]

Armed with a comprehensive education in both teaching and religious studies, McLeod began her career as a teacher in 1896 at the age of 21. She taught in a number of elementary schools and within a few years she married Albertus Bethune, an idealistic black schoolmaster. Together they moved to Florida and established the Daytona Normal and Industrial Institute for Negro Girls, which was quite successful and trained hundreds of black teachers over the next decades. In 1923 the school merged with another institution to become the Bethune-Cookman College. Mary Bethune then became president of the school and served in that capacity for over forty years.[13]

Both Laney and Bethune demonstrated remarkable strength and bravery in the face of racism in both the North and South. Their persistent vision would help to secure the foundations of black teacher education that had been established during Reconstruction. Although there was much left to be done, hundreds of African-American teachers like these two women helped to fuel a black educational revolution: in 1860 only about 3 percent of all black children ages five through nineteen had attended school (and this was primarily in a handful of southern cities and in the north); by 1880, that number had soared to over 33 percent.[14]

Jim Crow and Education: The Early Endowments

The revolution in black education stalled by the turn of the twentieth century, however. The dramatic rise in school attendance among African-American children during Reconstruction had leveled off, and even declined slightly to about 30 percent by 1900. In the face of persistent prejudice and a racist system of segregation, the great promise of black education during Reconstruction now seemed little more than a dream. In response to this growing problem, a number of philanthropic funds were created to encourage African-American and teacher education.

The first of these was the Slater/Peabody Fund. While not a new fund (it was originally established in 1880 and then expanded by the remnants of the Peabody endowment), its mission had been enlarged in 1911 by James Hardy Dillard to create secondary teacher-training schools for African Americans. By 1915 the fund had established eight such schools, and by 1929 nearly four hundred schools were supported by this fund.[15]

The second major endowment to aid African-American teacher education was established by Julius Rosenwald, head of Sears and Roebuck. Rosenwald was a generous, liberal-minded man who like many at that time was repulsed by the racism that pervaded society. Early in the century, Booker T. Washington had invited Rosenwald to his Tuskegee Institute and as a result of that visit Rosenwald pledged $5,000 to the school. Later, when Washington took Rosenwald on a tour of rural Alabama black schools, he was able to secure a pledge from him to help improve black education. That pledge, as it eventually evolved, required that individual communities match the funds that he provided. Although the plan was criticized by some (notably W. E. B. DuBois, who called it a "second tax" on African Americans) these funds did help to build five thousand teachers' homes and "Rosenwald schools" throughout the South. Later the fund was directed more toward teacher education and helped establish "university centers" in Washington, D.C. Atlanta Nashville and New Orleans.[16]

Even before the Rosenwald endowment was created, Anna Jeanes, a Quaker from Philadelphia, had established a fund of $200,000 to help educate black children in the South. She stipulated, however, that this money would be administered by Hollis Frissel, principal of the Hampton Institute, and Booker T. Washington of the Tuskegee Institute. These funds not only energized the training of teachers in the South, but because of Washington's philosophy of "vocational" education for blacks helped direct the nature of black teaching for the next two decades.

The Jeanes plan was very simple: exemplary teachers would be trained under the vocational philosophy of Booker T. Washington, and would then be assigned to remote schools throughout the South to assist teachers and serve as role models. Typically, Jeanes teachers encouraged vocational training and "domestic education" so that students could get a job once they completed their education. By 1930 it was estimated that over three hundred such teachers were working in rural schoolhouses throughout the South.[17]

The General Education Board

While the Peabody/Slater Fund and the Rosenwald and Jeanes endowments, as well as a host of other smaller funds, had a dramatic impact on the development of African-American teacher education during these years, the work of the General Education Board was also very important. The General Education Board was established by a congressional act in 1903 as a kind of clearinghouse for Northern philanthropic funds earmarked for the education of both black and white children in the South. Its creation was the result of the work of a group of reformers and philanthropists from the Southern Education Board, including Robert C. Ogden, George Peabody, and William H. Baldwin.[18]

Through the work of these three men and a host of others, including North Carolina's Walter Hines Page, the General Education Board gained the cooperation and generous donations of John D. Rockefeller Jr. Rockefeller's initial gift of $1 million dollars to the board grew quickly and by the end of the 1920s it had become a sizable endowment. This money was used for public schools and teacher education throughout the South.[19]

Equally important was the General Education Board's role as a kind of educational trust during these years. Eventually the board gained the cooperation (and sometimes the control) of most of the major philanthropic funds and in that capacity it inspected schools and monitored both funding requirements and educational progress.[20]

Booker T. Washington and W. E. B. Dubois

The Peabody/ Slater, Rosenwald, Rockefeller, and Jeanes endowments (as well as the work of the General Education Board) were the most important of the philanthropic funds established by liberal whites during the early 1900s to deal with the appalling lack of African-American teacher-training institutions in the South. While these endowments had an important effect on the state of black education, each in its own way reinforced a teaching model that emphasized vocational training rather than classical education. This model, championed by Booker T. Washington, was embraced by early-twentieth-century white reformers as a "safe" avenue of education. Blacks were to learn marketable skills in order to assimilate into (some would say "serve") white society. A classical education, on the other hand, was seen as dangerous and misguided. In his famous Atlanta Exposition address of 1895, for example, Washington noted that an academic education simply gave black children promises that could not be fulfilled. He made this point with reference to a young man who had just graduated from high school, who, "sitting down in a one room cabin, with grease on his clothing, filth all around him, and weeds in the yard and garden, engaged in studying French grammar."

Most white liberals of this period agreed and supported Washington. His idea was simple: in a nation built on slavery and racial segregation, blacks must work hard and get an industrial education in order to achieve a place in society. In this way, whites would be appeased and blacks could slowly climb the occupational ladder. In fact, for Washington, the way to improve the economic condition of African Americans in the South was clear. He emplored white entrepreneurs to "cast down your buckets where you are" and employ vocationally trained black workers.[21]

The counterargument, of course, was that if African Americans were "tracked" into vocational occupations through industrial education they would never be able to compete with whites for higher paying jobs and would permanently be locked into positions as common laborers or in menial service occupations. This argument was made most energetically by W. E. B. DuBois, the Harvard-trained historian and one of the founders of the NAACP. DuBois's philosophy of black education was one of confrontation rather than appeasement. He argued that education should disturb the status quo and not maintain it. Only through a rigorous academic education would blacks be able to rise to the educational level of whites and take responsible positions of leadership in industry, education, and politics.[22]

During the first two decades of the 1900s DuBois' ideas were not well received by the black community. But eventually the tide would turn. As we have seen in chapter 2, from the 1920s through the 1960s, African Americans began to demand more from the society in which they lived. As a result, the philosophies of appeasement and segregation gave way to notions of black pride, equality, and integration. The vision of W. E. B. DuBois gradually became the accepted model of education for African Americans.[23]

Self-Help Organizations: NATCS and the NAACP

DuBois's vision took decades to realize and resulted from the persistent work of black teacher organizations and the tenacity of individual black teachers. Among the most important of these organizations was the National Association of Teachers of Colored Schools (NATCS) formed in 1907. As might be expected, black teachers had traditionally been isolated and alienated from the National Education Association. As a result, they established the NATCS in order to improve black education. This new group began a vigorous campaign to reform the curriculum of black schools, and they called for increased salaries, improved teacher education, longer school terms, and better equipment, supplies, and facilities. They consistently argued that low teacher salaries were a major impediment to hiring and retaining competent black teachers. In early-twentieth-century

North Carolina, for example, they demonstrated that black teachers earned less than $20 per month, while in other parts of the South it was not uncommon for black teachers to earn as little as $10 per month.[24]

As a result of these abysmally low salaries, black educators often were forced to draw on the unbridled idealism of new black teachers. Fanny Jackson Coppin, for example, head of the Institute for Colored Youth in Philadelphia, continually tried to instill a kind of missionary zeal among her graduates. She urged her teachers to bring education to even the most remote regions of the country, noting, "The very places you are needed most are those where you will get paid the least. Do not resign a position in the South which pays you $12 a month . . . for one in Philadelphia which pays $50." This, of course, was a difficult path to follow.[25]

The NAACP also fought for equity in teachers salaries during this period. Beginning in the 1930s they initiated over thirty-five lawsuits demanding equal pay for black teachers. By 1941 nearly half of these suits had been settled in their favor. At the same time, the NAACP fought against segregation in public schools as a way to improve black education and achieve equal pay for black teachers. As we saw in chapter 2, the capstone of their efforts in this area was the favorable ruling by the Supreme Court in *Brown v. Board of Education of Topeka* in 1954.

Encouraged by this landmark ruling, building on the persistent work of the NATCS and NAACP and energized by decades of struggle for civil rights, both black education and the position of black teachers have slowly improved. Since 1900 the number of black children attending school has steadily increased. By 1930 the percentage of African-American children attending school had doubled to about 60 percent and by the mid-1950s that percentage reached 80 percent. Throughout the years of the civil rights movement and into the 1980s these numbers continued to climb, and today have reached the level of white children, at about 90 percent. Gains in teacher pay equity have paralleled these dramatic improvements.

Yet problems continue. In recent years a number of states have abandoned their commitment to affirmative action to recruit black teachers. Moreover, in their rush to improve the educational credentials of new teachers through more testing and stricter licensure requirements, the number of African Americans entering teaching has declined. Today only 8 percent of teachers are African American, despite the growing numbers of black students in the classroom. In short, while there has been some success in black education and teaching since the early days of Reconstruction, that success is bittersweet. There is still much more to do as America enters a third educational transition.

ETHNIC AND CULTURALLY DIVERSE TEACHERS
IN THE COLONIAL ERA

While the struggle of African-American teachers to enter the classrooms of the nation has been a monumental one, it has paralleled in many ways the story of ethnic/immigrant teachers over the years. From colonial times to the present day, ethnic minorities who have immigrated to America from all over the world have taught in variety of religious, private, and language schools. They also have struggled, with limited success, to enter the public school classrooms of the nation.

As we have seen, during America's colonial period the vast majority of schools had a religious and cultural orientation. The Dutch Reformed Church of New Amsterdam, for example, established schools in each of the original nine towns of the colony and hired Dutch-speaking teachers who also served as minor church officials. These early teachers were men, chosen because of their piety as well as their intellectual abilities. In addition to their teaching duties, they often read Scriptures during Sunday services, presided over the offering, maintained the grounds, and even rang the church bells.[26]

Quaker Teachers

Quakers were also quite active in education. They established an apprenticeship system for teachers that is considered America's first system of teacher education and also "licensed" teachers before allowing them to enter the classroom. This system was strictly enforced; colonial records show, for example, that Thomas Meking was censured by the Quaker Council of Philadelphia for teaching at a school without a license.[27]

As a result of both training and licensing, Quaker teachers were often quite capable and were typically able to instruct children in reading, writing, arithmetic, and bookkeeping as well as religion. Like other religious schools, the Quakers hired pious church officials as their teachers or in smaller communities expected the local minister to teach the children. In larger towns and cities like Philadelphia, on the other hand, teachers often were hired from other colonies or from Europe. The famous William Penn Charter School, for example, recruited teachers from outside the colony, such as Francis Pastorius, who taught the classics. Still, in all cases these male teachers were expected to be God-fearing members of the church.[28]

The Quaker tradition of excellence in teaching left a legacy for American education. In addition to teacher training and licensure, Quakers were active in the education of women, African-American slaves, and poor children. Colonial records indicate, for example, that in 1742

Anthony Benezet was hired to teach at a Friends (Quaker) school and he remained in education for the next forty-two years. In 1754 Benezet was appointed to head the girls school, and in 1782 he was granted permission to teach at the "Negro school," where he remained for the rest of his life. A few years later, English Quaker Joseph Lancaster continued this tradition of serving the less fortunate. With the support of the Friends and the British and Foreign School Society he established a number of "monitorial" charity schools in both England and the United States. While we will return to a discussion of these schools later, it is important to remember that the Quakers were the first to embrace diversity in education and carried the tradition of excellence in teaching into the modern era.[29]

Roman Catholic Teachers

While the Quakers were active in establishing schools for a diverse population and developing a tradition of excellence in teaching, Roman Catholics also pursued their vision of education. In a number of Northern and mid-Atlantic colonies, especially Maryland, Roman Catholics established several fine schools. For example, the Jesuits established a school in St. Mary's City as early as 1640 and another in Newton in 1673. Similarly, in 1684, New York governor Thomas Dongan was instrumental in establishing a Catholic school at Broadway and Wall Street in New York City.[30]

In the next century numerous other Catholic schools were established, including a Jesuit institution at Bohemia Manor, Pennsylvania, that operated for over a quarter of a century. Based on its success, fifteen additional Roman Catholic schools were created in the decades prior to the American Revolution.[31]

As we have seen, however, Roman Catholic schools were subjected to persistent repression during this period, and parishioners were routinely disenfranchised by Protestant society. In 1704 Maryland passed an Act to Prevent the Growth of Popery that forbade Roman Catholics to teach, board, or instruct children; violators were subject to deportation. And even after the American Revolution, only four of the original thirteen colonies gave Catholics the right to vote or hold political office. This repression would have an impact on the development of Roman Catholic schools, and, as we have seen in chapter 2, eventually led to a schism within the common school and the development of the first parochial school system in this country.[32]

Moravian and Mennonite Teachers

In addition to the Quakers and Roman Catholics, numerous other religious groups including the Moravians and the Mennonites had a long tradition of religious education. The Moravians, influenced by the pioneering educational work of Comenius in the 1600s, established a tradition of religious and liberal education for boys and girls, white and black. Similarly, while the Mennonite school curriculum focused on religious teaching and Bible reading, they also provided their young students with a broad academic program. We can get some sense of their curriculum from a letter written by Christopher Dock, a Mennonite teacher.

Dock immigrated to Pennsylvania in 1710 and taught in Mennonite schools most of his life. He described the day's lessons as consisting of singing a hymn and reciting the Lord's Prayer and the Ten Commandments, followed by lessons in reading and writing. The day concluded with individual recitation of the Scriptures. Dock then graded these assignments. If a student performed well, he indicated excellence by writing in crayon the letter "O" on the student's hand. If the student failed three times, he was called "lazy" by the class, and his name was inscribed on a slate with the heading "Lazy Pupils." Later, Dock published a treatise on schoolkeeping entitled *Schulordnung,* the first of its kind in this country. Although not all Mennonite teachers used these innovative techniques, Dock's curriculum and methods of instruction were probably similar to other Mennonite teachers' from the colonial period.[33]

In short, the colonial period offered ethnic, cultural, and religious "minorities " a variety of opportunities to teach. With the emergence of the common school in the nineteenth century, however, educational reformers made a clear distinction between the sectarian religious instruction of church schools and the academic instruction in the common schools. Moreover since the common-school curriculum eventually would embrace a nonsectarian pan-Protestant focus, there was little room in the classroom for either non–English-speaking immigrants or those individuals whose culture did not precisely match the Protestant norms of the 1800s.

TEACHER DIVERSITY IN THE NINETEENTH AND TWENTIETH CENTURIES

The common school, of course, was quite successful in providing young Americans of the early republic with a unified political culture and the skills necessary for their success in the new market economy; but the ethnic and cultural homogeneity of its pan-Protestant curriculum created major social conflicts and eventually spawned America's first private school movement with the exodus of millions of Roman Catholic children (see chapter 2).

Ethnic immigrants' children who did not have the unified political power of the Roman Catholics, typically attended public schools and were instructed in values and ideas that were often contrary to their culture or religion. Similarly, ethnic teachers who may have spoken with an accent or looked slightly different from others in the community were routinely barred from teaching through legal or cultural barriers or both.

Throughout the 1800s and into the early 1900s, many immigrant communities in rural and urban areas attempted to retain their cultural or religious heritage by teaching language and religion outside the public school. Jewish children often attended "Hebrew school" taught by a Rabbi or Jewish leader; Roman Catholics often attended Wednesday afternoon catechism classes, and other religious sects often established Saturday schools to reinforce their particular religious values. It was in these language or religious schools that ethnic minority teachers taught in obscurity. Public schools occasionally hired "foreign language" teachers, but typically they did not hire *foreign-born* teachers who had not totally assimilated into the wider American culture.[34]

In a few northern cities such as New York, Chicago, and Los Angeles, there was some support for "foreign language" instruction in ethnic, immigrant neighborhoods. In fact, governor William Seward of New York, in his address to the state legislature, January 1, 1840, recommended that Roman Catholic students "be instructed by teachers speaking in the same language as themselves." Similarly, in some of these diverse neighborhood schools, language instruction was quietly integrated into classroom instruction. In these cases, however, there was no *official* policy regarding dual-language instruction, and teachers were simply responding to the needs of their students.[35]

These informal attempts to include dual-language instruction in the schools ended abruptly during World War I. In an attempt to generate support for America's involvement in the Great War, the Committee on Public Information was created. That committee, headed by George Creel, a journalist from Denver, launched a massive propaganda campaign to convince Americans of the threat of the "Hun" and demonstrate how horrible life would be under the control of Germany. In addition, the Creel Committee also sought to eliminate all foreign influences from the schools.[36]

Before long most schools had banned the teaching of German because, as one pamphlet noted, it was a "language that disseminates the ideals of autocracy, brutality, and hatred." German measles became "liberty measles," sauerkraut became "liberty cabbage" and music by German composers was routinely banned. Teachers with German surnames were often fired from their jobs, and other ethnic teachers were harassed. Soon the prejudice would spread to other groups. For example, the loyalty of some

Irish teachers was questioned because Ireland had remained neutral during the war. Spanish-speaking teachers also were suspect because of the notorious Zimmerman Telegram that suggested Germany might return land to Mexico if Mexico supported Germany in the war. And, of course, following the Russian Revolution in 1917, many Russian and Slavic teachers were dismissed because of their imagined links to communism.[37]

The hysteria that swept across America during and immediately following World War I had a devastating impact on ethnic people in this country for decades to come. As we have seen in chapter 2, during the 1920s the United States essentially "closed the door" to immigration for the first time in its history with a series of immigrant restriction laws. This, of course, had a chilling effect on ethnic teachers. Speaking in a language other than English became dangerous, even in classrooms that were full of non–English-speaking immigrant children. These formal and informal policies were reinforced during the difficult era of the Great Depression, during World War II, and through the "Red Scare" of McCarthyism in the 1950s. Forced assimilation had once again become common in the multicultural classrooms of the nation.[38]

During the 1960s, a more open attitude toward immigration gradually emerged in the wake of the Great Society programs. For example, in 1965 Congress passed the Immigration and Naturalization Act, which restructured our immigration policy from one based on "national origins" to one that reflected the economic needs of the nation as a whole. In addition, a series of Cold War–inspired refugee acts passed between 1961 and 1980 opened our doors to immigrants fleeing communist countries. The result of this was a dramatic increase in legal immigration from the non-English-speaking nations of Asia, Central America, and Mexico, and more recently southeastern Europe. And of course, in addition to these legal immigrants and refugees there were thousands of undocumented immigrants from all over the world.[39]

ETHNIC TEACHERS TODAY

In the wake of the greatest levels of immigration to this country since the early 1900s, teachers throughout the country have been challenged once again. The growth of bilingual education over the last three decades has led to a growing demand for teachers who are proficient in both English and another language, especially Spanish (see chapter 3). As the number of Limited English Proficient (LEP) and non–English-speaking students has increased, the demand for immigrant teachers has also grown. As a result, the legal and cultural barriers to the profession have eased somewhat, and school boards throughout the country have slowly begun to recruit and hire Hispanic, Asian, and other ethnic teachers. Yet despite the growing demand for their services, entry into the teaching profession has been slow.[40]

The National Coalition of Advocates for Students (NCAS) recently issued a report on the state of immigrant education in this country and clearly articulated many of the problems that educators must face in this regard. These include issues of language acquisition, harassment by the white community, the difficulties of overcoming the memories of violence in their countries of origin, and the growing reaction against educational programs that are designed to help immigrant children learn. Using figures published in their review of state laws regarding bilingual education in 1988, we can see that of the fifty states, twenty-six do not require education, with one state (West Virginia) actually prohibiting the practice altogether. Eleven states have mandated bilingual education while another twelve "permit" the practice without any legal protection.[41]

The NCAS recommendations are inclusive and encourage vigorous action from the U.S. Immigration and Naturalization Service, the U.S. Department of Education, and state and local educational agencies. In the area of teacher education they recommend that schools "face the new reality in U.S. schools," and expand their efforts to hire bilingual teachers recruited from the immigrant community. They also recommend that federal, state, and local officials help all teachers understand the difficult problems and issues facing immigrant children and remove barriers that prevent foreign-born Americans from becoming teachers.[42]

In short, while schools have begun to recruit immigrant teachers, like women and people of color before them, they, too, will not readily be admitted into the profession. Because of widespread cultural stereotypes and latent prejudice, they will have to push their way into America's classrooms with all the determination they can muster—individually and collectively—in order to produce social change. Considering the political climate today, their struggle is just beginning.

As we approach our third educational transition it is clear that as a nation and as a people we must do much more to recruit and retain African American and ethnic minority teachers. The United States desperately needs a diverse corps of teachers to match our diverse student population. These teachers will provide important role models for black and immigrant children. Their presence in the classroom will help children develop the self-esteem they need to enter the American economy and society as full and equal members.

Moreover, we must resist the parochial policies of English-only classroom instruction. These policies have failed in the past, they are failing today, and they will fail in the future. Rather, we must recognize that America's ethnic bilingual teachers are one of our greatest hidden treasures. Far from being a cultural problem to be "legislated away," these young men and women will provide a cultural bridge between the old and new worlds for America's newest arrivals. They are essential if we are to build a stronger, more diverse nation.

An Old Schoolhouse Near the End of its Long Service, Albany County, New York, 1937. While the image of the "Little Red Schoolhouse" persists to this day, many were actually white frame, brick, or stone structures. This handsome building was probably one of the nicer schools of its time. (Courtesy of Library of Congress, Prints and Photographs Division, FSA-OWI Collection.)

A Speech Class in a Colorado School, circa 1910. Here children learn the pronunciation of the phonetic sound "ch" by playing "choo-choo train." Teachers often used creative methods to teach subjects that may have been boring for young children. (Courtesy of Library of Congress, Prints and Photographs Division, Detroit Publishing Company Photograph Collection.)

History Lesson in a Tuskegee Institute Classroom, 1902. The Tuskegee Institute was both the intellectual center of the African American community and the premier black teacher training college of the "Jim Crow" era. (see chapter 5) (Courtesy of Library of Congress, Prints and Photographs Division, African American Odyssey Collection.)

Teachers Convention, Cambridge, Massachusetts, 1910. Teachers began to organize during the early 1900s, demanding smaller class sizes, higher wages, more autonomy and greater professional status. That struggle continues to this day (see chapter 9). (Courtesy of Library of Congress, Prints and Photographs Division, Panoramic Photographs Collection.)

New Sumner High School, 1911. This classic, turn-of-the-century high school was a massive three-story structure with administrative offices in the center, flanked by an auditorium and gymnasium at either end of the building. Note the skylights and large windows that provided light for classroom instruction. (Courtesy of Library of Congress, Prints and Photographs Division, Panoramic Photographs Collection.)

Interior of a "Little Red Schoolhouse," Crossville, Tennessee, 1935. Until recently, there were many one-room schoolhouses still in existence. Here a teacher works with six students while others complete their lessons on school benches. Note the heating stove in the center of the classroom. (Courtesy of Library of Congress, Prints and Photographs Division, FSA-OWI Collection.)

Conducting School in a Church at Gees Bend, Alabama, 1937. Excluded from public schools, African Americans often conducted classes in their churches following services. This tradition dates back to the colonial era. Here the teacher points to a makeshift blackboard with his assistant standing by. Note the potbellied stove, the only source of heat, and the oil lamp, the only source of light in the building (see chapter 3). (Courtesy of Library of Congress, Prints and Photographs Division, FSA-OWI Collection.)

Raising the Flag, Irwinville, Georgia, 1938. Patriotic nationalism has been an important component of the public school curriculum since the 1800s. Here the entire student body of a school in Georgia participate in an assembly honoring the American flag. (Courtesy of Library of Congress, Prints and Photographs Division, FSA-OWI Collection.)

Playground Scene, Irwinville School, Georgia, 1938. Children clowning around during recess on a homemade "monkey bar." (Courtesy of Library of Congress, Prints and Photographs Division, FSA-OWI Collection.)

Teaching the Only Second-Grader in a One-Room Schoolhouse in Grundy, Iowa, 1939. In this photograph, a teacher in a one-room schoolhouse helps a second-grader with his arithmetic while other students work independently. Notice the absence of black students in this and other classroom scenes. (Courtesy of Library of Congress, Prints and Photographs Division, FSA-OWI Collection.)

Schoolroom, San Luis Valley Farms, Colorado, 1939. As the population of young children grew in this Colorado town, temporary classrooms were set up in the community building. Here the teacher helps one child as others, for the most part, work independently. (Courtesy of Library of Congress, Prints and Photographs Division, FSA-OWI Collection.)

Mary McLeod Bethune, 1949. This photograph was taken near the end of Ms. Bethune's long and productive life as an educator. She represents an important chapter in the struggle for education among African-American children and the preparation of black teachers. In 1904 she opened the Daytona Normal and Industrial Institute for Girls, later to become Bethune-Cookman College (see chapter 5). (Courtesy of Library of Congress, Prints and Photographs Division, Carl Van Vechten Collection.)

6

The Struggle for Control
of Instruction and Curriculum

In the early 1800s, Memorus Wordwell, a Hercules in the wilderness of words, "could read any word in his speller." But as one of his classmates tells us, "he did not know [at all] what the sounds he uttered meant." Today, educators use a variety of approaches to teach reading with a primary emphasis on comprehension, rather than simply parroting words from a book. And yet, local and state political pressure to control the basic reading curriculum (such as *legislating* the phonics method) continues to this day. At the secondary level, this kind of micromanagement may not be as apparent but is reflected in the selection of textbooks, in the direct censorship of reading material, and in the continued pressure to incorporate politically popular courses into the curriculum.[1]

The New England Primer

Since the early colonial period, teachers have struggled to control both their curriculum and methods of instruction. As we have seen in chapter 2, the selectmen of colonial New England controlled virtually every aspect of primary schooling. This was accomplished by mandating particular readings that eventually were collected in the *New England Primer*.

In the early decades of the settlement, from the 1630s to at least the 1670s, there was no standardized reader or catechism for Puritan children. As a result, church leaders often developed their own materials for basic reading and religious instruction. Reverend-teachers such as John Davenport, John Cotton, John Norton, Richard Mather, and many others produced what Cotton Mather later called "the most judicious and elaborate catechisms published." Yet religious leaders continued to search for a common catechism that would help unite the colony and provide a standard set of instructional materials for Puritan children. The search eventually led to the creation of the *New England Primer*.[2]

While we do not know the exact date of publication for the first edition of the *Primer* (no copy of the book exists today), it probably was introduced sometime between the late 1670s and mid-1680s. We do know, however, that a second impression of the *Primer* was printed in 1690 and that by 1700 it had become the standard catechism reader of the region. In fact, the *Primer* was reissued numerous times with different titles to appeal to other colonists. For example, it was published as *A Primer for the Colony of Connecticut,* the *New York Primer* and following the revolution as the *American Primer* and the *Columbian Primer.* So popular was this little volume that by the end of the 1800s it had sold over three million copies.[3]

Although the style and content of these primers changed slightly over the years to meet the specific needs of the communities that used them, their basic components remained the same. Each primer began with the letters of the alphabet, vowels, consonants, "Double Letters" (archaic letter combinations like *fs* that represented *ss*), "Italiek Letters," and "Italiek Double Letters." Following these were the "Great English Letters" (essentially Old English), "Small English Letters," and the "Great Letters" (capital letters). Then came a section on phonetic syllables (called "Easie Syllables for Children"), which included a total of 140 combinations. These were followed in order by words of one syllable, two syllables, three syllables, four syllables, five syllables, and sometimes six syllables.[4]

Following this "syllabarium," as it was called, the typical *New England Primer* then presented the famous twenty-four pictures with accompanying alphabetical rhymes. (Curiously, the letters *I* and *V* were not included). Here we find the well-known phrases "In Adam's Fall We Sinned all," "The Cat doth play And after slay," and "The Idle Fool Is whipt at School." These phrases were followed by a number of short pieces to memorize including "The Dutiful Child's Promises," "The Lord's Prayer," "The Creed," the books of the Bible, and both the Roman and Arabic numerals from 1 to 100. The *Primer* ended with the story/poem of Mr. John Rogers, "the first Martyr in Queen Mary's Reign, [who] was burnt at Smithfield, February the fourteenth, 1554. . . ."[5]

In addition, the original *New England Primer* also contained "The Shorter Catechism," which consisted of questions and answers concerning the Puritans' interpretation of religion. One selection included the following, for example: "Q. What is God? A. God is a Spirit, Infinite, Eternal and Unchangeable, in His Being, Wisdom, Power, Holiness, Justice, Goodness and Truth."[6]

In addition to its great popularity for over two centuries, the *New England Primer* also prescribed the methods of reading instruction for nearly 150 years. The focus of this instruction was a three-stage memorization process. It began with the learning of the alphabet, and other letter combinations such as those of vowels and consonants. Once the student mastered the "abs," as they were sometimes called, he was then expected to memorize a cacophony of phonetic sounds, what the *Primer* referred to as "easie syllables." When that formidable task was completed the student would then begin to memorize short and long reading passages sometimes in poetic and sometimes in prose form.

While the passages to be memorized varied from reader to reader to meet the particular needs of the community, the instructional process was essentially the same. Students were to commit to memory stories, verses, or religious/moral selections and then recite those materials verbatim to the teacher. This remained the standard method of reading instruction from the colonial times well into the 1800s.

CHANGES IN INSTRUCTION AND CURRICULUM

While memorization would continue to be a central component of reading instruction for years to come, the democratic and market revolutions that swept across America in the late 1700s and early 1800s would alter both the curriculum and methods of instruction. As the American Revolution transformed the thirteen independent and squabbling colonies into the United States of America, our diverse colonial educational experiments were called into question. Patriots from all over the country soon recognized that the potpourri of educational approaches used during the colonial era simply would not provide the basis of a coherent nation, nor would they help instill the values of patriotism and nationalism seen as necessary for our development.

While each of the colonies had created their own unique educational institutions to reflect the diverse culture and religious orientation of their settlers, now the nation demanded a common set of values from the youth of America. Education was no longer seen as a luxury of the wealthy; our new democratic experiment demanded that education be within the reach of all Americans, both rich and poor (see chapter 1).

These dramatic changes paralleled the emergence of the "market economy." As we have seen, this new economy, based on the exchange of cash for goods and services as opposed to the self-sufficiency and barter of earlier years, gave many Americans their first taste of the new consumer culture. In addition, it restructured their social roles and provided them with an exciting vision of what the new nation could become. Together, the American Revolution and the market revolution would fundamentally change our attitudes toward education, propel us into our first educational transition, and provide support for the creation of the common school.

American teachers and educational reformers of the period soon recognized that changes in the curriculum and methods of instruction were also necessary. Students would need to learn the values of patriotism and national pride. No longer would love of God, family, community, and state be enough; now a love of country was necessary if our nation was to endure. Moreover, in order to succeed in the new competitive market economy, students would have to learn to appreciate the values of hard work, determination, and achievement. In short, a love of God and country had to be balanced with intense individualism in the humble setting of the common school. Teachers had their work cut out for them.

God and Country

While the common-school classrooms throughout the country continued to reinforce religious values through daily prayer and readings from the Bible, children were also instructed in a set of pan-Protestant values that were acceptable to most Americans. Early readers like the first McGuffey series of 1837, of course, included religious content. About one in four lessons in the first two of McGuffey's *Eclectic Readers,* for example, made some reference to God or the Bible.[7]

Yet these readers typically did not promote religious and moral teachings specific to a particular denomination. As we have seen, educators of this period wanted to incorporate Christian values into the curriculum, but most recommended that they find a common cultural ground. That common ground was pan-Protestantism.[8]

While the nature of religious instruction in the classroom had begun to change in the common school, teaching patriotic nationalism was seen as essential by most common-school teachers. This sentiment was clearly reflected in the readers of the day. The early instructional readers used in the common schools, for example, typically portrayed the American people as the most virtuous in the world and showed that others were often cruel or ignorant. For example, the *Juvenile Mentor*, a popular reader of the early 1800s, included several stories that described the cruelty of Spaniards as a national character trait. And even when other nationalities were seen in a positive light, that light reflected the values of Americans. A good example of this is William Tell, the Swiss patriot. In this story, William Tell shoots the apple off the head of his young son. This is portrayed as an act of intense nationalism and something that should be emulated by all good American boys and girls.[9]

In addition, the early readers helped to reinforce students' patriotism by including many reading selections about such founding fathers as Alexander Hamilton, Thomas Jefferson, George Washington, Benjamin Franklin, and others. The rousing tales of their accomplishments and inherent values, like Washington's truthfulness to his father in the famous cherry tree story, became an essential component of common-school curriculum. In that tale, a young George Washington "tried the edge of his new hatchet upon his father's favorite cherry tree [but later confessed] 'Father, I cannot tell a lie, I cut the tree.'"[10]

Other readers used the actual or imagined words of the founding fathers to inspire patriotism in students. McGuffey's *Fifth Eclectic Reader*, for example, included an imagined speech by Daniel Webster about the bravery and heroism of John Adams at the time of the American Revolution. Part of this passage read, "Sink or swim, live or die, survive or perish, I give my hand and my heart to this vote. It is true that in the beginning we aimed not at Independence. But *'there's a divinity that shapes our ends.'"*[11]

In fact, an important part of the common-school education of the 1800s was the memorization and dramatic delivery of these famous political speeches. Teachers often included in their reading instruction lessons on how to bow formally to the audience and teacher before and following a presentation. As one common-school student noted, the primary objective of reciting memorized materials was to display the appropriate classical gestures, "read fast, mind the stops and marks and speak up loud." Such was the nature of patriotic training in the common schools of the 1800s.[12]

Market-Based Curriculum

While teachers continued to instill the values of God and country in their young students, educators had also begun to recognize the importance of preparing them for the new market economy. Among the first of these was Joseph Lancaster, whose method, sometimes called the "monitorial system" because of its use of monitors to teach small groups of students, was firmly embedded in the values of the marketplace. The system had a number of important elements. Lancaster grouped students according to their abilities, thus anticipating the graded school movement that came later in the 1800s. He employed "simultaneous instruction," wherein groups of students were taught by monitors rather than each student reciting memorized material to the teacher as others read silently. Lancaster also developed a system of motivation (see chapter 8) that encouraged student achievement by praising them and awarding them prizes for academic success and good behavior but used shame and humiliation when they either failed academically or broke school rules. And finally, he introduced a form of competency examinations that students were required to pass in order to advance to the next level.[13]

Although Lancaster's formal system of instruction eventually fell out of favor among mid-nineteenth-century educational reformers including Horace Mann, many of his ideas were embraced by common-school teachers throughout the nation. In fact many teacher-training manuals of this era promoted Lancaster's market-based instructional strategies—especially his emphasis on student motivation and evaluation. Two of the most important of these manuals were Edwin C. Hewett's *A Treatise on Pedagogy for Young Teachers* (1884) and Charles Northend's *The Teacher and the Parent* (1853).[14]

Both Hewett and Northend recognized the role of positive motivation rather than physical punishment in promoting a student's punctuality, hard work, and achievement. For example, Hewett noted that the student's conscience was the basis of all action and should be appealed to in order to improve attendance, deportment, and grades. Both educators also vigorously defended the use of examinations to evaluate students' progress. For Hewett, examination marks were an important "written record of the teacher's estimate concerning the relative success of the pupils efforts." Similarly, Northend saw examinations as an important "auxiliary in the great work of education." These new ideas concerning the motivation and accountability of students were based on the values of the emerging market economy. By incorporating them into a curriculum that was rooted in patriotic and nationalistic readings, the nature of teaching had begun to change.[15]

THE PERSISTENCE OF TRADITIONAL INSTRUCTION

In the early 1800s, however, basic instructional methods were controlled by the local community and, as a result, students in the early common schools would continue to learn through memorization and recitation. Though the reading materials had changed and new methods of instruction were gradually making their way into the classroom, "memorization and recitation" continued to be the accepted method of instruction and local communities expected their teachers to carry on that tradition. If they did not they were either fired, or more likely simply not rehired the following term.

Memorizing "Abs" and "Little Words"

Once students had mastered the letters of the alphabet, the "abs" and the short rhymes associated with the alphabet, they were expected to silently read and memorize passages from their readers while each of their classmates recited their memorized lessons *individually* to the teacher. When students learned to spell words from their Webster's *Blue Backed* speller, for example, they were encouraged to memorize them with little consideration of their meaning. As Warren Burton recalls, "It never entered . . . the heads of . . . parents [or] teachers that words and sentences were written . . . to be understood."[16]

Even Burton's favorite teacher, Mary, was obliged by the customs of the community to teach reading to her summer term students the "old way." As Burton reminds us, this was because at the end of the term, *both she and her pupils* would be examined by the school commissioner and other prominent members of the community, and her continued employment was contingent upon her pupils successfully reciting the alphabet, combinations of vowel and consonant sounds, and numerous selected passages.[17]

Burton remembers these awful lessons vividly: "The severest duty I was ever called upon to perform was sitting on that little front seat" reciting abs as well as vowel and consonant combinations. The lessons, he complains, "conveyed no ideas, excited no interest. . . ." And yet, he recalls that Mary presented the material with such "sweet demeanor" that the "unmeaning string of sights and sounds were bound forever to my memory by . . . gentle tones and looks."[18] In short, Mary was a good teacher!

Isaac Phillips Roberts also recalls the lessons of his youth. "The details of my early school life," he explains, "will scarcely interest you since my studies did not interest me." As "crude" as they were, however they taught him to "commit to memory many things, sad and gay, solid and trivial which were expressed in rhyme and taught me to speak somewhat easily on my feet."[19]

Clearly, the routine of the common school, though punctuated by a spelling bee or a visit from the school commissioner at the end of the term, could be quite boring for young, active boys and girls. Students spent hours each day silently reading, writing, figuring and/or memorizing while others recited their lessons for the teacher. Except for a few minutes a day when the teacher listened to *your* lesson, there was very little individual attention. In Laura Ingalls Wilder's winter class, the typical day consisted of "a shivering walk to the cold school shanty; then the usual round of recitations . . . with recess and noon, breaking it into four equal parts."[20]

During those seemingly endless periods between morning recess, lunch, afternoon recess and dismissal, a student's mind might wander. Roberts recalls how during the summer term, his legs "served as roosts for flies while [he planned] how to catch that chipmunk" just outside the schoolhouse window. In the winter, with his "feet at least four inches from the floor," he thought about how comfortable the "big boy" was with his "Windsor chair" covered with a "soft wooly sheepskin." Such were the typical school daydreams of the future dean of agriculture at Cornell University![21]

When the "little ones" had mastered their ABCs, the long process of "learning to read" began in earnest. Students would start by memorizing "an expanse of little syllables" eventually reciting "ab, eb, ibs as fast as he possibly [could,] naming each one after the voice of the teacher as he hurrie[d] along." Once the young scholar was able to articulate "each [of these] lifeless and uninteresting objects" he graduated to learning individual words "of one syllable," out of context, that were listed in his speller.[22]

Spelling Bees

When their spelling words were memorized, students often were called upon to match their skills with others in the class during regular spelling bees on Friday or Saturday afternoons. These competitions were the highlight of the long school week. No matter how dull the school may have been, the spelling bee was exciting. Warren Burton recalls that the thrill of competition seemed to bring out the best in every student, "whether he is at the head or the foot of the class." It was "something like a tug of strength in the wrestle, something of the . . . hope and fear in the game of chance."[23]

Yet as we have seen, in early common schools, students often memorized the spelling of words without knowing their meaning. Burton often struggled with his spelling words but typically failed because he had "the lamentable defect of mind not to be able to commit to memory, what I did not understand." But this mattered little to those students who eagerly embraced the spelling competition. And it mattered even less to parents, members of the school board or others in the community who attended these spelling bees. The important thing was that words were spelled correctly, even if their meaning was unknown to them or the speller.[24]

Simple Readings without Comprehension

As students progressed, they were introduced to simple readings, but as might be expected, the emphasis in these early common schools was not on "comprehension." It meant little what was read, simply *how well* it was read. Lost in the process were "the ideas hidden in the great long words and spacious sentences."[25]

One of the reasons for the emphasis on recitation rather than comprehension was that in some early classrooms (especially in frontier communities) there were few standard readers, and so students read whatever books were available. As such, it was virtually impossible for the teacher to discuss with individual students the meaning of a selected passage even if she wanted to do so. In Laura Ingalls Wilder's first winter school on the frontier, one student read from an almanac while another from the family Bible. Still another pair, Ruby and Tommy, shared a book as Laura and her sister had done years before. Ruby read from an earlier section of the spelling book while Tommy did his best to read a lesson later in the volume. As Wilder explains, "They were not studying the same lessons in the book but they could hold it open in two places. Leaning to one side, Tommy could study his lesson, while Ruby . . . could study hers." Cooperation rather than comprehension was apparently the operating principle in these early schoolhouses.[26]

The primary reason for this convoluted approach to reading and spelling, however, was to *entertain* parents and other members of the community. The end-of-year "examination," like the spelling bee, was more a showcase of a student's dramatic talent and less a "test" of his comprehensive abilities. Students were expected to recite a poem or patriotic speech with expression and the appropriate classical gestures. How well they performed before parents and other members of the community often determined whether the *teacher*, not the student, would return the following term. Similarly, the regular spelling bees that were part of the life of most common schools were also important social events for the community. In a world where there were few diversions from the routine of work, the spelling bee was an exciting event indeed. Families often traveled miles by wagon to see the spelling matches and the great spellers like Memorus Wordwell.

READING FOR COMPREHENSION

Toward the end of the 1800s, however, two interrelated developments slowly began to change the nature of instruction from memorization to understanding. The first was the publication of a new generation of standardized readers that had become available for use in the district school, and the second was the emergence of America's first educational reform movement that emphasized understanding rather than memorization and subordination to authority.

Standardized Readers

With the widespread publication by the mid-1800s of William McGuffey's *Eclectic Readers* as well as dozens of other lesser-known reading books, common schools throughout the country finally had *standardized* works available to them for reading instruction. Of course, not all students read from "Old Guff's," as these readers were called by the children of the day, but millions did. In fact, by the time of McGuffey's death in 1873, fifty million copies of his *Readers* had been sold, read, and reread by generations of young Americans. By the early 1920s, that number had soared to an estimated 122 million copies.[27]

Although the entire series consisted of five readers plus a Primer, the first two usually provided the core of the reading curriculum for most common schools. In addition to the reading material itself, the key difference between the McGuffey readers and those of the colonial era, such as the *New England Primer*, were the "discussion questions" that appeared at the end of each lesson, beginning with the second reader. Unlike earlier readers that had no commentary on selected passages, the graded McGuffey readers provided both students and teachers with questions that encouraged thinking and comprehension.[28]

In his "Suggestions to Teachers" that prefaced the reading lessons, McGuffey noted that "nothing can be more fatiguing to the teacher than a recitation conducted on . . . verbatim answers." This method, he argued, "would be little more than an exercise of memory to the neglect of the other faculties. . . ." Rather, he suggested that the teacher "try the *conversational* mode of communicating instruction and training the mind. Let [the teacher] use the questions, furnished in the book, as the basis of this method." With these discussion questions, teachers were now able to engage their students more directly, rather than simply listening to their memorized lessons. In short, the McGuffey *Readers* helped teachers gradually shift their instruction from memorization and oral presentation to reading comprehension.[29]

Educational Ideas of Rousseau and Pestalozzi

In addition to a gradual shift in emphasis from "reading with expression" to "reading comprehension," educational reformers of the late 1800s began to embrace the education ideas of Jean-Jacques Rousseau and Johann Pestalozzi, most notably their emphasis on the development of intellect among children.

In his influential novel *Emile*, written in 1762, Rousseau argued that young children did not have the ability to reason until adolescence, a stage of development he called "the age of social reasoning." As a result, he felt that primary education should be based on the child's experiences and his need to know and understand. Rather than forcing a child to memorize reading passages at a young age, Rousseau argued that reading instruction should begin when the student saw it as necessary; only then would it be successful. For example, the character Emile received several invitations to parties but was unable to read them, nor could he find anyone who would read the invitations to him. As a result, Emile developed the need to read, and so he did.[30]

Yet Rousseau's concept of the child went beyond reading instruction alone. His understanding of child development fundamentally challenged prevailing attitudes toward the nature of childhood itself. More traditional visions of the child, like those of the colonial period in this country, held that a child was born into a state of "original sin." As a result, the purpose of education was to restrain the child from evil and to subordinate him to a greater authority. Rousseau, on the other hand, saw children as inherently good but corrupted by a society that was rife with sin.

This "romantic" vision of the child was also the basis of Pestalozzi's approach to education. Like Rousseau, he argued that children were not equipped to reason until much later in life and as a result, early education should focus on the objects and activities of the real world, presented to the child with love and nurture.

Pestalozzi presented his ideas concerning education in two novels, *Leonard and Gertrude* (1781) and *How Gertrude Teaches Her Children* (1799–1804). These novels centered on how Gertrude used everyday items as the basis of learning, and on the importance of the teacher's love in learning. In his first novel, for example, the character Gertrude teaches children arithmetic by having them count "the number of steps from one end of the room to the other" the "threads while spinning, and the number of turns on the reel when they wound the yarn into skeins."[31]

In his second novel, Pestalozzi expanded these ideas and demonstrated how the mother (and by extension, the female teacher) could develop a conscience in the child by her nurturing love. For Pestalozzi, the "first instruction of the child" should be the "business of the senses . . . of the mother." Only when this was achieved could instruction move to the development of reason.[32]

Pestalozzi's instructional methods (and his new approach to discipline, which we will discuss in chapter 8) were popularized in this country by a number of educators. The first of these was John Griscom, an educational and social reformer of the early 1800s who toured Pestalozzi's school in Yverdun, Switzerland, in 1805. In his *A Year in Europe* (1808), Griscom enthusiastically reported on Pestalozzi's methods. He wrote that Pestalozzi's school (a class of ninety young boys) had only one teacher, who instructed without books and was "constantly with a child, always talking, questioning, explaining and repeating." Griscom came away from his tour with a great deal of respect for these methods, especially what he called their "moral charm." He wrote that they were superior to other forms of instruction in producing an intelligent and moral citizenry.[33]

As a result of Griscom's early support, Pestalozzi's ideas were gradually embraced by educational reformers and innovative teachers in this country. During the early 1800s they were successfully adapted by Charles Mayo, who employed them in his "infant schools," and later were embraced by Friedrich Froebel as the basis of kindergarten instruction. And by the late 1850s, Edward Sheldon, the founder of the Oswego State Normal School in New York, adopted Pestalozzi's methods of teacher education. Moreover, for the rest of the century Pestalozzi's ideas were popularized in a series of public lectures known collectively as the Oswego movement.[34]

By 1900 the use of familiar "objects" both in and out of the classroom had become an accepted part of the elementary school curriculum. Map reading, for example had become a standard component of both the history and geography curriculums. Primary schoolteachers typically used physical objects like desks, chairs, and windowpanes to help children learn to count, just as Pestalozzi's Gertrude had done a century before. Similarly, nature walks where students identified plants and animals often supplemented traditional biology texts. Finally, as we shall see, Pestalozzi's nurturing approach to education (the role of love) gradually was accepted as an important instructional and disciplinary model in public schools.

Despite these advances, however, older instructional methods based on rote memorization persisted. Most common-school teachers literally were forced by the community to cling to more traditional forms and were slow to change. When sociologist Lester Frank Ward recorded his experiences as a schoolteacher in 1860, for example, he revealed his reliance on "individualized instruction" and memorization: "The exercises this afternoon were as follows. First I heard the little ones, then the pieces [recitation], then 15 minutes recess. Then the composition papers were read and the exercises ended in a spelling match." When Ward deviated from these accepted methods, however, he was fired midway through his first term! This persistence of traditional methods recently has been seen as a function of a conservative teacher culture. However, the demands placed on teachers by both the community and administration must also be considered. Teachers often have little choice.[35]

These antiquated methods of instruction took their toll on generations of young Americans. As is the case today, young students came to school with varying degrees of "emergent literacy." During the 1800s most children had little preparation and struggled throughout their short school terms trying to memorize obscure reading passages and wincing from the lash of a "ferule" (ruler) or pointer. Typical of this kind of student were the older boys and girls that Warren Burton referred to as the "Anaks." These were the "slow" children of the 1800s who never seemed to progress far enough in the short winter term to make real headway in their studies. After about eight weeks of silent reading, daydreaming, severe discipline, and the humiliation of having to read and recite poorly before the teacher, the term finally ended. Then came a full summer of hard work. By the following winter term many of these boys and girls had forgotten much of what they had learned the year before. And then, faced with yet another teacher, their prospects for academic success were bleak indeed.[36]

Others, like Isaac Phillips Roberts, already knew how to read when he first stepped into the schoolhouse. This lucky young man recalled that "his mother taught [him] to read . . . before the winter daylight broke by the great fireplace, while she was knitting. . . ." And though his mind may have wandered during those long days on the hard benches of his school room, he was well prepared compared to some of his school chums, who had little in the way of nurturing home environment.[37]

Unfortunately most children of the 1800s did not have this kind of support at home. And as today, teachers were expected to educate these children and help them enter a world that was becoming increasingly complex. By the end of the nineteenth century reformers had begun to recognize that fundamental changes in the nature of instruction were needed.

LATE-NINETEENTH-CENTURY EDUCATIONAL REFORMERS

By the late 1800s and early 1900s teachers began to improve instruction by introducing innovations into the classroom that were based on scientific educational research. Among the most important of these were Johann Herbart's lesson plan, William Heard Kilpatrick's project method, Edward Thorndike's educational measurement and John Dewey's enormous contributions of the "laboratory school" and concepts of "learning by doing." Each of these powerful figures in their own way contributed to a virtual revolution in teaching.

Herbart and the Lesson Plan

Johann Herbart (1776–1841) was a German psychologist whose ideas concerning the structured "lesson plan" continue to have a major impact on teachers to this day. Although Herbart was a disciple of Pestalozzi, especially with his emphasis on "learning through the senses" and the use of objects as learning tools, he took a step further by detailing how students actually "assimilated knowledge." Very simply, Herbart argued that when the "interests" of the child were stimulated, learning would take place. Similar to Rousseau's ideas in *Emile,* Herbart argued that the key to learning (what he called "mental assimilation") was the child's desire and need to understand.[38]

As a result, the proper sequencing of material was critical. By building on materials that were of interest to students, new ideas and concepts could effectively be introduced. Herbart's emphasis on sequencing led him to develop the five-step lesson plan that included preparation, presentation, comparison, generalization, and application. During preparation and presentation, students reviewed materials of interest to them and then new material was introduced that was related to those interests. Comparisons were then made between previous knowledge and the new material. Finally, students learned to generalize on the basis of old and new materials and apply the main ideas to other situations.

Herbart's innovations were successful for both pedagogical and organizational reasons. Teachers liked them because they were built directly on the important work of Pestalozzi and they also appealed to administrators of the emerging system of the graded school. It just made good sense to school principals and superintendents (mostly men) that teachers (mostly women) should prepare detailed "lesson plans" each week that could then be inspected and evaluated. This kind of "quality control" in education in fact was at the very heart of the corporate school model and further reinforced its hierarchical nature (see chapter 9).

Kilpatrick's Project Method

Although very different from Herbart, the methods of William Heard Kilpatrick were also eagerly embraced for their pedagogical innovation and because they reflected the perceived needs of society at the time. Developed in the late 1910s and early 1920s, Kilpatrick's "project method" became extremely popular among educators. Very simply, the project method involved student learning by means of a "socially purposeful act." Like most progressive educators of this period, Kilpatrick felt that the modern world had fragmented the lives of Americans, that we had become disconnected from the larger society. The answer to this predicament was to reestablish those connections through the schools. By involving students in projects like making a dress or putting out a newspaper from start to finish, teachers could direct student learning to socially useful ends and strengthen the connection to the larger society.[39]

William James: Stimulus-Response

While Pestalozzi, Herbart, Kilpatrick, and Dewey (to be discussed later in this chapter) revolutionized our ideas of instruction, William James (1842–1910) introduced the concept of "stimulus-response" to explain *how* children learned. As a proponent of what we now call "behavioral psychology" or behaviorism, James argued that children learned by developing habits in response to external stimulation. His classic example of this process, published in his *Principles of Psychology* in 1890, involved a baby who reached for a candle's flame as a result of a normal reflex. When the baby's fingers were burned, however, she learned not to repeat that behavior because the consequences were too painful. For James, all learning was similar to the baby burning her finger and developing the habit of not doing it again.[40]

Edward Thorndike: Standardized Tests

Edward Thorndike (1874–1949) was James's student and he applied some of James's theories to the classroom. Thorndike also focused his attention on the measurement of students' progress and developed some of the first standardized intelligence tests. Thorndike is sometimes referred to as "the father of educational psychology" because of this work. In his classic statement on learning, published in his *Educational Psychology* in 1913, Thorndike argued that intelligence was a product of "connectionism," or the connections between "stimulus-response." The more often a child made the connection between stimulus and response and the more gratification she achieved by choosing the correct responses, the greater the learning. This "fundamental law of change" was the basis of his learning theory. [41]

Thorndike, however, went beyond theories of learning. He wanted all instruction to be based on the scientific method and all results to be evaluated by scientific instruments. For Thorndike, educational testing would help teachers choose the most effective instructional methods. Moreover, teachers could use standardized tests to direct students to their "most useful role" in society. Those who excelled in math, for example, might be tracked toward careers in engineering or science, while those with advanced social and communication skills could be directed to careers in social work or teaching.

These ideas were eagerly embraced during this period (and continue to be popular) for several reasons. First, Thorndike's emphasis on the *scientific* basis of instruction and testing appealed to some educators as an efficient way to evaluate students and guide them toward useful careers in the business world. Second, Thorndike's idea that intelligence was inherited appealed to those who saw certain groups such as African Americans, and southeastern Europeans, and women as intellectually inferior. Certainly Thorndike's ideas in this regard have been used by some to justify policies of both racial segregation and vocational tracking that were popular during this period (see chapter 2). Today some of these ideas are being resurrected in books such as *The Bell Curve*.[42]

John Watson and B. F. Skinner: Behaviorism

While James and Thorndike pioneered the use of the scientific method in educational research, instruction and testing, it was John Watson (1878–1958) and B. F. Skinner (1904–1990) who popularized educational psychology by broadening its appeal. Their approach, called *behaviorism*, had an enormous impact on education. Watson's research with infants, for example, demonstrated that the *environment was more important than heredity*. He showed that through education and training, any normal child could become an athlete or a doctor; this notion appealed to many teachers. Skinner's early work with rats focused on the effect of rewards in the learning process. He gave rats food when they successfully completed a task. Later he demonstrated that the process was similar for humans. Out of this research came the basis of "programmed learning" that in turn provided the foundation of today's computer-aided instruction. While these applications have been criticized by many humanistic scholars over the years, behaviorism has had a major effect on the development of educational research and teaching in the last half century.[43]

THE BASAL READER

The ideas of Pestalozzi, Herbart, Kilpatrick, James, and Thorndike certainly did not make their way directly into every classroom in the nation. However, their collective influence clearly can be seen in reading instruction, especially with the development of "basal readers" in the early 1920s. Emerging from the important education research of this period, the basal reader represented a revolution in reading instruction. These readers incorporated Pestalozzi's and Herbart's ideas of distinctive developmental levels through the use of a "controlled vocabulary." They used Kilpatrick's idea of drawing on the "interests" and experiences of students by providing familiar settings for the readers. They drew on Herbart's idea of the lesson plan in terms of the presentation and review of materials; they employed Pestalozzi's idea of objects in the form of vivid illustrations of everyday life; they borrowed the concept of measuring the progress of student comprehension from Thorndike; and they drew on Herbart's concepts of sequencing reading materials. The basal readers were the first textbooks based on scientific educational research.

Dick and Jane

As early readers (such as the McGuffey series) were replaced with basal readers (like the classic *Dick and Jane* series, popular from the 1920s through the 1970s) the gradual shift to comprehension was virtually complete. Basal readers provided students with graded reading and spelling material accessible for each developmental level. Rather than a first-grade student being required to read (and memorize) a patriotic speech from the 1770s, materials were "graded" so that students actually understood what they had read.

From their introduction in the 1920s, the *Dick and Jane* basal readers were the trendsetters in reading instruction. It has been estimated that these books eventually were used in 85 percent of the elementary schools across America, and during their half century of use they helped teach millions of children to read. In the progressive, scientific tradition of education, the *Dick and Jane* series was created by a team of educational researchers including William Gray, a reading specialist; Zerna Sharp, a reading consultant; Eleanor Campbell, an illustrator; and other educators, writers, illustrators, and editors. These specialists pooled their expertise in reading research, methods, instruction, child development, and child psychology to develop these readers. The series was then revised every five years to reflect changes in style, innovations, and social conditions such as updating the illustrations to reflect current clothing styles and newer-model cars and the inclusion of a black family in the 1960s.[44]

Stories used a "controlled vocabulary" based on the developmental level of students. This technique introduced a set of new words for each story, repeated them and then built on these learned words in subsequent stories. Sentences were kept short and the stories employed a syntactic simplicity that paralleled the child's development. And since the choice of words was determined by the developmental level of the student, reliance on phonics (typical of most other readers up to this time) was not necessary. Instead, the series utilized the "look-say" method, sometimes referred to as the "whole word" method. In this technique, students learned to recognize words on sight, rather than "sounding out" each new word. The authors of the series understood that when the child had to apply a phonics rule in order to "read" each word, comprehension was slower. Words could be "parroted" but not necessarily understood.

The content of the *Dick and Jane* stories was also designed to match the experiences of young (middle-class, white) children. The famous pair lived in an idealized, yet vaguely familiar middle-class community. They had a spacious two-story white house with a well-trimmed yard. Their family consisted of Mother and Father, Dick and Jane, baby Sally, the dog Spot, and Puff the cat.

Family members reflected commonly held gender and class stereotypes. Father went to work in a suit and mowed the lawn on weekends in more casual clothes. Mother, on the other hand, always wore a dress as she took care of the household. Her domestic duties included washing and drying clothes, cooking and baking, cleaning and sewing. Like other boys of his age, Dick was very active. He rode his bike, played ball, and climbed trees. Jane, on the other hand, was more passive and typically played with her dolls, jumped rope, and helped her mother take care of her little sister, Sally. The children were always well behaved, and Mother and Father never yelled or scolded.

Dick and Jane usually remained at home but they occasionally interacted with others. Sometimes they saw a community worker, like the policeman who served as a crossing guard at school, or the fireman who once rescued Puff from a tree. When Dick and Jane and the family ventured out of their community, they visited their grandparents who lived on a farm. On the farm, Dick and Jane had adventures like riding a pony and feeding chickens, and Spot was chased by a rooster. Other than that, however, Dick and Jane seldom left their sheltered homogeneous environment.

These short, upbeat stories were a dramatic contrast to darker stories that generations of children had read before them. One of the first lessons in the *New England Primer*, for example, was a rhymed alphabet that contained the lines, "In Adam's fall, we sinned all." and "The idle fool is whipped at school." Similarly, the McGuffey *Readers* often had a dark side. One story told of a young boy who became an alcoholic by the age of ten and died in a poorhouse. Another told how children frightened their friend who was traumatized and ended up an idiot! [45]

The *Dick and Jane* basal reader series was among the first to include a separate teachers manual. These "teachers editions" were extremely popular. Derived from ideas first presented by Herbart, they provided detailed lesson plans and even included teaching "scripts" for less experienced teachers to follow. There were four carefully labeled steps for each lesson. The first was *preparing for reading*; teachers were given suggestions to interest children in the story, to introduce new words on the blackboard or via word cards ("flash cards"), and to use new words in sentences. The second step was *interpreting the story;* this involved examining the illustrations, discussing what was happening, and then encouraging students to make predictions about what might happen next. The story was then read aloud or silently, followed by comprehension questions. The third step involved *extending skills and abilities;* here the teacher might incorporate some phonics skills into the lesson (if mandated by the school board) and help individual children with their comprehension skills. The final step focused on *extending interest;* at this stage the teacher might read a poem or story related to the topic, or suggest a game related to *Dick and Jane*'s activities, like jumping rope. These four steps are similar to the "directed reading lesson" common in basal readers today. [46]

Illustrations also played an important role in the *Dick and Jane* series. Like Pestalozzi's objects, these illustrations were designed to stimulate the child's interest. They typically were large and covered most of the page. They were very colorful, printed on glossy paper, contained detail, and were carefully designed to "tell the story"—teachers encouraged children to tell the story based on these illustrations. They might ask questions like, "Look carefully at the picture; what is Jane doing? What is Dick doing? What is Dick wearing? Can you tell what season it is?" Workbook pages also encouraged children to read and interpret the illustrations. For example, an exercise might ask the student to list the things in the picture with which he could play. This emphasis on interpreting illustrations was seen as a reflection of the more visual world as television became a popular leisure entertainment, but it was clearly also rooted in Pestalozzi's idea of using familiar objects as the basis of learning.

The instructional materials that accompanied these basal readers also contributed to their enduring popularity. In addition to the student text and the teachers's manual, the core components of the series included workbooks and worksheets with answer sheets, as well as tests to determine the child's progress. The inclusion of testing materials in these readers reveals the powerful influence of Edward Thorndike. Schools could also purchase some attractive supplementary instructional aids, like word cards, word charts, and tape-recorded stories. Today these supplementary materials continue to enhance the popularity of contemporary basal readers and include "big books," videotapes, small picture books, CDs, cassette tapes, wall charts, phonics cards, easels, and oversize writing tablets. The workbook and worksheets have become so popular, however, that they tend to dominate reading instruction.[47]

Finally, the *Dick and Jane* series introduced the "scope and sequence" chart. This chart illustrated the range of skills and competencies by grade level. The teacher could see the grade at which a particular skill should be introduced, when it should be retaught, and when it should be tested. Skills and subskills were usually classified in broad categories and ranged from simple to complex.[48]

The *Dick and Jane* basal reading series was so popular (and so lucrative for the textbook company Scott Foresman) that it became the standard for reading instruction. Soon Row, Peterson and Company came out with *Alice and Jerry*, Ginn introduced *Susan and Tom*, and D.C. Heath developed *Ned and Nancy*. Many others followed suit. Today basal readers are big business, and a handful of publishers dominate the market. These include Harcourt Brace; Houghton Mifflin; Macmillian/McGraw-Hill/SRA; Open Court; Scholastic; Silver, Burdett and Ginn; D.C. Heath; and Holt, Rinehart, and Winston.

JOHN DEWEY AND THE PROGRESSIVES

As the basal reader made its way into the classrooms of America in the 1920s, other innovative reforms were also being introduced by socially progressive educators. While there were dozens of important progressives who had an impact on education, John Dewey stands alone. Although his enormous contributions were not always embraced by the educational community during his early career, Dewey's work can be seen as a critical link between the ideas of Pestalozzi, the social progressives of the early 1900s, the instructional and curricular innovations of the 1960s and some of the more innovative programs of today.[49]

John Dewey clearly was influenced by Johann Pestalozzi—especially the latter's use of objects in the classroom as an instrument of learning. Like Pestalozzi, Dewey felt that learning could not take place in the abstract. He argued that students needed to connect the objects of a lesson with the ideas behind them. From this notion Dewey developed his idea of "learning by doing." Rather than learning each aspect of the operation of a grocery store like buying, selling, and making change in the abstract, Dewey argued that students should learn the entire operation of the facility by working in a simulated (or "play") grocery store. By actually running the store, the connections between each of the abstract elements of its operation (buying, selling, and making change) would become clearer, and learning could take place.[50]

For Dewey, however, the abstract nature of teaching, so common in schools at that time, reflected deeper problems. He noted that as a result of rapid industrialization in the 1800s we had lost our sense of how our individual actions related to the larger society. Americans, he wrote, had once been involved with the production of complete products on the family farm or in the craftsman's shop and as a result they understood intuitively the interdependent role they played in society. With industrialization, however, we had become little more than individual cogs in the wheel of industry and had lost our sense of wholeness and community.[51]

As a result, Dewey argued that the primary role of the school should be to help reacquaint students with the fundamental interdependency of society. For Dewey, no man was an island, despite America's ongoing love affair with "rugged individualism." As a result, he favored an "open classroom" environment in which students could work in groups, learn to cooperate with one another, and grapple with real social problems in the context of classroom activities.[52]

In the famous "lab school" established by Dewey and his wife, Alice Chipman Dewey, at the University of Chicago, younger students, typically age five, worked together on household projects such as preparing their own breakfast. Later they might establish a simulated grocery store to learn cooperation as they developed their skills in math and reading. At age six children would build a farmhouse and barn from blocks and would then "play" farmer. In this way they would not only learn about that important occupation but would be introduced to more abstract ideas like weather and the growing conditions suitable for particular crops. By age seven children began their study of world history, the centerpiece of the lab-school curriculum. Students were introduced to various civilizations in the past through the people and their occupations. They would immerse themselves in the subject by "becoming" weavers, printers, or farmers in different historical and geographic settings. In so doing, they were better able not only to understand the critical importance of different occupations but also how each related to one another in society. Finally, at each level, students were evaluated to determine how well they had mastered important concepts. In short, the lab school was not just a special place of learning but a kind of human laboratory where educational theories could be tested scientifically.[53]

CURRICULAR INNOVATIONS OF THE 1960s AND BEYOND

The Deweys' emphasis on innovative, socially responsible group instruction linked to rigorous scientific evaluation became the basis of the progressive education movement of the 1920s and 1930s. In turn, many of the socially progressive instructional experiments that emerged from that movement provided the foundation of curricular innovations of later years, from the 1960s to the present. Of these, inquiry-based instruction, individual contracting, preschool education, multi-age grouping, differential staffing, flexible scheduling, team teaching, and the open classroom are the most well known. Each of these innovations owes an intellectual debt to the progressives.[54]

Inquiry-based instruction, through which students learn via experimentation (often in a laboratory setting), for example, was enthusiastically supported by the Deweys in their lab school and by most progressives during this period. Similarly, individual contracting (quite popular in the 1960s and still used today) also has a direct link to the progressives. Here, students and teachers developed "contracts" that specified exactly what was expected of each in the learning process. A more informal contracting arrangement was used by progressive Helen Pankhurst in her now famous Dalton Contract Plan of 1919.

Helen Pankhurst was a student of Maria Montessori, who pioneered preschool education in her native Italy. Montessori worked in the tradition of progressive education, though she was not well accepted by many educators at the time because of her foreign birth, her Roman Catholic religion, and her feminist perspective. Montessori, like many progressives of her time, was influenced by Pestalozzi, especially his emphasis on learning through the senses. She understood that children learned by manipulating objects in an open classroom setting. She also recognized that children should be allowed to choose learning activities that matched their interests. Finally, Montessori pioneered the concept of multi-age grouping, based on a three-year age span, realizing that children of different ages could effectively help one another. She noted that while a teacher may have difficulty explaining an important concept (such as *sharing*) to a three-year-old, a five-year-old might be able to communicate that idea "with the utmost ease."[55]

Montessori sought to configure the physical learning environment of the child to achieve these goals. She was the first to devise "child-size" furniture, which is now commonly used in preschool and primary-grade classrooms. She also developed a number of instructional materials for younger children, such as "frames" for lacing and buttoning, "sticks" for counting, and cards with sandpaper letters. These innovations emerged from her ideas on the importance of using the senses in learning. (Feeling the sandpaper letters, for example, reinforced the shape of the letter through the sense of touch.) Many of these ideas and innovations were popularized during the 1960s and are still used today in progressive Montessori schools and in public kindergartens throughout the nation.

The concepts of differentiated staffing and team teaching, both important innovations popularized in the 1960s, were also pioneered by the progressives. Today the idea of drawing on the expertise of educational experts like counselors, psychologists, reading specialists, and others is commonplace. Similarly, team teaching, especially in the area of reading instruction, has become widely accepted as an effective way to reach students at a variety of levels of "emergent literacy" and monitor their progress over a period of years. In other team-teaching situations teachers share curriculum planning and instruction. In one North Carolina classroom, we observed Dennis Jenkins, a science/math teacher, and Debbie White, a social studies/language arts teacher, teach a class of fifth graders. One lesson focused on the life of Thomas Edison. Students learned about this important historical figure and then performed some simple science experiments dealing with electricity and the light bulb.[56]

The open classroom, popularized in the 1960s by Charles Silberman in his classic *Crisis in the Classroom*, also has its roots in progressive education. Silberman argued that the open classroom environment, widely used in Great Britain since World War II, might be an effective method of instruction for primary-grade children in this country. Today, the open classroom continues to be an important instructional strategy in such programs as Head Start, progressive preschools, kindergartens, and some primary grades. Here again we can see the influence of John Dewey and Alice Chipman Dewey, whose open classroom centered on meaningful group activity. And once again, while the Deweys' emphasis on important social issues is not always part of open classrooms today, this important instructional method persists.[57]

Whole Language

Finally, even relatively new instructional programs such as the "whole language" method are rooted in the ideas of the social progressives, especially those of John Dewey. In this case, however, the developers of whole language have effectively blended the approaches of behaviorists with those of the progressives. As we have seen, behaviorists understood the acquisition of reading skills as a case of stimulus-response in which the text provided the stimulus and the reader responded by decoding letters into sounds, combining the sounds first into words and then sentences. Progressives, on the other hand, argued that the reading process began with the reader, who brought experiences and knowledge to the text in order to obtain meaning. They also argued (following Dewey) that reading should not be an abstract process but a holistic one that consists of the text, the reader, and the social context of the student. Moreover, since reading, spelling, handwriting, and the like were learned in the same way that children develop oral language, these subjects should be taught as a whole and not fragmented into isolated subject areas. Whole language, therefore, embraced both the progressive and the behaviorist approaches to reading instruction by recognizing that students anticipate text based on experience and knowledge of the topic but then sample it using decoding skills and conduct self-checks for meaning.[58]

In the whole-language curriculum, speaking, listening, reading, and writing are integrated into the experiences and prior knowledge of students. Diane Baker, a teacher in the North Carolina public schools, recorded what her students saw on a field trip to the zoo and then helped them formulate ideas and compose sentences about their experiences. She wrote the student-composed sentences on the blackboard so that students could perceive the relationship between what they saw and what she wrote down. She then read the sentences aloud so that her students could begin to understand that reading is actually "talk written down," that their speech could be recorded into words and those printed words could be read back.[59]

Whole-language approaches can also integrate more traditional forms of instruction in, say, punctuation skills and phonics. For example, Mary Lane, a second-grade teacher, introduced the use of quotation marks to her class while reading a big book entitled *The Little Red Hen.* She "set off" with quotation marks what each character in the story said and then read to the class: "The Little Red Hen said, 'Who is going to help me plant these seeds'? 'Not me,' said the rooster. 'Not me,' said the goose," and so on. Here, learning proceeds from "whole to part" as opposed to "part to whole," as with the memorization of rules of grammar. Later Ms. Lane had the children bake bread (just as the Little Red Hen had done) in the school kitchen as part of the total learning experience. She also integrated phonics into the lesson to help students decode especially difficult words. Throughout the process, however, she connected her instruction in writing and reading and reinforced it in a holistic environment.[60]

THE RECENT STRUGGLE TO CONTROL INSTRUCTION

When first-grader Johnny Peters forgot his lunch box, his mother dutifully delivered it to his rural school; but when she peeked into her son's classroom, she was horrified by what she saw. None of the children were in their seats quietly working. Children were clustered in small groups around the classroom and were involved in a variety of activities ranging from painting and singing to writing and illustrating stories. She stormed to the principal's office and complained for nearly thirty minutes that "this wasn't education, this was chaos." Ms. Peters was not alone.[61]

As teachers embraced innovations such as the basal reader, the open classroom and programs like whole language over the years, they paid an enormous *social* and *political* price. As we have seen, parents of the nineteenth century were often inspired by the "spectacle" of their young children reading a piece of classical literature, or reciting, from memory, a famous speech by one of the founding fathers. Moreover, the routine observation of their children's progress in the year-end "examination" validated the educational experience for them. With the emergence of the graded school, however, direct parental observation and evaluation gradually became more limited. Other than the annual open house or the occasional school play, parents had few opportunities to see what was actually happening in the classroom. When they did, like Ms. Peters, they often were puzzled or annoyed by what they saw. The simplified language of the basal readers appeared remedial to many parents. (This was not classical literature!) Similarly, the apparent cacophony and lack of structure in the open classroom often irritated parents like Ms. Peters. (How could learning take place in such a chaotic environment?) More recently, the emphasis on writing and expression in whole language, where spelling words correctly is less important than the expression of ideas, seems remote and abstract and suggests a "dumbing down" of material. (How can children learn to read and write when they always seem to spell words incorrectly?)

By the early 1970s a broad-based educational backlash (discussed in chapter 1) had begun. Some traditionally disadvantaged groups like African Americans and ethnic people, who had for decades felt alienated from what they saw as a "white curriculum," demanded that schools return control to the local community. Some teachers were perceived as being out of touch with the values of ethnic and black people. Similarly, some administrators were hostile to new instructional programs like "black history," ebonics, or even English as a Second Language. In short, schools were often seen as simply carrying out the mandates of a white-dominated racist society.

Then, as the cost of education continued to rise (due in part to the extension of services and programs to disadvantaged children) and as standardized test scores continued to fall (due in part to the larger and more diverse groups of students actually taking those standardized tests), many others were outraged and demanded fundamental changes in education. For example, by the 1970s, many conservatives rejected some of the more innovative progressive-based educational programs initiated during the 1960s (and discussed in this chapter). They argued that these sorts of programs lacked rigor and academic credibility and that as a result, the United States could not compete in the emerging "global economy." Of course, American workers were the most productive in the world during this period (and they continue to be so today), but the sluggish economy of the late 1970s seemed to validate their criticisms.[62]

Others argued that the solution to our "educational crisis" was greater student accountability through "competency-based" instructional programs rooted in the behaviorist psychology of B. F. Skinner and Edward Thorndike. Still others rejected the basal reader and instructional methods like whole language and demanded (and in some cases actually *legislated*) phonics, and memorization as the primary methods of reading instruction. Some schools even resurrected "Old Guff," requiring the McGuffey *Readers* as the basis of reading instruction.

Another proposed solution to our education malaise was to link education more closely to the world of business. President Richard Nixon's commissioner of education, Sidney P. Marland, for example, advocated this kind of "back to basics" education in the early 1970s, rejecting many of the recent classroom innovations. Marland vigorously supported vocational education over general or "liberal" educational policies. These suggestions were clearly reminiscent of the vocational education movement of the early 1900s; nevertheless, they were embraced as a "fresh" approach to our educational "problems."[63]

By the 1980s, the educational backlash reached a crescendo. Irritated by the National Education Association's support of Jimmy Carter for president in 1976, some politicians engaged in a kind of anti-intellectualism by bashing "liberal teachers," claiming they were out of step with the values, ideals, and instructional methods deemed "best" by the American people (see chapter 10).

These political attacks gained a degree of legitimacy with the publication of *A Nation at Risk* in 1983. This controversial document warned the American people that "for the first time in the history of our country, the educational skills of one generation will not surpass, will not equal, will not even approach those of their parents."[64]

The apocalyptic language of parts of this report alarmed the American people and added further momentum to the educational backlash. By the end of the decade, many political leaders were calling for wide-ranging reforms in education, such as "privatization." In the early 1990s, for example, as part of his America 2000 initiatives, President George Bush brought business leaders together to form the New American Schools Development Corporation (NASDC) to "unleash America's creative genius to invent . . . the best schools in the world . . . to achieve a quantum leap in learning."[65]

This group, composed almost exclusively of businessmen, was convinced that they could create a "privatized" system of schools that would outperform any public institution in the country. To that end Christopher Whittle, the chairman of the group, launched the Edison Project, so called because these schools would be superior to public schools as a light bulb was to a candle. This project was to create hundreds of private schools that would quickly demonstrate their superiority to public institutions.[66]

Of course, the initial enthusiasm for this plan quickly faded when examined in detail. Nevertheless, state legislatures throughout the country were energized and initiated a cacophony of educational "reforms." Recently, for example, the North Carolina legislature demonstrated its distrust of professional schools of education and teachers in general by requiring schools to use phonics as the primary method of reading instruction. The legislature mandated that this method must be used in every primary classroom in the state, and schools must verify that they are in compliance with this directive through annual reports to the Department of Public Instruction. And as Steven Stahl has recently shown, North Carolina is certainly not the only state to act in this way.[67]

The micromanagement of the curriculum by local communities and state legislators may appear less obvious at the secondary level, but enormous political pressure exists nontheless. For years, local communities and state legislators have mandated that schools include politically popular subjects in the curriculum. These have included drug abuse education and sexual abstinence education programs instituted throughout the country. In 1995, for example, the North Carolina legislature mandated that sex education programs throughout the state would focus exclusively on "abstinence from sexual activity until marriage." This approach, according to state law, "is the only certain means of avoiding out of wedlock pregnancy, sexually transmitted diseases and other associated health and emotional problems." Yet beyond the issue of disease prevention, this law also required teachers to inform sixth- through eighth-grade students that the only valid relationship was "a mutually faithful monogamous heterosexual [one] in the context of marriage." As with other curriculum mandates, the state allows individual school districts to adopt a more "comprehensive" sex education program only when public hearings have been held, and only when objectives and instructional materials are made available to parents for review. Needless to say, only one school district in the state has opted for the more comprehensive approach. In all fairness, it should be remembered that North Carolina is certainly not alone: states throughout the nation have also attempted to micromanage the school curriculum through the legislative process.[68]

And of course, pressure to ban certain books from school libraries and from use in the classroom has long been a reality in our schools. Classics like William Shakespeare's *Romeo and Juliet*, Mark Twain's *Huckleberry Finn*, and Nathaniel Hawthorne's *The Scarlet Letter*, as well as a host of more contemporary works like J. D. Salinger's *The Catcher in the Rye* and all of Judy Blum's books have been banned in some elementary and secondary school libraries throughout the nation. Other schools simply remove the "dirty words" or controversial material from these and many other books and return them to the library shelf. Some groups have even criticized certain Disney characters, like the Lion King, as sending anti-Christian messages to children, or have identified certain traits of the Public Broadcasting System's "Teletubbies" as promoting homosexual values.[69]

These kinds of actions, of course, have been challenged over the years by the vigorous action of professional educational organizations as well as informed exchange within the field of education itself. From the work of the Progressive Education Association earlier this century through the publication of the Seven Cardinal Principles in 1918 and synoptic curriculum texts beginning in the 1930s, to Tyler's Rationale in the late 1940s and the humanistic studies of the 1960s and '70s, the secondary (and elementary) educational curriculum has been shaped and reshaped by professional educators. Sometimes these reforms have been implemented in response to critics of the curriculum and sometimes they have been made in anticipation of that criticism. For the most part, however, these changes are grounded in educational research and not the whims of the political establishment.

In recent years, however, the persistent criticism of elementary, secondary, and even higher education by "reformers" such as Allan Bloom, Dinesh D'Souza, and William Bennett, as well as the political demand for more accountability in education, has led to the forced introduction of what William Schubert calls "an ever capricious bandwagon of curricular novelties."[70]

These movements are very disturbing to most teachers, but they clearly suggest that we have passed the threshold of yet another educational transition. It is perhaps ironic that as the federal government increases its role in education through national achievement and credentialing standards teachers will slowly gain greater autonomy as they are relieved of parochial political pressure that often requires the adoption of specific instructional techniques like phonics and sexual abstinence education, and that physically removes certain books from school libraries.

As this happens, we will reach a kind of "educational compact" in which national academic achievement standards will be established and teachers will gain more autonomy to help students achieve those standards. In this environment the growing pressure to conform to ineffective "curricular novelties" will certainly diminish. The judgments of the teacher rather than the politician will become the basis of curricular change. Moreover, in this new environment, beleaguered professional schools of education and university-trained professionals, in consultation with the U.S. Department of Education, will help to define educational standards and, indirectly, the curriculum. The control of the curriculum, in short, will finally shift from the parochial judgments of the local community and state legislature to the professional educator, with virtual control assumed by the federal government.

Moral Education

As Americans read their morning papers or listen to the evening news, they are bombarded by a seemingly endless stream of horror stories about how children are "running amok": drug use, illegitimate births, racial hatred, vandalism, and violence now appear to be part of the fabric of schools—even *elementary* schools—throughout America. More recently, we have witnessed horrific shootings at a number of schools across the nation.

While the nature of this problem clearly has changed over time, the fact is that there have always been grave concerns about the values and morals of our young people. From the declining religiosity of Puritan schoolchildren, the lack of civility among common-school students, the juvenile delinquency of the 1950s, illegal drug use in the 1960s and 1970s and school violence in recent years, Americans have always been concerned—some might even say *obsessed*—with the behavior of children both in and out of school.[1]

In the past, educators dealt with these problems by aggressively teaching their students a set of moral values; but now moral education has disappeared, squeezed out of the curriculum by a singular effort to improve individual academic achievement, and expunged by administrators who have built a virtual wall between church and state. Today a teacher's future often depends on how well his students perform on regular achievement tests, while some administrators, fearful of reprisals from both the Left and Right, refuse to include in the curriculum anything that might be construed as having a moral, religious, or ideological focus. This, of course, has not always been the case.

MORAL EDUCATION DURING THE COLONIAL PERIOD

In colonial times, the centerpieces of moral education were the family, the community, and the church. Supplementing this basic education were denominational church schools that developed as places of learning almost as a secondary function to religion. As we have seen, religious schools sat-isfied the diverse needs of colonial Americans. Even in New England, where a relatively homogeneous population of Puritans allowed the great experiment in "public schooling," education and religion went hand in hand. Most American communities during this period were diverse in terms of both ethnicity and religion. As a result, religious education and moral training specific to each denomination made a great deal of sense.

The basis of the instructional methods of these schools typically focused on learning the catechism that provided a basic moral guide for young children. In a series of formalized questions and answers, children would learn correct individual behavior as well as basic moral and civic virtues. The original *New England Primer,* for example, contained "The Shorter Catechism" that consisted of questions and answers concerning the Puritans' interpretation of religion. One selection included the fol-lowing, for example:

Q. What is the duty which God requires of Man?
A. The duty which God requires of man is obedient to his revealed will.
Q. Where is the moral law summarily comprehended?
A. The moral law is summarily comprehended in the ten com-mandments.[2]

In addition, The *New England Primer* also was a reading book. And yet, as we have seen, moral lessons often were woven into the fabric of these books. The famous twenty-four pictures with accompanying alpha-betical rhymes used to teach reading in the *Primer* (see chapter 6) incor-porated phrases linked to moral behavior. For example, the letter A included the sentence "In Adam's Fall We Sinned all." For the letter F, was the sentence "The Idle Fool Is whipt at School." Following these alphabetical rhymes, students memorized a number of religious tracts like "The Dutiful Child's Promises," "The Lord's Prayer," "The Creed," and the books of the Bible.[3]

For those unable to attend school in colonial times, religious and moral teachings were expected to be a part of a young person's appren-ticeship training or acquired through informal associations within the community. Apprenticeship was more than simply learning a trade; it was seen as a period of moral education during which the master would teach a young man the values of obedience, hard work, persistence, and of course, fear of God. For a young girl, these lessons would be introduced in the family kitchen or while she performed domestic tasks with mothers, sis-ters, and grandmothers. Similarly, members of the community at large were expected not only to act responsibly and morally in their relations with children and young adults but also to assertively provide them with moral lessons when appropriate. Learning these life lessons from the local shoemaker, blacksmith, or storekeeper was a natural and essential component in promoting the moral basis of the community of God. Indeed, it did take a village to raise a child!

MORAL EDUCATION AND THE COMMON SCHOOL

While the family, church, and community would continue to promote morality and values, the nature of moral education began to change following the American Revolution. During this exciting period of nation building, Americans began to recognize that colonial religious schools were not able to provide the basic social and political cohesion for the nation as a whole. No longer would these narrow denominational approaches to education serve the needs of a growing United States of America. Now a "common" educational experience was seen as necessary. Gradually, during the early to mid-1800s, a consensus concerning the content of instruction and moral education began to emerge. The common school embraced a set of pedagogical principles that emphasized the importance of individual achievement developed through memorization and recitation and measured through competitive "bees" (like spelling bees) and, later, oral and written examinations. In addition, early school reformers recognized the need to teach students a set of moral principles that reflected their new roles in American society.

As we have seen in chapter 1, the American Revolution shattered the basis of traditional authority that had centered on deference to an individuals ascribed position (e.g. noble birth). Whether it was in politics, social relationships, or the workplace, deference was part of the traditional, hierarchial order. In this new aggressively democratic nation, however, Americans (including American children) would no longer automatically defer to an individual simply because of their status at birth; that individual now had to *earn* that respect.

The market revolution also helped to weaken the basis of traditional authority. One's status in society was no longer based on who one *was*, but rather what one *did*. In a society where competition in the marketplace routinely sorted out "winners" and "losers," achievement and success also had become the basis of respect and authority. Individualism was rapidly becoming the primary value of American society

While this brash egalitarianism and individualism were cherished hallmarks of early America, they were troubling to many parents. Children, cut loose from traditional restraints, often appeared rebellious and stubbornly independent. Moreover, misbehavior both inside and outside the classroom seemed to be a growing problem. The solution was a "balanced education" that would encourage the marketplace values of hard work, persistence, and achievement but would also demonstrate to children the importance of respecting the wider community and nation. While many commercially minded Americans of this era embraced the values of the marketplace, they also recognized the inherent dangers of unbridled individualism. As the editor of *Harper's* noted in an 1856 editorial, heaven had given Americans "the instincts of property and they must be satisfied." But, he continued, for the greater good "it is widely ordered that in acquiring wealth we should promote the welfare of the human family." Educational reformers of this era quickly recognized that only in the common school could younger Americans learn to balance individualism with a greater sense of God and country.[4]

The Balanced Curriculum

The idea of a "balanced curriculum" was clearly expressed by Noah Webster in his essay "On the Education of Youth in America." Common schools, he argued, should not only develop a student's knowledge base but also an understanding of his "moral and social duties." Similarly, Samuel Harrison Smith, in his "Remarks on Education," argued that the "two great objects of correct education [were] to make men virtuous and wise." Wisdom would aid in individual development while virtue would help equip him to serve the commonweal.[5]

In his important book on teaching, *The Teacher and the Parent,* Charles Northend argued that the primary aim of the common school should be to demonstrate to a student "his true relation to God and his fellow beings and . . . obligations laid on him by these." And Alanzo Potter in his classic *The School and the Schoolmaster*, wrote that simply imparting knowledge was not enough. Education should also help students develop "a power of self control and a habit of postponing present indulgences to a greater . . . good."[6]

Virtue-Centered Morality: God and Country

Religion, of course, would continue to play a role in the moral education of American children well into the 1800s. As we have seen, many common school classes recited a short, nonsectarian prayer at the beginning or end of the day. Yet religion was not the centerpiece of the curriculum; rather, it emphasized the importance of becoming a useful citizen and balancing one's individualism with a sense of community. Early lessons in common school readers such as the McGuffey series focused on one's individual responsibility to the community. Then in more advanced lessons, students were instructed in the values of patriotism.

McGuffey's *Second Reader*, for example, included the story, "The Boys who did Mischief for Fun." In this selection, two boys, William and Edward, tie a grass rope across a path and watch as several people trip and fall down. Discussion questions following the story ask students, "Was it not wicked for them to do such things?" and "When we do mischief can we tell where we shall stop?" Similarly, in the selection "Robbing Birds' Nest," a little boy takes a bird's nest from a tree and then rejoices "at his good fortune." When his sister explains to him that what he has done is wrong, the boy "yielded to the sweet impulse of humanity," and returns the nest. In the discussion questions following this story, students are asked, "Are we not too likely to forget that animals can suffer in feeling as well as we?" Clearly, these stories and many others taught children that *just because something pleased you did not necessarily make it right.* This idea became a central value of the common-school curriculum.[7]

Thus, when McGuffey and his brother selected materials for these readers, they did so with an eye to the contemporary values of mid-1800s America, namely a nonsectarian, pan-Protestantism integrated with a strong commitment to civic virtue. These readers included some direct readings from the Bible but typically scriptural materials were reduced to simple axioms of life that had a clear message for impressionable young boys and girls. The vast majority of the lessons, moreover, focused on civic virtue, presented in a secular context. Students were taught through rather dramatic examples the importance of subjugating their own selfish impulses to the good of their family and community. Once these values were learned, later lessons focused on civic virtue and patriotic nationalism.

The importance of teaching the core values of "God and country" were almost universally expressed by the educational reformers of this time. Their work, published as pedagogies and teacher training manuals were used extensively in the premier teaching institutes of this era as well as in hundreds of academies and normal schools that trained teachers for the common schools. Even those teachers who had little formal training were affected by these pedagogical ideas through independent reading and the emulation of these principles passed on informally from generation to generation of teachers. In turn, it was common-school teachers of the 1800s who transmitted these values to their students on the hard benches of the old schoolhouse.

The Virtuous Schoolteacher

The final component of moral education in the common school was the virtuous schoolteacher. As we have seen in chapter 2, from the very beginning of the common-school movement in the early 1800s women were seen as ideal teachers. They were willing to work for about half the wage of men and since they had few employment opportunities outside of teaching, they routinely were called upon to work far from home, board with strangers and teach in cramped, unheated shanties, log cabins, or converted barns. Among the most important reasons for their employment, however, was their virtuous character.

By the mid-1800s there was a growing consensus that women were more qualified than men to teach younger children. In his important educational treatise *The School and the School Master,* published in 1842, for example, Alanzo Potter argued that women "have a native *tact* in the management of very young minds which is rarely possessed by men." With these words, Potter echoed the general belief among educational reformers of the day regarding women. As part of the commonly held ideology of "separate spheres" (i.e., the "proper" places for male and female), women were seen as particularly suited to teach and nurture young children; it was seen as their "natural mission." As a contemporary of Potter put it, men had been drawn into the demanding and difficult world of the marketplace while women provided a shelter from this growing storm. "While *he* is summoned into the wide and busy theatre of a contentious world where the . . . love of gain . . . tyrannizes over the soul, *she* is walking in a more peaceful sphere."[8]

Because of a woman's unique position in society, many educational reformers felt that the character of common-school students could effectively be shaped by the gentle hand of the female teacher. As Potter noted, they would improve students' "manners and morals in school since females attach more importance to these than men." And as we have seen, Pestalozzi's ideas concerning the importance of "nurturing love" in education certainly had an impact on the acceptance of women in the common school.[9]

In his *North American Reader*, Lyman Cobb included an essay by Gannett that clearly articulated this idea. He wrote that "the sensibilities and affections are the strength of women's nature. She has an instructive sympathy with the tender . . . and the poor. We expect from her examples of goodness." Others felt that the female approach to teaching was superior to that of men because women were presumably better able to encourage students to achieve. As Potter noted, women teachers had a "peculiar power of . . . inspiring [children] with a desire to excel." In short, women teachers not only could nurture children more effectively than men but they also were better teachers, especially in the primary grades.[10]

Mothers also supported women as teachers. As Americans migrated in great numbers from farms to cities; from east to west and from county to county during the 1800s, families were often separated from grandmothers, sisters, and aunts. Without the important child rearing provided by these women, many mothers felt better about having their children taught by a woman rather than a man.[11]

Horace Mann echoed these ideas in his *Fourth Annual Report* of 1840. In this important message to the Massachusetts Legislature he noted that "good behavior and morals" were essential characteristics of a good teacher. Extreme care should be taken by school boards, he said, to assure that "no teacher ever crosses [the school's] threshold, who is not clothed . . . in garments of virtue." Clearly, most educators of the period agreed that women in their "more peaceful sphere" could effectively nurture children in primary common schools and provide them with a moral environment. Their "peculiar power" in this area, moreover, made them ideally suited for the important work of moral education.[12]

By the end of the 1800s, fundamental changes in the American society and economy had, once again, begun to transform the structure and administration of schools as well as the nature of instruction. The consensus over virtue-oriented moral education in the common school was also challenged. The simple moral lessons of the McGuffey *Readers* that focused on God and country seemed appropriate for a relatively homogeneous rural nation of the 1800s. By the end of that century, however, America was neither homogeneous nor rural. Rapid immigration and urbanization had changed the social landscape while the second industrial and corporate revolutions had transformed our economy (see chapter 1).

THE PROGRESSIVE APPROACH TO MORAL EDUCATION

As a result, progressive educators began to question the very nature of moral education. Many argued that the complexity of modern life had made traditional moral codes obsolete. Simple, rigid rules of behavior, they argued, were too arbitrary to deal with the complexities of our rapidly changing modern world. As John Dewey noted in his influential 1909 work *Moral Principles in Education*, "moral principles are not arbitrary . . . they are not 'transcendental.'" What was needed, progressives argued, was a more flexible approach to moral education.[13]

These ideas were summarized in an important report from the Character Education Committee of the National Education Association's Department of Superintendence. Presented during the depths of the Great Depression, it urged that *relativity* rather than *absolutism* should be the guiding principle of moral education. This relativity did not "mean that each generation must repudiate the system of values of its predecessors. It [did] mean, however, that no such system is permanent. . . ."[14]

John Dewey and Moral Education

John Dewey clarified the emerging progressive perspective on moral education by making a distinction between an individual's personal behavior and his civic responsibility. Like other progressives he noted that traditional, virtue-centered moral education focused too narrowly on "moral habits" such as the consumption of alcohol, church attendance, or sexual behavior. This "goody-goody" approach, as Dewey called it, was misdirected. It specified a set of moral codes and did not allow individuals to respond to a range of ambiguous moral dilemmas that they certainly would face in their lives. Rather, Dewey and the progressives favored a more civic-oriented approach to moral education with special emphasis on developing a "social intelligence" in the "service of social interest and aims."[15]

As in chapter 6, Dewey, like many other progressives, was concerned about the effect of rapid industrialization on Americans. He noted that prior to industrialization in the early 1800s, Americans had a direct connection to their society through the world of work. Farmers, for example, understood their important role in providing food for a hungry nation. Similarly, artisans understood their direct connection to society through the products they produced. Whether that product was a pair of shoes or a handmade suit, the artisan created the complete product for market. In the modern industrial age of the late 1800s, Dewey argued, that "connectedness" had disappeared and Americans had lost their understanding of the interdependence of society. Gradually we had become a nation of individuals, mere "cogs in the machinery of life." As such, we had become more isolated and estranged from the communities in which we lived.[16]

Dewey's solution to this predicament, as discussed in chapter 6, was classroom instruction that would help reconnect American children with their communities. Paralleling this was a system of moral education that would help children develop skills to deal creatively with the many problems facing the nation. Rather than simply presenting children with a rigid set of moral codes and rules concerning individual behavior, progressive moral education emphasized solving social problems based on scientific reasoning in a democratic context. Like other aspects of Dewey's educational philosophy, moral education would not be separated from other areas of instruction. Children would receive both a basic pedagogic and moral education through an experience-based, group learning environment.

The Social Education Association

In 1906, Colin Scott organized the Social Education Association to promote these and other progressive educational ideas. Like Dewey, Scott favored self-organized group activities in the classroom, where children would learn their basic lessons and receive a moral education to prepare them for a socially purposeful life. The Social Education Association was instrumental in promoting these ideas through their influential journal *Social Education*, books, and prepared activity plans.[17]

One of the most important of these approaches was William Heard Kilpatrick's "project method," discussed in chapter 6. Through it, Kilpatrick embraced the progressive method of instruction in what he called the "socially purposeful act." Beyond instruction, Kilpatrick was also concerned about the moral education of students. Like most progressives of the time he felt that the development of a civic morality must be integrated into the context of learning. He wrote that the student who "regulates his life with reference to worthy social aims meets at once the demands for practical efficiency and of moral responsibility." By working on socially purposeful projects in a group setting, students would develop cooperation, begin to understand the interdependency of society and appreciate the importance of the community.[18]

Progressive Moral Education's Mixed Legacy

The progressive approach to moral education represented both the possibilities and problems of any democracy. Students who experienced these new approaches to moral education certainly were more flexible in their approach to social problems. They were less likely to submit to arbitrary authority, and they were much more able to abandon traditions when necessary. They were more likely to try new things and they were more willing to experiment. Perhaps most important, they were able to understand the relative nature of morality inherent in the emerging multicultural society. The lesson was simple: not everyone had the same moral code.

On the other hand, the "relativity" of progressive moral education tended to weaken parental authority and often left students more vulnerable to peer influence and contemporary fads. This was especially true for emotionally immature and troubled children. In the absence of an "absolute code of morality," immature students often found it difficult to make the "right" decision about their personal behavior. Similarly, some troubled students understood this approach to moral education as little more than "anything goes." In short, while progressive moral education could be empowering it could also be bewildering and disorienting.

The legacy of progressive moral education, therefore, was mixed. For some students, it fostered a sense of moral ambiguity by introducing to them the difficult concept of relativity in morals. On the other hand, it represented an important transition in morals education. By rejecting the traditional, virtue-centered morality code approach in favor of one that respected independent thinking, it gave students a greater appreciation of diversity and a better understanding of the importance of the community *and* the individual. In short, it helped young Americans deal more effectively with the complexities of the emerging modern world.

Because of these problems, the progressive approach to moral education was not universally adopted by educators during this period. Of course, some schools systems eagerly embraced the new progressive ideas of Dewey's "group learning" or Kilpatrick's "project method"; but others, fearful of the very idea of "relativity" in progressive moral education, clung to the virtue-centered approach. The continued popularity of the McGuffey *Readers*, with fifteen million copies sold between 1890 and 1920, testifies to the persistence of virtue-centered moral education well into the twentieth century. Finally, many school boards adopted some parts of progressive moral education but retained elements of the traditional virtue-centered approach. In these cases, students often were exposed to contradictory set of signals regarding morality, at once both liberating and punitive, creative and authoritarian.

CHARACTER EDUCATION

In addition to the progressive and traditional virtue-centered approach to moral education was a third alternative: character education. Character education emerged in the late 1800s and early 1900s in response to the same forces that spawned the progressive movement. Like the progressives, character educators recognized that changes in the nature of our society and economy would require new approaches to education, especially in the area of moral education. And like the progressives they rejected traditional virtue-centered moral education.

The supporters of this approach established the Character Education Association (CEA) to promote their ideas. The CEA recognized the benefits of the group activities approach to learning because it prepared students for the corporate world that they soon would enter. By understanding the importance of cooperation and teamwork in the classroom, students would be better able to function effectively in the new world of business. They also recognized the importance of the "civic approach" to moral education as a way to develop habits of community responsibility and patriotism.[19]

But character educators parted ways with the progressives over the question of "relativity" in the area of moral education. Like their lineal descendants today, such as William Bennett, they argued that all students must be provided with one absolute moral code with which to direct their life activities. This code could be reinforced through peer influence and group work. The perfect vehicle to promote these values, therefore, was the student club.

Student Clubs

Inspired by the great success of the Boy Scouts of America and other clubs like 4-H established in the early 1900s, character educators recommended the creation of student clubs within the schools to promote specific codes of morality and reinforce them through pledges and oaths. One of the most popular of these "pledges" was the "Children's Morality Code," written by William Hutchins as part of a competition sponsored by the Character Education Association in 1917. Similar to the Boy Scouts' oath (A Scout is trustworthy, loyal, helpful, friendly, kind, obedient, brave, etc.) this code specified "ten laws of right living" that centered on mental and physical hygiene as well as moral development. Attracted to the simplicity of the "code," public schools throughout the country adopted it as part of their moral education program. Similar codes, such as the one developed by *Colliers* magazine a few years later, also became very popular. Many of these codes were used in the creation of student clubs like the influential national Uncle Sam's Boys and Girls Clubs or local clubs like Boston's Courtesy Club, Prompt Club, and Thrift Club.[20]

The influence of the Character Education Association was far reaching and even made its way into the NEA's landmark report *Cardinal Principles of Secondary Education* in 1918. The important principles articulated in this report focused on citizenship, the development of an ethical character, vocational preparation, health, the "worthy use of leisure time," and the need to develop among students the primary elements of democracy: specialization and unification.[21]

In response to the cardinal principle of *unification*, "the democratic ideal that brought people together and provide them with a common set of ideas," for example, educators were encouraged to establish extracurricular activities like school newspapers, social and academic clubs, and intermural sports like football and baseball. These activities were seen as an effective way to promote important democratic principles of social cooperation and teamwork among students. Similarly, school sports would help nonparticipating students develop "school spirit." And of course, where appropriate, these clubs and organizations required specific pledges and oaths for their members.[22]

Educators were also encouraged to support the development of student government associations. Like other extracurricular activities, student government would help diffuse the energies of young high school students. In addition, however, these "model governments" would pro-

vide students with serious lessons in applied civics and instruct them in
the workings of state and federal governments. In short, the extracurricular activities movement that began in response to the publication of the
NEA's *Cardinal Principles* was reminiscent of the character education movement of this era. Through their involvement in clubs and organizations,
grounded in a set of moral codes, students would not only learn lessons of
social cooperation and teamwork but would also be guided by absolute
rules of moral behavior.[23]

THE SEARCH FOR COMPROMISE IN MORAL EDUCATION

The dramatic changes in the social and economic organization of America in the late 1800s and early 1900s led to a dramatic shift in moral education. Variations on both progressive and character education would
continue to dominate the public schools' curriculum on moral education
for the next half century. Although neither approach would be adopted
universally, each would provide the philosophical and pedagogical basis
of more contemporary programs of moral education that defined America's third educational transition.

Through America's experiences in World War I, the Great Depression, and World War II, educators continued to search for a consensus over
an appropriate moral education curriculum for public schools. In the wake
of these three monumental crises, the National Education Association, in
conjunction with the American Association of School Supervisors, issued
a report entitled *Moral and Spiritual Values in the Public Schools*. This report,
published in 1951, attempted to synthesize the progressive and charac-
ter-education approaches and reach a compromise. It recognized components of "character education" by recommending that schools transmit a
"generally accepted body of values" to their students. On the other hand,
the report reflected the progressive orientation by recognizing that these
values could not be presented as universal or absolute. As a result, they
recommended that members of the local community, working with groups
of teachers and parents, develop an appropriate moral agenda for their
schools. While the report failed to satisfy anyone completely, it did represent a kind of uneasy compromise between the two major directions in
moral education. That consensus, like others over the years, however,
would soon disappear.[24]

THE FALL AND RISE OF MORAL EDUCATION IN AMERICA

In the 1950s and 1960s, support for *both* the progressive and character
education approaches to moral education began to collapse. There were

three reasons for this collapse. The first was the growing demand for more academic subjects in the curriculum. The second centered on the rise of anticommunism during the Cold War and the exclusion of other moral issues from the curriculum. And the third was the growing chasm between "sectarian-religious" and "secular-humanist" moral educators.[25]

Academic Subjects

In the years following World War II, and then accelerating during the 1950s, American educators and political reformers began to recognize the need to expand the school's scientific and technical curriculum. In the wake of major scientific advances and the growing demand of colleges for greater academic skills of students, the curriculum of both the elementary and secondary schools began to change. The addition of more academic subjects to the curriculum, however, tended to "squeeze out" the school's traditional emphasis on moral education. There simply were not enough hours in the day to teach everything.

Anticommunism

In addition to the growing number of academic subjects in the curriculum, however, was a dramatic change in the direction of moral education itself. Beginning in the late 1940s a series of international events reignited America's fear of communism and triggered yet another phase of our Cold War. In 1949, China underwent a major communist revolution and emerged as the Peoples' Republic of China. As a result, one of the largest nations in the world had become our "ideological enemy." Then in 1950 the Soviet Union detonated its first nuclear device, thus ending our short-lived monopoly on that devastating weapon. That same year, civil war broke out between communist North Korea and South Korea, the latter supported by the United States. That conflict rapidly escalated into the Korean War and eventually led to the deaths of over 36,000 Americans and millions of Koreans.

In the midst of these serious international events, Senator Joseph McCarthy whipped the country into a frenzy by declaring publicly that communists had infiltrated virtually every area of government and society. In fact, McCarthy said that he had a list of hundreds of individuals who were part of a communist conspiracy. What came to be known as the McCarthy era was a difficult period in America and led to a growing hysteria about the "red menace" in America. We now know that McCarthy had dramatically overstated the "problem," that he *never had* a list of communists, and that his political witch-hunt was designed primarily to advance his own faltering political career. Nevertheless, the "McCarthy era" had a dramatic influence on both domestic and foreign policy during the 1950s.

In addition, McCarthyism refocused the entire moral education curriculum in our schools. Under the renewed threat of communism and the possibility of thermonuclear war, schools throughout the country repackaged their morals education curriculum into a comprehensive anti-communism. This is not to suggest that other issues of moral education, like personal morality or local civic responsibility, were jettisoned, but simply that these issues were subsumed by a pervasive anticommunist crusade. (The observant student might consider other "crusades" in the schools like patriotism during World Wars I and II or today's drug/tobacco education and sexual abstinence initiatives.) There seemed to be no place in the curriculum for these other moral issues as Americans appeared to be caught up in a fight for their lives.

When Joseph McCarthy was found to be little more than a dema-gogue and was formally censured by Congress, the hysteria over communism began to decline. And by the mid-1960s the Cold War had slowly begun to thaw (ironically, despite our growing involvement in the Vietnam War, a war that we fought, ostensibly, to combat communist aggression). As a result, however, our singular emphasis on anticommu-nism as the basis of moral education also began to unravel. By now, both the progressive/civic-responsibility approach to moral education as well as traditional character education had both been virtually abandoned in the schools. In addition, other issues of the period had encouraged edu-cators to avoid the entire area of moral education in the schools.

America's Culture War

The increased number of academic subjects in the curriculum and the Cold War certainly undermined moral education in the schools. In addi-tion, a growing culture war in America that pitted conservative religious sectarian reformers against liberal secular humanists virtually eliminated moral education from the public schools. America's culture wars may have become most recognizable during the 1980s the early 1990s, but the ori-gins of these conflicts can be seen in the Supreme Court's rulings two decades earlier over mandatory prayer in the schools (*Engle v. Vitale*) and the issue of women's reproductive rights (*Roe v. Wade*). In addition, the sexual revolution, the growing use of drugs, and the apparent decline in the morals of young Americans during this period outraged conservative educators, who renewed their call for a new moral agenda for the schools.

These new conservatives, most effective at the local level, typically demanded narrow religious-sectarian approaches to moral education, often pressuring local school boards to allow Bible reading or promoting a specific moral code such as the Ten Commandments. Even today many conservative groups continue to demand that schools post the Ten Commandments in every classroom.[26]

School administrators responded to the growing power and pressure of conservative religious groups by distancing themselves from any sort of moral education in the curriculum and by drawing a clear line between the public and private spheres of education. This line became so sharp, however, that the school curriculum was "sanitized"of any traces of moral education whatsoever. By eliminating any discussion of moral issues in the classroom, they reasoned, political controversy could be avoided. As a result, by the end of the 1970s moral education was virtually nonexistent in America's public schools.

THE NEW RISE OF MORAL EDUCATION

But rumors of the death of moral education in America were highly exaggerated. Even as administrators jettisoned its last remains from the classroom, a new generation of moral education had quietly begun to emerge in this country. Two distinctive approaches began to appear during this period, each with roots earlier in the century. The first was a "neoprogressive" approach and included the "values clarification" movement and the "cognitive-based values development" of psychologists such as Lawrence Kohlberg. The second approach was a resurrection of traditional character education based on a virtue-centered moral education reminiscent of the 1800s.

Values Clarification

The values clarification movement began with the publication of *Values and Teaching* by Louis Raths, Merrill Harmin, and Sydney Simon in 1966. This volume not only provided a comprehensive theory concerning the importance of moral education in the schools but also included practical ideas and activities to include them in the classroom. In the 1970s the movement spread to public schools throughout the country. Like the progressive moral educators before them, values clarification theorists recognized the "relative nature" of values in a rapidly changing society. They argued that moral education should help students develop a process to help them make choices and decisions that were "positive, purposeful, enthusiastic and proud."[27]

Like the progressives, values clarificationists also rejected the memorization of certain moral rules. Instead they argued that moral education could be achieved through intensive "dialogue" with teachers to discover meaningful individual values; through the use of "value sheets" on which students would respond in writing to ambiguous moral dilemmas, and through "group discussions" organized around movies or the media. In each of these realms, teachers were to guide rather than indoctrinate students in making their own ethical decisions. For example, rather than simply demanding that her students support America's involvement in the Vietnam War, Sara Whitfield used a form of values clarification in her eighth-grade history class to explore with students their personal feelings about the conflict and help them make their own ethical decisions about the war. In the same way, she helped students examine the very personal issues of prejudice, racism, and sexism through the values-clarification process. In her literature class, Ms. Whitfield had students read *Roll of Thunder, Hear My Cry* by Mildred Taylor. This award-winning book focuses on the life of a young black girl, Cassie, growing up in the segregated rural South in the 1930s. Cassie experiences racism, prejudice, and sexism for the first time in her life. Ms. Whitfield explored these episodes with her students, who then confronted their own feelings on these subjects. This process was very effective, and helped her students grapple with difficult issues that they would face later in life.[28]

Although values clarification was popular among many teachers during the 1960s and 1970s and continues to be so today, it also has received its share of criticism. Some saw the process as encouraging a form of ethical relativism while others felt it represented a subtle form of indoctrination. Similar to the criticisms of progressive moral education fifty years before, conservatives mistakenly argued that values clarification simply encouraged students to believe that all moral positions were valid. This, they said, was dangerous for society. Others asserted that values clarification was, by its very nature, a form of indoctrination. For example, William Casement noted that one of the values clarification values sheets asked students to list ten things they could do for the environment. Casement said that this exercise was a form of indoctrination because it was built on the assumption that protecting the environment was a positive good![29]

Cognitive Moral Development

The other important neoprogressive approach to moral education was cognitive moral development. The most influential advocate of this approach was Lawrence Kohlberg, who articulated his ideas in a series of articles beginning in the mid-1960s. Kohlberg fused educational theory on the cognitive development of students with theories of psychological growth. He argued that children evolve through six distinctive stages of moral reasoning during which they move from total self-orientation to a moral perspective that is based on principles. The movement from one cognitive moral stage to the next was achieved through conflict in the form of debate and vigorous discussion concerning ethical questions.[30]

As with the values clarificationists, Kohlberg recommended vigorous discussions to achieve greater awareness of one's own ethical values. This method, he argued, was essential in moving from one cognitive moral level to another. Unlike the values clarificationists however, Kohlberg argued that his cognitive moral stages had nearly universal validity. Kohlberg did distinguish his cognitive approach based on principles from the traditional values-centered education, which he saw as being centered on rules. Rules, he argued, like the Ten Commandments, simply specified certain kinds of behavior (however exemplary that behavior might be) while *principles* provided universal guides with which to make moral decisions.

Over the years, Kohlberg's ideas have been criticized both by conservatives who perceive a strong liberal bias in his cognitive levels, and feminists, who argue that his model does not recognize gender differences in moral decision making. Nevertheless, his approach has helped educators understand that moral reasoning is not entirely an abstract process but can be rooted in rigorous scientific research. As such, his work has provided us with an exciting new direction in the development of moral education.

The Neoconservative Reaction

While the neoprogressive approaches to moral education (values clarification and cognitive moral development) have had a major impact in the resurrection of moral education in America over the last few decades, traditional character education also has resurfaced as a conservative alternative to these approaches. In addition, a growing minority of Americans, demanding a denominational religious education for their children, have rejected each of these approaches and have begun to send their children to Christian day schools. Others have embraced home schooling.

This "new" character education emerged in the 1970s as a conservative reaction to the perceived "moral ambiguity" of both values clarification and cognitive moral development; the "movement" included two distinctive groups. The first were the traditional character educators who supported the work of the American Institute of Character Education (AICE). The AICE had developed a comprehensive character education curriculum for grades K–6 that included instructional materials and manuals for classroom use. The second group were "new" character educators who emerged from the short-lived conservative revolution of the 1980s. These conservatives had a more political agenda that included a return to the virtue-centered morals education of the late 1800s. Led by William Bennett, secretary of the Department of Education under Ronald Reagan, the movement sought to create a comprehensive curriculum of moral education from elementary through secondary education that would not require new courses but would integrate moral values into the existing curriculum through the use of literature. Bennett's highly profitable *The Book of Virtues* is a collection of these kinds of stories that encourage and develop what he has called "moral literacy."[31]

While these "new" conservative approaches to character education appeal to some Christian parents and educators today, others see Christian religious education or home schooling as an alternative. (Of course, not all home schooling enthusiasts are part of this conservative Christian movement.) Between 1965 and 1990, the number of students enrolled in Christian day schools more than tripled, from about 800,000 to nearly 2.8 million. These schools often adopt the Accelerated Christian Education Program, a "comprehensive" set of instructional and moral education materials for grades K–12. These materials are "individual learning packets" (workbooks) that students complete at their own pace, after which they take tests on the material. Each lesson has a moral and Christian focus that reflects an evangelical/fundamentalist interpretation of the Scriptures. These lessons also have a clear, rigidly conservative agenda condemning socialism, liberalism, and humanism and sometimes even denigrating Catholicism and Judaism. Moreover, since these lessons are "individualized" there is little classroom instruction, and teachers (who typically are not certified) simply monitor student progress in their workbooks.[32]

AMERICA'S THIRD EDUCATIONAL TRANSITION AND MORAL EDUCATION

The future of moral education remains unclear. As the achievement test gradually becomes the sole measure of the worth of education, emphasis on moral education will continue to struggle for a place in the curriculum. Our exam-driven curriculum today has little room for moral education except for an emphasis on competitive individualism and the occasional politically popular crusade like drug, tobacco, alcohol, or sexual abstinence education. We seldom find a systematic inclusion of the values of civic virtue in the primary or secondary school curriculum. It is no wonder that some students have little appreciation of how their actions might affect others. The focus is on *me* and not *we*.

As we have seen, the major causes of the decline of moral education are local control of schools and their demand for sectarian approaches to morality and the more recent move toward accountability. Since local communities have often demanded a narrow sectarian approach to moral education, reformers have virtually jettisoned the entire concept of a "values curriculum" in order to achieve a separation of church and state. In their headlong attempt to secularize the schools, however, administrators have forgotten that there are important societal values like civic virtue and individual responsibility that can be taught in schools without violating an individual's religious freedoms. Similarly, as political pressure for accountability in education (typically measured by multiple-choice examinations) has mounted, teachers have been forced to shift their attention from values education to academic achievement. Taking time to demonstrate complex ideas of civic virtue in the classroom, for example, may seem "counterproductive" for teachers today since these ideas will *not* be included on standardized achievement tests.

However, as we move to a more global economy, and as our classrooms become even more culturally diverse, the need for a new system of values education is becoming apparent. If history is our guide, this new system will transcend narrow sectarian religion and focus on an emerging consensus of national and international secular values. Toni Marie Massaro's recent call for a "constitutional literacy" that emphasizes our nation's "perpetual struggle to balance multiple competing concerns" represents an important new direction in moral education. While this kind of approach will not be achieved without vigorous opposition, it appears to be the direction we are headed. Two things are certain: first, we must learn from our past and once again recognize moral education as an integral part of the school curriculum; second, we must abandon our attempt to "sanitize" the curriculum of its moral component in response to the parochial judgments of local and state interests.[33]

Discipline

Just as the *New England Primer* helped to define the methods of reading instruction for nearly two hundred years during America's colonial period, the infamous whipping posts of New England schoolhouses symbolized the severity of student discipline during the 1600s and 1700s. In fact, this corporal approach to discipline had a long history and reflected generally accepted attitudes toward children. As those entrenched attitudes changed in the context of America's educational transitions, however, the common forms of discipline also began to change.

Traditional attitudes toward discipline were rooted in the Judeo-Christian idea of "original sin." Given this biblical assumption, children were seen as "stained," and as a result severe discipline and corporal punishment were often deemed necessary to wrest them from the influence of the devil. The imperative "Spare the rod and spoil the child" first appears in Proverbs 23: 13–14, where it reads, "Withhold not correction from the child . . . for if thou beatest him with a rod . . . thou shalt deliver his soul from hell."[1]

This attitude toward discipline was commonplace in English public schools of the 1500s and then spread to the colonies in the early 1600s. Richard Mulcaster, tutor to Princess Elizabeth, teacher at London's Merchant Taylor's School and respected pedagogue, reflected this general view when he wrote his influential manual *Training Up of Children* in 1581. While he felt that whipping children because they had failed "in learning" was "worse than madness," he wrote that the "rod may no more be spared in schooles, then the sworde may in the Prince's hand."[2]

COLONIAL-ERA DISCIPLINE

Physical punishment, often administered before the other students, was seen as valuable for a number of reasons. First, the errant student would learn to obey the school rules or to apply himself to his lessons. Second, those witnessing the punishment would, in theory, remember the episode with terror and think twice about making the same mistake. John Robinson, a New England schoolmaster from Plymouth Colony, made his position on discipline very clear when he wrote "there is in all children . . . a stubbornness and stoutness of mind . . . which must in the first place, be broken down and beaten down." And even the legendary teacher Ezekiel Cheever, renowned for his patience and love of students, would use corporal punishment when he felt it was necessary. One of his students, John Bernard, recalled his early school days with Cheever at the Boston Latin School. Bernard wrote that he "was often beaten for my play and my little roguish tricks"[3]

By the end of the 1700s disciplinary methods had changed little, though an occasional teacher might spare the rod on his young charges. More typically, however, the daily school routine of silent reading, memorization, and recitations was interrupted by the explosive sound of the ferule (ruler) across the hand or the shrill cry of admonition and the sobbing of a young student. In fact, keeping order through the use of corporal punishment in the classroom was as much a part of teaching as was the daily reading lessons, the recitation of spelling words, or the cacophony of alphabet and syllable drills. In 1785, for example, Joseph Eaton complained to the selectmen that his son had "received unsuitable correction" (a severe beating) from Mr. Clark of the writing school Queen Street. But the selectmen vigorously supported the disciplinary techniques of Mr. Clark and instructed him to continue to use them to maintain the "reputation of the school."[4]

DISCIPLINE IN THE EARLY REPUBLIC

The use of corporal punishment in schools was, of course, not confined to New England. Throughout the colonies and states of the early republic physical violence was routinely used to discipline students. Because his upstate New York schoolhouse could often be a place of disciplinary terror, Warren Burton remembered vividly the restraint and patience of his beloved teacher, Mary Smith. As you will recall, her methods of discipline were based on gentle persuasion rather than corporal punishment. When Burton or his young schoolmates became sleepy during a lesson, for example, Miss Smith would "lay [them] across the seat for a nap." Similarly when students talked in class, she quieted them with a gentle admonition or a knowing look.[5]

But Mary Smith's methods of discipline were the exception at the beginning of the 1800s. Although some teachers were gradually abandoning corporal punishment, classroom discipline was often quite severe. This fact certainly did not escape young Warren as he awaited his first school term, with vivid images of the schoolmaster's "frowns and ferulings" looming in his head. He often had heard Ben, son of the hired man, describe the "direful punishments" (of some teachers), the "tingling hand, black and blue with twenty strokes." And his fears seemed to be realized when the minister and new schoolmaster visited his home the fall preceding his first winter term. Burton remembered his new teacher "as stiff and unstooping as the long kitchen fire shovel and as solemn of face as a cloudy . . . day."[6]

Though they varied from teacher to teacher, methods of "keeping order" continued to be quite severe in the first decades of the 1800s. Burton recalled with horror one of the "stricter teachers," Mehitabel Holt, who was "very popular with . . . parents." Miss Holt "was not lovely," he noted, and she differed "from . . . dear Mary as much as all that is sour does from the quintessence of sweetness." Children who whispered during her class were often locked in a "windowless closet." And those who fidgeted or squirmed in their seats were "tied to her chair-post for an hour." Miss Holt also twisted ears and snapped children on the head with her "thimbled finger." Even during the five-minute recess, children were threatened with punishments if they raised their voices above "quiet conversation."[7]

John Dean Caton, future chief justice of the Supreme Court, sometimes used a more primitive form of justice in his classroom during the 1820s. In his *Memoirs and Observations,* he wrote that he seldom resorted to corporal punishment but recalled the day that one student challenged his authority and he "resolved to settle the question as to who was master." On his way to school he "cut several birch whips about five feet long and as large as my thumb at the butt." When he arrived at the school he "commanded" the "delinquent" to "stand forth" and "applied the birch about ten blows as hard as [I] could lay it on." He then "struck him over the head and face with [my] whip which was [by then] well worn up." Not sensing sufficient remorse from his student he "took a fresh whip and laid on perhaps fifteen lashes with [my] best efforts. The cotton from [the student's] shirt sleeves actually flew across the house in bits."[8]

While not all teachers used such force with students, Warren Burton's "Master Particular" had a long list of regulations and spent the good part of the school day dealing severely with offenders. For minor offenses, he required that children sit under or on top of their desk. He also required boys to sit on the girls' side or girls to sit on the boys' side of the classroom. His punishments for more "severe" infractions of the rules included "ferruling on the hand[s], whipping with a rod on the back, pulling hair, tweaking noses pinching and boxing ears and locking offenders in the closet." Other punishments, however, were akin to torture. The offending child was required to "hold out at arms length the largest book which could be found." If the arm bent or drooped the child received a "knock of the ruler on the elbow." Burton recalled that one of his classmates fainted during this punishment. Another favorite of "Master Particular" required that the offender stoop over and place his finger on the head of a nail on the floor. As the blood rushed to the head, students would become dizzy and would either faint or fall to the ground. [9]

Yet another teacher, John Vance Cheyney, routinely resorted to violence. Cheyney recorded in his *Autobiography* that he had difficulty maintaining order in his classroom in West Rupert, New York. The students had all "turned against" him until one day he "chucked the shortest of them under his bench . . . with [my] feet on his neck." Apparently that was an insufficient deterrent to "misbehavior" because one "strapping dullard" continued to look out the window. As a punishment, Cheyney "struck him across the jugular vein with the back of a solid book." By week's end he "had but one pupil left in his class." No wonder![10]

As might be expected, these kinds of punishment sometimes backfired. Though some parents were delighted that teachers provided an ordered classroom environment, they were less than enthusiastic when severe discipline was inflicted on their own children. And occasionally, students themselves rebelled. During his tenth winter in school, Warren Burton's new teacher was a former "inferior officer aboard a privateer in the late war" (the War of 1812). Although Mr. Augustus Starr was "genteelly dressed and gentlemanly in his manners," he was a harsh disciplinarian. On one occasion, "he knocked [a] lad down [and] hurled a stick of wood at another." His temper was so volatile that "the scholars were terrified and some [parents] kept their younger children at home."[11]

One fateful day Starr hit John Howe on the head with a ruler giving him " a cut . . . which drew blood. The dripping wound and the screaming boy were a signal for action." John's older brother, Thomas, and another boy, Mark Mouten, ran to "our privateer," wrested the ruler from his hand, and with the help of several others, they carried him out of the schoolhouse "kicking and swearing." The boys then brought him to the crest of the hill, "smooth and slippery as pure ice from a recent rain . . . [and] . . . pitched him over the side."[12]

Starr slid down the hill "until he fairly came to the climax . . . of his pedagogical career." The Captain lay still for a while, then looked up at his "mutinous crew, great and small, male and female, now lining the side of the road next to the declivity from which most of them had witnessed his expedition." Following a brief and violent encounter with some of the older boys he "gathered up his goods and chattels and left the schoolhouse." The next day he "sailed out of port," never to be seen again.[13]

A CHANGE IN DISCIPLINE

Augustus Starr, of course, had no idea that the little rebellion of his students symbolically represented the end of an era. During the early to mid-1800s, important changes in classroom discipline were taking place. These changes were initiated by the forces of both the American Revolution and a fundamental alteration in the material conditions of Americans brought about by the market revolution. America's first educational transition would witness a gradual transformation in classroom discipline for the new nation.

As discussed in chapter 1, the 1700s were a period of dramatic change in the American colonists' attitudes toward religion. Although the changes were in some ways contradictory, together they helped alter the colonists' attitudes toward discipline and punishment of both adults and children. The first of these changes was the first Great Awakening, and the second was the growing secularization of society as part of the Enlightenment.

As we have seen, the Great Awakening essentially was a challenge to the prevailing Calvinist doctrines of the northern colonies and the Anglicanism in the South. From the 1720s until the eve of the American Revolution, evangelical preachers from a variety of denominations brought religion to colonists in back-country camp meetings and city churches alike. The clear message of the revivals was that salvation did not depend on formal religion; rather, it was a personal matter. Ordinary people, touched by these charismatic preachers, gradually began to embrace these new religious denominations not because of the formal training of the clergy but because of their persuasive power and message of personal salvation. This created an environment that was not only more tolerant of religious diversity, but one that gradually helped to erode the "fire and brimstone" vision of the basic depravity of humankind as well as the idea that most were predestined to hell.

This new vision, moreover, called for a more humane approach to the discipline of soldiers, sailors, prisoners, and of course, children in school. In the late 1700s and early 1800s, for example, flogging in the military as the primary means of punishment began to decline in Great Britain and the United States. At the same time, the corporal punishment of criminals, such as whipping and pillorying, gave way to the more humane penitentiary, where lawbreakers were imprisoned and rehabilitated rather than beaten. New progressive institutions like Sing Sing prison in upstate New York were built in the first decades of the 1800s. And in the humble schoolhouses and classrooms throughout the republic, a new attitude toward discipline also was emerging.[14]

In addition to the Great Awakening, there was a parallel decline in the role of religion in the lives of many colonists. This secularization of society was not *necessarily* a rejection of the existence of God, but a recognition of the central importance of rational, scientific, "natural laws" in their lives. Influenced by the great scientific discoveries of the 1600s and 1700s by Isaac Newton, William Harvey, René Descartes, and Francis Bacon, as well as the new secular philosophies of John Locke, Voltaire, Jean-Jacques Rousseau and others, American colonists had begun to change the way they understood the nature of their world.

John Locke

In his influential *Essay Concerning Human Understanding* (1689), for example, John Locke rejected the prevailing Calvinist doctrine of predestination and argued that humankind had the capacity to learn and to improve; by extension, society could also be improved. Then in 1737, the Abbe de Saint-Pierre wrote his famous *Observations on the Continuous Progress of Universal Reason*, which introduced Europeans and Americans to the idea of human progress through scientific and rational thought. Denis Diderot also developed these and other ideas. In his *Encyclopedia,* for example, Diderot helped popularize the notions of equality, liberty, and the rights of man and at the same time was highly critical of organized religion. The message of these and other philosophers was clear: if Americans embraced science and rationality, they, too, could achieve "enlightenment."[15]

This new conception of the individual challenged the traditional beliefs concerning the inherent depravity of mankind and reinforced the basic notion of human dignity and perfectibility. These ideas were reinforced by John Locke in his influential volume *Some Thoughts Concerning Education*, in which he introduced his ideas of psychological discipline. Sharply breaking with more traditional notions on the subject, Locke perceived young children as "white paper, void of all character," rather than permanently stained by original sin. Since children were malleable and able to change, he recommended vigorous training with an emphasis on development of rational attitudes, especially by denying them short-term gratification. For Locke, praise for correct behavior and humiliation for failure and misbehavior were two ends of the same approach.[16]

Jean-Jacques Rousseau

While John Locke argued that the child was a blank slate (*tabula rasa*) and could effectively be disciplined through psychological motivation, Jean-Jacques Rousseau saw the child as essentially good though sometimes corrupted by society itself. While Rousseau's vision of childhood was different, his emphasis on psychological rather than corporal discipline paralleled that of Locke. As we have seen in chapter 6, Rousseau argued that the most effective method of instruction was one that allowed the child's natural curiosity and needs to guide learning. If the child understood that he needed to read, learning would begin and proceed quickly.

Similarly, in the area of discipline, Rousseau felt that children should be allowed to do as they wished as long as they understood and experienced the consequences of their actions. Those consequences, however, should not be corporal punishment but rather psychological motivation. If a child broke a toy in anger, for example, she should not be beaten but made to understand that the toy would not be replaced. The limits of her actions would then be learned. Similarly, if the child told a lie to his parent or teacher, he should be made to understand that he would not be trusted in the future. In short, punishment was individualized on the basis of a specific offense but was never meted out with physical violence.[17]

These ideas were eagerly adopted by progressive families in Britain and the colonies during the late 1700s, and by the early 1800s they had been embraced by Americans who were having fewer children, but were investing more time and energy in their children's development and education. Numerous "advice books" of the 1800s were read by the growing middle class of urban America. Similarly, agricultural journals like *The Cultivator*, written for the new commercial farmers of the era, promoted these revolutionary ideas of psychological discipline among rural Americans.[18]

THE MERIT-BASED SOCIETY

While the ideas of Locke, Rousseau, and a host of lesser-known educators and reformers of this period had an important influence on changing attitudes toward discipline, the market revolution of the late 1700s and early 1800s provided the material conditions that made sense of these philosophies. As the market economy and the merit-based society associated with it emerged during this period, a new rationale for discipline had become necessary. Traditional deference (respecting and obeying your "betters" because of their noble birth) was gradually abandoned as the basis of one's status shifted from inherited social position to one of merit and achievement.

As Augustus Starr had discovered the hard way, students of the 1800s (like others in this society) would not automatically defer to the authority of an individual simply because of his ascribed status. Rather, mutual respect between teacher and student was becoming more common in the aggressively democratic and market-oriented society of young America.

Michel Foucault has shown in his *Discipline and Punish* that a new rationale for obedience had begun to emerge in the wake of the market revolution. This new "disciplinary power" was based on supervision, establishing norms of achievement, and the written examination. Constant supervision in the classroom encouraged students to obey the rules of behavior. Standards of achievement drew children into a competitive environment while the examination measured their performance and helped reinforce the "disciplinary power" of the teacher. Through constant supervision of students and by controlling the content and administration of the exam, teachers were able to establish their positions of authority in the classroom and maintain order.[19]

By linking the new "secular culture of Discipline" with what remained of traditional deference, common-school teachers, both male and female, had a powerful tool with which to maintain discipline in the classroom; no longer would the whipping post be the primary method of classroom discipline. Now, psychological forms of motivation, combined with constant supervision and a system of grading and evaluation, would become the new tools to encourage proper behavior.

Joseph Lancaster

One of the first educators to systematically apply these revolutionary ideas of discipline in the classroom was Joseph Lancaster. As we saw in chapter 6, Lancaster developed his monitorial system of instruction to facilitate the education of large numbers of students in his Boroughs Road school in England. With two hundred or three hundred students in one classroom, Lancaster desperately needed a system of discipline that would keep order. But as a Quaker and a gentle man, he opposed the use of corporal punishment with his beloved students. Rather, he favored "constant activity and proper motivation."[20]

Lancaster's basic motivational technique was a system of material rewards for both academic excellence and good behavior. In addition to an elaborate system of badges of honor, he awarded tickets that students could redeem for balls, tops, and books. In 1803 alone, for example, he distributed five thousand little toys, seven dozen books, twenty-five engraved medals, three star medals, eight silver pens, and thirty-six purses.[21]

In addition to motivating students to do well and behave in the classroom, Lancaster used humiliation for those who broke the school rules. Offenses such as truancy or "repeated or frequent" idleness and talking were punished by placing a small log around the students neck. Students who disobeyed parents or the teacher were required to wear a paper crown with the school infraction written on it (an early dunce cap?). And for coming to school with a dirty face or hands, boys were subjected to the most humiliating of punishments: being washed in public by a girl.[22]

Psychological Motivation: Praise and Shame

Although Joseph Lancaster's career was cut short when he was trampled to death by a runaway horse in New York City on October 23, 1838, his ideas on motivation for both instruction and discipline had a lasting impact on educators in the new United States. As noted in chapter 6, many of these ideas were popularized by educational reformers in this country. Edwin C. Hewett in his *A Treatise on Pedagogy for Young Teachers*, and Charles Northend, with his *The Teacher and the Parent,* for example, spent a great deal of time discussing motivation. Hewett recommended that teachers understand the importance of promoting the value of desire among their students to encourage discipline and achievement. And in his seventh "principle" of teaching he stated "it is a general law that desire precedes acquisition."[23]

Northend also wrote that the love of approbation, "the desire to gain the favor of the wise and good and the approval of their teachers" could be used as an "inducement to good deportment and diligent applications." By praising students when they acted responsibly in the classroom, teachers could effectively maintain order. Northend related the story of a "young lady," a former pupil who had once "caused trouble" in the classroom. Then suddenly her behavior changed, and she became one of the most well-behaved and best students in the class. Years later the "young lady" told Northend what had happened: "I remember what first induced me to alter my course. You praised me. I found I had met your approbation and I [was] determined to deserve it."[24]

But while both of these important educational pedagogues recommended the use of positive motivation as a tool in maintaining classroom discipline, they also saw shame and humiliation as useful motivational techniques. For example, Hewett noted that the power of conscience, "that which makes us feel that we ought to do what we think is right and let alone what we think is wrong," was one of the principal components of training. In order to improve deportment, he noted, the teacher must "make frequent appeals to the child's conscience." In so doing, students would be encouraged to "do the right thing" and behave in the classroom.[25]

The New Readers and Discipline

By the middle of the 1800s, the accepted method of discipline in the classroom had quietly shifted from corporal punishment to psychological motivation. Educational reformers, influenced by the philosophical and economic changes associated with America's first educational transition, had begun to promote a more humane approach to discipline and punishment. These new approaches, moreover, were reinforced in the classroom by a new generation reading materials, such as the McGuffey *Eclectic Reader* series first published in 1837. As we have seen, these readers, like many others of this period, developed the idea of subordination of individual interest to a higher authority. By first providing a rationale for children's obedience to parents, students were in a better position to understand the idea of obedience to other secular authorities, including the teacher.

In McGuffey's first *Reader*, for example, five selections demonstrated to students why obedience to parents was important. These lessons did not command students to obey (in the biblical sense) but rather provided logical reasons why children should act responsibly and curb their own self-interests to the authority of their parents. Once this value was embraced it was a short step to obeying the teacher.[26]

Thus, by the mid-1800s the intellectual revolution regarding discipline launched by Locke and reinforced by the market revolution had begun to take hold in middle-class households throughout the countryside and cities. New attitudes toward children encouraged "psychological" approaches to discipline rather than corporal solutions. In the schoolhouse this shift from whipping post to dunce cap was becoming much more common (though certainly not universal) and was reinforced by a "secular culture of discipline," with lessons on obedience and civic responsibility carefully integrated into the early readers.

REACTION OF LOCAL COMMUNITIES

As many teachers of this era began to change their disciplinary methods in the classroom, some members of their communities responded with both anger and frustration. The teaching experiences of Benjamin Gue, for example, reveal a number of problems associated with his more modern disciplinary policy. During his last year as a teacher in upstate New York, Gue boarded with the Hawley family. Mr. Hawley routinely told Ben that he should change his teaching methods in one way or another. One day he complained that he "did not whip enough." Gue responded that "no scholar had refused to mind [and that he] had no occasion for whipping." In a huff Hawley retorted that he "thought it was a good plan to whip sometimes."[27]

Not whipping enough actually ended the careers of many young teachers during this period. A good example was Lester Ward. Though generally a good teacher, young Ward had the usual minor disciplinary problems in his first classroom. On Monday, December 24, 1860, he recorded, "I did not have a very good school today. The pupils are beginning to hate me." Three days later he recorded that "the day passed but not without a little trouble. I made Emerson Bull [and William Drake] stay after school. I talked to them a little and let them go." The following day he contemplated more drastic measures, noting, "I got a whip this morning but I hope I shall have no occasion to use it." And he did not.[28]

But Ward's restraint cost him his job. He wrote in his diary on January 5, 1861, that although he had been "in authority all day [and had] a very agreeable morning, *I am shut out from the school.*" In just a little over a month into his first teaching assignment he had been dismissed by the local school board. Ward noted that Mr. Smith, the school trustee, "took me outside to tell me that . . . he was sick of hearing so many rumors and complaints against the order in the school."[29]

The difficulties that Ben Gue and Lester Ward faced as teachers, though common, were perhaps even more pronounced for women teachers. Mary Augusta Roper of Templeton, Massachusetts, for example, experienced severe criticism for her progressive methods of discipline. Following completion of her teachers education at Hartford Institute, her first teaching position, at the age of nineteen, was in Mill Point, Michigan. Roper conducted the school the way she had been trained and "never used the rod unless a scholar refused to obey." Nevertheless, some parents demanded her removal because she "don't *lick* them at all."[30]

As we saw in the case of instruction (see chapter 6), more modern teaching methods were often slow to be adopted by classroom teachers because of the parochial interests of the community. When an enlightened teacher sought to use newer psychological methods of discipline rather than the ferule or whip, she often was second-guessed by members of the town and sometimes was fired or simply not rehired for the next term. As a result, though some teachers of the mid-1800s abandoned whipping as the routine method of keeping order in the schoolroom, severe corporal punishment, sometimes akin to torture, continued. Successful teachers had to be able to balance classroom discipline with the "mores" of the community, however twisted those mores may have appeared to them at the time. They were required to "whip enough" to satisfy the more primitive instincts of some parents but they also used reason, kindness, praise, and the "knowing look" to maintain the respect and devotion of their students. The shift from "whipping post to dunce cap" had begun in earnest.

DISCIPLINE AND THE SECOND EDUCATIONAL TRANSITION

As the graded elementary school and high school of the late nineteenth century became the standard form of education in this country, the dunce cap symbolically replaced the whipping post throughout the nation, and psychological modes of discipline became more accepted. Yet while corporal punishment gradually fell from favor in most areas of the country, schools (especially urban schools) were faced with a new set of problems. The rapid immigration of people from Europe and the migration of rural Americans from the country to the city during this period led to an extraordinary increase in enrollment in urban schools. The growing number of new students strained the resources of these schools and challenged teachers as never before.

In order to deal with this relatively new problem, educators adopted the corporate model of organization with a new administrative structure, a new school architecture, and new ideas on student regimentation and discipline. In larger schools, for example, principals or sometimes assistant principals assumed the role of formal disciplinarians of last resort and were often called upon when classroom teachers were unable to control unruly students. Being "sent to the principal's office" was (and continues to be) a terrifying event in a student's life; it could result in a severe tongue lashing, suspension, or in some cases, a paddling.

Similarly, new approaches to classroom organization were developed in order to deal with the sheer numbers of new students. In the late 1800s, for example, school architect C. B. J. Snyder created what would become the standardized classroom of the twentieth century. It consisted of symmetrical rows of identical desks (with attached chairs) securely bolted to the floor, facing the blackboard and the teacher. Typically there were forty-eight desks for grades 1 through 4; forty-five desks for grades 5 and 6, and forty desks for grades 7 and 8. The vast majority of all secondary school desks also were permanently fastened to the floor and would remain so for much of the next century.[31]

William Bagley and the Industrial Model of Discipline

While the terror of the disciplinarian and the rigidity of the bolted-down desk provided the *structure* for discipline in the large schools of the late 1800s and 1900s, new methods of student discipline and regimentation were also demanded to keep order in the classroom. Responding to this demand was William Bagley. In his extremely popular *Classroom Management*, first published in 1907, Bagley developed a system of student management that was used by hundreds of thousands of teachers over the next quarter century.[32]

For Bagley, the primary purpose of the school was to establish and nurture habits compatible with industrial society. Upon leaving school, the student should be able to quickly adapt to the rigors of the industrial assembly line. The teacher's role, therefore, was to enforce strict discipline and regimentation. Bagley noted, for example, that he could judge the efficiency of a teacher simply by observing "the manner in which lines pass to and from the room." In fact, he recommended that students move through the halls of the school quietly and in lockstep, similar to Lancaster's monitorial school students a century before.[33]

Even the bodily functions should be regulated. Students would silently march to the restroom, remain in line with "head[s] erect, eyes turned toward the teacher." At the signal, a group of four or five students would enter the lavatory, relieve themselves, and exit to another line. This process would continue until "toilet recess" was completed.[34]

When students were in the classroom, they were to remain silent and still with their hands folded, "feet flat on the floor." At the call of "attention" by the teacher (sometimes with a clap of the hands) the students were to adjust their bodies "in a certain definite posture" and prepare for the work of the day. In this way, the maintenance of classroom discipline was not simply an adjunct to learning, but the central component of learning itself.[35]

Bagley, of course, was not the only proponent of the structured, regimented, industrial model of discipline. E. W. Elmore, professor of education at the University of Wisconsin, took a slightly different approach to this method with his "Squads for Discipline." For Elmore, writing in 1923, the military organization of squads in the classroom was the solution to all discipline problems. He suggested that each row of the class become a "squad" complete with a permanent nickname and leader who would sit in the front seat. This leader (drill sergeant?) would be in control of the entire squad in the classroom and on the playground. Using the group conformity concept of the military, Elmore recommended that the misbehavior of one "squad" member would result in punishment of the entire group. He felt that this would lead to peer pressure on individuals to behave.[36]

The new industrial/corporate approach to the classroom was a popular one, especially among ambitious school administrators, members of local school boards, and the business community. Classrooms were quiet, students were docile—they marched lockstep in straight lines—and graduates became accustomed to the new industrial discipline of rigid punctuality and order. This model was consistent with both the "vocational education" movement of the early 1900s and the new instructional methods of this era. In short, many schools during this period embraced a new ethos of social efficiency, organization, and "scientific management" compatible with the modern economy.

Behavior Modification Techniques

While this industrial model of discipline was popular, it lacked intellectual credibility. That credibility was supplied by the behaviorists. As noted in chapter 6, John B. Watson had a profound influence on education as a result of his behavioral studies and experimentation at the beginning of the 1900s. Watson argued that all human behavior was a response to external conditioning and could, effectively, be molded. What came to be known as "behavior modification techniques" soon captured the imagination of educators and became a powerful force not only in instruction but also in discipline.

While Watson introduced the concepts of stimulus-response to the intellectual community, B. F. Skinner popularized them with his early work on the scientific basis of behaviorism. In his classic, *Science and Human Behavior,* first published in 1951, he noted that the primary goal of the behaviorists was to "predict and control the behavior of the individual organism." He noted further that the "'cause and effect relationships' in behavior—are the laws of science [that could] yield a comprehensive picture of the organism as a behaving system."[37]

Reinforcements

Skinner gradually developed the idea that *reinforcements* in the form of rewards could shape behavior. In a more recent reformulation of his position he noted that "by carefully constructing certain 'contingencies of reinforcement,' it is possible to change behavior quickly and to maintain it in strength for long periods of time." He argued, moreover, that the teacher must *consciously* discipline students, lest they be influenced by other factors such as the media or their peers. In fact, as Skinner noted in his popular book *Beyond Freedom and Dignity*, students were not free to choose because their behavior was a function of what had happened to them in the past. As a result, Skinner recommended subtle manipulation of the students' environment through reinforcement in order to achieve goals of classroom discipline.[38]

The idea of reinforcement through prizes and badges for good behavior and achievement had, of course, been a part of the classroom since the early 1800s beginning with Lancaster and others. However, Skinner differed from most traditional forms of discipline in that he rejected punishment, even in its psychological form of shame and humiliation. In fact, as behaviorists have argued over the years, any form of punishment actually works against the development of good behavior. Rather, Skinner argued that the best policy was for teachers to ignore a student's bad behavior as much as possible (to avoid sending the wrong signals) but to reward good behavior quickly and vigorously.

Over the years, however, Skinner became more and more frustrated with the direction of modern education, and he routinely chided educators for their unscientific approach to teaching. As a result, he often promoted the idea of "teacher-proof," programmed learning materials with which students could work independently and learn concepts, ideas, and facts through a system of repetition and reinforcement. As we have seen in chapter 6, this kind of "teacher-proof" education has been embraced by many schools, including Christian day schools' Accelerated Christian Education curriculum.

Skinner also wrote a novel that was designed to demonstrate how the principles of behavioral psychology could operate if they were rigorously adopted by schools. The fruit of that effort was his controversial *Walden Two*, published in 1974. In this ideal community, children were peaceful, cooperative, happy, and above all, demonstrated self-control. His conclusion was that social problems could be eliminated if schools and communities would adopt his behavioral conditioning techniques. By establishing scientifically designed institutions that continually reinforced only those values that were beneficial to the larger society, moreover, the world would be a much better place. While many argued that *Walden Two* was simply a conservative reaction against the outspoken language and excessiveness of young people in the 1960s, the book was very influential.[39]

Despite the rather grandiose claims of Skinner, behaviorists continue to influence modern disciplinary techniques. So called "neo-Skinnerians" such as Fredric Jones and Lee and Marlene Canter have modified these ideas and suggested a variety of reinforcements that can be used in the classroom. Some have emphasized the importance of using traditional verbal signals such as praise, graphic rewards like gold stars, and actual prizes such as books and free time to reinforce correct behavior.

Neo-Skinnerians: Frederic Jones and Lee and Marlene Canter

In his *Positive Classroom Discipline*, published in 1987, Fredric Jones' focused his attention on the importance of nonverbal methods of communication such as body language, facial expressions, eye contact, and physical proximity as important methods of discipline in the classroom. He has also suggested that teachers reconfigure the classroom seating, if possible, to allow easier access to students and vice versa. Each of these strategies, he argued, could be effective in producing positive behavior in the classroom. And for Lou Ann Ryan, who taught in an urban elementary school in North Carolina, Jones' disciplinary approach worked.

Gary D. was a large and unruly third-grade boy who often bullied others and distracted his classmates. Nothing seemed to work with Gary. Finally, Ms. Ryan placed Gary's desk next to hers. The close proximity to Ms. Ryan kept Gary's disruptive behavior under control, and teacher and student actually bonded over the course of the school year. While Ryan understood that this procedure does not always work, she was willing to try anything to solve this particularly difficult discipline problem.[40]

Lee and Marlene Canter also developed a comprehensive program of discipline in their *Assertive Discipline* (1976) and *Succeeding with Difficult Students* (1993). Their program, packaged for use in classrooms, presented a "competency-based" approach to discipline. This model suggested that teachers assume an assertive "take charge" attitude in the classroom to deal with all disciplinary problems. For the Cantors, "assertive teachers are empowered teachers" who insist on having their needs met first before learning can begin. The basis of their model was a clearly articulated student discipline plan ("limit setting") that rewarded good behavior but forbade any activity that interfered with learning. The Cantors broke with Skinner by recommending punishments for misbehavior. However, they followed Skinner by recommending that teachers place "marbles in a jar" as a signal of good behavior and reward the class with additional recess minutes or reading a story at the end of the day.[41]

When Barbara Taylor took over a fourth-grade class during the spring semester of the school year, she found her students to be "wild and out of control." After a difficult first few days she implemented a version of the Cantor Assertive Discipline program. She created a large bulletin board and wrote every student's name on it. Next to each name she placed a paper pocket. Each student was then given ten paper stars on Monday morning. If a student exhibited good behavior, such as working quietly or remaining his seat, he was awarded an additional star. For misbehavior, a star was removed. At the end of the week, the five students with the most stars were rewarded with a pizza lunch. Competition was intense, and within a week classroom discipline had improved significantly. Although the system was time consuming and often interfered with classroom instruction, it did solve the problem for Ms. Taylor.[42]

The legacy of social efficiency discipline and behaviorism continues to the present day. It can be seen in programs that promote school uniforms, require formal student responses like "yes, sir" and "yes, ma'am" (such as Louisiana's Yes Sir Law), and in systemwide programs like the Cantors'. Even in schools where these formal programs have not been implemented we can see the residual elements of the social efficiency approach. In recent observations of several elementary schools, we found that "toilet recess," straight lines in the halls, and sometimes even a kind of lockstep marching was alive and well, nearly a century after William Bagley proposed them. Moreover, the behavior modification techniques of neo-Skinnerians, in which positive reinforcement plays a central role in both classroom instruction and discipline, continues to have an impact on teachers. Virtually every elementary and middle school bulletin board we observed was adorned with arrays of gold and silver stars, smiley faces, papers with words of praise, and certificates of achievement—all used to reinforce student behavior. Neo-Skinnerism is alive and well.

THE PROGRESSIVE/HUMANISTIC APPROACH

Beyond what might be called the industrial/behaviorist model of discipline is another important direction in classroom management and instruction that might appropriately be called the progressive/humanistic approach. This method recommends greater communication between teacher and students, with an emphasis on *preventative* discipline and the judicious use of *corrective* discipline. It also recommends the development of a more democratic environment in the classroom and greater emphasis on nurturing self-esteem among students.

This approach emerged from the work of the progressives at the turn of twentieth century who were appalled by the new organization and regimentation in the schools proposed by Bagley and others. They argued that by suppressing natural curiosity in the name of "keeping order," intellectual development had also been suppressed. A quiet classroom was *not* necessarily a place where *learning* would take place. A classroom organized in a symmetrical pattern with immovable desks was *not* necessarily a place where students could experiment or effectively work in groups. Moreover, the subtle manipulation of students in the name of reinforcement represented a kind of authoritarianism that had no place in the classroom.

Pestalozzi and Rousseau

Many of the progressive ideas concerning instruction and discipline were derived originally from the writings of Johann Pestalozzi and Jean-Jacques Rousseau in the late 1700s and early 1800s. As we saw in chapter 6, both Pestalozzi and Rousseau saw constant activity based on familiar objects and interests of students as a kind of *preventative* form of discipline. From Pestalozzi came the idea of the child-centered approach to education; that is, the focusing of attention on the individual needs of students rather than forcing them into a rigid instructional/disciplinary regime. Although children were taught together, the child-centered approach was flexible enought to address individual variations in learning. Moreover, the interests of the students themselves often became the focus of instruction.

Taking advantage of student interests such as the anniversary of a special event, a newspaper story, or their personal experiences, the teacher could mold the curriculum and facilitate learning.

Perhaps more important in the context of discipline, however, was Pestalozzi's ideas regarding the importance of love of children. Like his child-centered curriculum, which focused on the individual needs of students, his emphasis on the importance of love and affection for each child was central to his ideas on discipline. The character Gertrude, in his famous educational novel *Leonard and Gertrude*, had boundless love for her students, and her discipline was a natural product of that love. For Pestalozzi, mental and moral order were interdependent and represented the essence of his educational ideas. Mental order was achieved by doing practical work. In Gertrude's school (her home) that work was spinning and weaving cloth. Moral order, on the other hand, was achieved through love for each of her students. This individual love created a kind of inner peace among "her children" that in turn led to contentment and freedom.

From Rousseau came a slightly different approach toward individual discipline of the child. As we have seen, Rousseau believed that children were basically good but often were corrupted by their social environment. In the opening paragraph of his novel *Emile*, he made his position on this issue very clear: "All things are good as they came out of the hands of their Creator, but every thing degenerates in the hands of man." This view, of course, differed from the more traditional vision of the child as inherently evil from birth. As a result, Rousseau rejected violence against the child as a means of discipline, favoring a more rational approach that demonstrated to children the consequences of their misbehavior and reinforced the idea of individual responsibility. This approach would quietly reinforce the importance of self-control and clearly demonstrate the link between the child's actions and the consequences of those actions. What might be seen as subtle manipulation, therefore, was the essence of Rousseau's method of discipline. Without impinging on the freedom of the child, the teacher would manipulate experiences so that lessons could be learned. In book 4 of *Emile*, Rousseau discussed this form of manipulation in the context of children learning "coarse words" and "unpleasant ideas." He noted that "you do not forbid the child to say these words or to form these ideas; but without his knowing it you make him unwilling to recall them."[43]

Francis Parker

By the end of the 1800s, Francis Parker had begun to implement a number of these new instructional and disciplinary ideas in the classroom. Under his guidance, the public schools of Quincy, Massachusetts, adopted a program of education that was in many respects "progressive" before that term had been used in the educational setting. Lelia E. Patridge reported on the Quincy Methods in 1885. She noted that in these schools, the "child was the objective point and not the courses of study, examinations, or promotions." In addition to innovative instructional methods such as grouping students and the introduction of new subjects such as drawing, modeling, coloring, and natural history, the classroom was a "joyous" place built on the "comradeship of teacher and pupils." In this "atmosphere of happy work" teachers were not concerned about disorder in the classroom; nor did they scold, snub, or spy on their students. Rather, they promoted a classroom based on mutual "courtesy and respect." These ideas were the basis of the emerging democratic classroom of the twentieth century.[44]

John and Alice Chipman Dewey

In their University of Chicago lab school, John and Alice Chipman Dewey adopted many of these ideas. As discussed in chapter 6, their goal was to develop a sense of community and cooperation among their students through an activities-based approach to learning. Those activities focused on developing what the Deweys called the "social value" of knowledge. By simulating occupations from the past and present, students learned about the interdependence of individuals in the larger society and how those indivduals worked together.

As we saw in chapter 7, John Dewey argued that as a result of the industrial revolution of the 1800s and the corresponding rise of individualism we had lost our sense of community. Over the years, Americans had placed greater and greater emphasis on achievement and individual success but had somehow forgotten the broader community of which we were all a part—we had developed *Me* at the expense of *We*.

For these reasons, Dewey rejected the "social efficiency" industrial form of discipline (such as Bagley's *Classroom Management*) in favor of one that would help students reestablish their connections to society. If students understood that they were an important part of their community, they would have a greater stake in it and would be less likely to become alienated. Moreover, through academic group work that centered on knowledge that was socially important, students would develop moral habits and social cooperation in the classroom and later in their communities.

Like most progressive educators, the Deweys' notion of discipline in the classroom was directly tied to instruction. By creating a classroom environment of constant activity where lessons of social cooperation were reinforced continually in group work, students would not only learn their academic subjects but would develop disciplinary habits of social cooperation. This emphasis on the importance of group dynamics would become a powerful tool for educators over the next hundred years.

Other progressive schools in the first decades of the 1900s followed that general tradition. Marietta Johnson's School of Organic Education, for example, adopted the progressive model of instruction and discipline with special emphaisis on the ideas of both Pestalozzi and Rousseau. For example, she emphasized the importance of a child-centered, individually paced curriculum where learning tasks were not arbitrarily assigned but selected by the student and the teacher. The child-centered curriculum was reinforced in a loving and nurturing classroom environment. Students learned to behave not by traditional disciplinary techniques but by recognizing the consequences of their actions. This was reinforced through group pressure and the gentle but firm persuasive power of the teacher. Junius Merriman's lab school at the University of Missouri adoped a similar curricular and disciplinary program that included more flexible time schedules for classes, an interest-centered curriculum and a disciplinary regime that emphasized the democratic responsibilities of both students and teachers.[45]

The Cottage School, located in the planned suburban community of Riverside, Illinois, outside Chicago, and the Little School in the Woods in Greenwich, Connecticut, also used preventative forms of discipline centered on the activity-based curriculum. Through socially constructive simulations in a "play" format, students learned cooperation and the rules of behavior from peers and encouragement from teachers.[46]

While students in these progressive schools were highly motivated and often needed little corrective discipline, these schools represented a distinctive shift from regimentation and corporal punishment to a child-centered, democratic classroom. In each of these cases, students developed what educators today refer to as self-esteem. Children were given freedom to act and learn (within the limits discussed above) rather than being regimented into passive submission. Such was the emerging ideal of the progressive classroom of the twentieth century.

MODERN DISCIPLINARY TECHNIQUES:
PREVENTATIVE APPROACHES

While progressive educators of the late 1800s and early 1900s adapted the ideas of Rousseau and Pestalozzi and effectively challenged the traditional use of corporal punishment and regimentation as methods of discipline in the classroom, other educators and psychologists expanded their vision and contributed greatly to our understanding of modern disciplinary methods.

Rudolph Dreikers

Rudolph Dreikers, for example, centered his attention on the importance of democratic teaching in his *Discipline without Tears.* This book, completed by P. Cassel when Driekers died in 1972, demonstrated that the most effective classroom was one in which mutual respect and democracy replaced the traditional autocratic environment. Rather than the teacher demanding adherence to a set of arbitrary rules, students were invited as a group to have input into the process. By understanding the rules of behavior and the consequences of their actions, students tended to behave more responsibly.[47]

Cathy Lee Gates, a fifth-grade teacher in an urban school, was impressed by these ideas. On the first day of school, she worked with her students to develop a set of classroom behavior rules. Everyone had input into the process, and there was a general agreement that these rules were important. Throughout the school year students had the opportunity to add to the list. The class voted on each proposed new rule. Ms. Gates found that this approach gave her students a "stake" in classroom management and as a result there were fewer cases of misbehavior. Students, moreover, tended to "monitor" the actions of their classmates.[48]

Following Dewey and other progressives, Rudolph Dreikers felt that the group was the most effective basis of both instruction and discipline. He argued that the genuine goal of all students was to belong to the group but that trouble began when a student could not achieve a sense of belonging. Typically these isolated students sought attention by "clowning around," refusing to obey the teacher, seeking revenge through vandalism, spreading lies, or simply by withdrawing emotionally from the class. Each of these "mistaken goals," as Dreikers called them, was the basis of misbehavior in the classroom. Yet by drawing students into the group through individual counseling and peer nurturing, these problems could be resolved.[49]

Jacob Kounin

Directly influenced by Dreikers, Jacob Kounin focused on the role of the group in understanding disciplinary problems; but Kounin also offered specific instructional strategies to prevent disruptions in the first place. Like other progressive educators, Kounin argued that the most effective method to prevent behavioral problems in the classroom was constant activity. In his *Discipline and Group Management in the Classroom,* published in 1971, Kounin placed special emphasis on lesson momentum and effective transitions from one subject to another to keep students "on track."[50]

Kounin also introduced a concept he called "with-it-ness," or the ability to have what Ms. Gates called "having eyes in the back of your head."

Kounin argued that when the teacher knew everything that was going on in the classroom, students would be less likely to disrupt the class. Moreover, they would respect the teacher who understood the actual causes of specific classroom disruptions (such as a personal problem with one of the students) and the primary instigators of trouble. If the teacher did not have "with-it-ness" and did not understand what really was "going down," she would lose the respect of the students.[51]

Kounin also noted the importance of "overlapping"; that is, being able to deal with several individuals or groups at a time. By remaining aware of the diverse activities in the classroom through a kind of "eternal vigilance," a teacher demonstrates to her students that she is concerned with everyone and not just a chosen few. This reinforces the democratic nature of the classroom and encourages proper behavior.[52]

Haim Ginott

While Dreikers and Kounin each focused on the importance of preventing disciplinary problems by creating a democratic classroom and demonstrating the importance of the group in shaping individual behavior, Haim Ginott emphasized the role of effective communication and building self-esteem among students. Beginning with his popular 1965 book *Between Parent and Child* through his classic *Between Teacher and Child* (1971), Ginott demonstrated that the way we communicate with children is the most important factor shaping discipline. He argued that disciplining a student was a series of "little victories" over time and not a single event, such as yelling or screaming to achieve momentary silence. By maintaining their own self-discipline and modeling that behavior before the class, teachers could also mold the behavior of their students. Ginott also felt that by sending "sane messages" to students (notably the use of *I* rather than *you*), effective communication could be achieved.[53]

Amy Prescott, a sixth-grade teacher in an urban school system, had success with this method and incorporated it into all her classes. Instead of isolating a "problem" student by saying "Johnny, *you* are always out of your seat," Ms. Prescott preferred to say, "Johnny, *I* would like you keep your seat during the lesson." In this way, Johnny was not humiliated and the correct behavior was "telegraphed" to him. Johnny recognized the specific thing he must do to please Ms. Prescott.[54]

Finally, Ginott recommended the use of "congruent communication." Teachers, he argued, should avoid labeling students and should focus on the specific issue or problem at hand and not generalize. Rather than saying "Johnny, you always do that!" or "Why can't you learn to listen?" congruent communication would limit criticism to the specific incident or problem. Once again, Ms. Prescott would say: "Johnny, I would like you to reread your math book on fractions," or "Johnny, what did we say about fractions in our lesson today?"

Despite their cool swagger and the appearance that they just don't care, Ginott emphasized, most students are very sensitive to what the teacher has to say. By being sarcastic, by labeling students, by attacking their character and by using "you" messages rather than "I" messages, students will be hurt and will either withdraw or misbehave as a method of revenge. By inviting cooperation and demonstrating respect for them as individuals, teachers can slowly and surely help students build their self-esteem and direct them toward acceptable classroom behavior.

Ginott had an important impact on modern theories of classroom behavior. He was the first to establish the link between the ways that teachers (and administrators) communicate with students and the manner in which students respond. Moreover, by focusing on the need to develop self-esteem in students in order, to achieve self-control in the classroom, he built on the work of the early progressives and demonstrated the psychological basis of behavior. Today we recognize that one of the primary causes of classroom disruption (as well as low achievement) is the lack of self-esteem among students. Ginott's work essentially completed the long shift from traditional corporal forms of punishment to modern behavior modification.

MODERN DISCIPLINARY TECHNIQUES: CORRECTIVE APPROACHES

While each of these progressive/humanistic approaches to discipline proved to be effective, each was *preventative* rather than *corrective*. And as powerful as each was in keeping students on track in order to avoid discipline problems in the first place, there are always those disciplinary problems that seem insoluble. Beginning in the mid-1960s however, William Glasser built on these ideas and developed a corrective approach that complemented them very well.

William Glasser: Reality Therapy

In his first two books, *Reality Therapy: A New Approach to Psychiatry* (1965) and *Schools without Failure* (1969), William Glasser introduced a radically new approach to psychiatry that essentially rejected Freudian psychology. Freud had argued that the key to mental disturbances, especially neurosis, could be found in past experiences of psychic trauma, or unresolved conflicts. By unlocking those repressed memories, individuals could recognize their problems and presumably solve them. Glasser rejected this approach; he reasoned that individuals could do little to change past events but did have the ability to modify their behavior and make productive prosocial choices about their future.[55]

Before introducing "reality therapy" into the classroom, however, Glasser argued that schools must become a "good place to be" where teachers and students show respect for one another; where students feel that they are important, have a degree of democratic power; where "one frequently hears laughter," where rules are reasonable and understood to be for everyone's benefit, and where administrators support the entire disciplinary approach. Once this environment is created, reality therapy can successfully be implemented to deal with specific discipline problems.[56]

Glasser identifies a number of steps through which student behavior will improve. The first is to secure student involvement in the process. Teachers begin by asking a "problem child" to identify his own misbehavior. Glasser notes that while it is much easier to simply tell the student what he has done wrong, this does not allow him to take responsibility for his behavior. Also, it is not the role of the teacher to uncover the presumed psychological basis of the problem (what Glasser sees as excuses) by asking *why* the student misbehaved. Rather, the teacher should focus on what actually was done. Once the student has identified his problem behavior, he must clearly express why that misbehavior is a problem. Again, while it is easier for the teacher to clarify this to the student, this strategy subtly shifts responsibility from the student to the teacher. Also, moral judgments should not be acceptable: the student should not be allowed to say that the reason that he misbehaved was because he was "bad."[57]

Once students have recognized that they have done something wrong and why they did it, teachers should let them develop a plan to change that behavior. Although the teacher may have to make subtle suggestions at first, students must take individual responsibility and plan a course of action. Having done that, teachers must get a commitment from the student, preferably in writing, that specifies that plan of action. Glasser concludes by recommending that teachers accept no excuses from students regarding the reasons for their misbehavior, that they do not punish them and thereby destroy the trust that has developed in the school and classroom, and finally, they should *never give up*. His recommendation is to "hang in there longer than the student thinks you will."[58]

Today, while teachers recognize the need for a comprehensive, child-centered disciplinary policy (whether it is based on the behaviorist or progressive humanistic model) public humiliation continues to be the primary form of discipline in many classrooms throughout the country. But this technique often backfires. Children who come from homes where violence is common, or who lack the self-esteem necessary to achieve successfully, act appropriately in the classroom, or care about either, will probably not respond to archaic forms of discipline. In fact, their punishment will certainly disrupt the entire classroom. Over the years we have learned that some students cannot achieve or behave because of physiological, sociological, or psychological problems. These basic issues must be addressed first. Others fail or misbehave because their basic needs of security or belonging have not been met. In each of these cases traditional humiliation-based forms of discipline will have little effect on their behavior and may actually make things worse.

In some cases active intervention though counseling and testing in conjunction with intensive programs to promote self-esteem, improve remedial skills, or develop conflict-resolution strategies might be part of a comprehensive intervention plan. Moreover, temporary placement of these students in special schools may also be an appropriate strategy of last resort.

Our ideas regarding discipline have changed greatly since the early years of our nation's history. In colonial times, children were seen as inherently corrupt because of the stain of original sin. Only through corporal punishment could teachers correct this condition and wrest students from the great deceiver, Lucifer. In the wake of America's first educational transition in the early 1800s, however, these traditional attitudes toward children began to change. Gradually young people came to be seen as either inherently good though sometimes corrupted by society, or alternatively, as a blank slate (*tabula rasa*) that could be molded through vigorous intervention. As a result, the whipping post gradually gave way to more humane psychological methods of discipline that emphasized incentives and rewards for good behavior and achievement but shame and humiliation for poor deportment, laziness, or poor grades. As we approached our second educational transition in the early 1900s, society's attitudes toward children had changed once again. While some were alarmed by the great numbers of immigrant children pouring into public schools and devised industrial and vocational approaches to discipline and instruction, children in general gradually came to be seen as having unlimited potential and were valued as individuals like never before. The response to this new perspective was the development of disciplinary programs that were democratic in focus, hinged on mutual respect, and recognized the importance of developing self-esteem among children.

We are now moving rapidly toward our third educational transition, with greater teacher autonomy juxtaposed to national standards for student achievement. In this new environment, teachers have reinforced their authority and *preventative* classroom discipline through effective communications and by creating a democratic classroom where students understand the consequences of their actions in the context of the group. Moreover, as teachers have helped students balance their own individualism with a sense of community and recognize the direct consequences of their actions, discipline in the classroom has gradually improved.

In fact, contrary to the impression that may have been created by extensive media coverage of tragic school shootings in Colorado and elsewhere across the nation, these modern disciplinary techniques are working. Students today have higher school enrollments; more are involved in college preparatory work; they have higher levels of volunteerism as compared to their grandparents' generation of the 1930s or even their parent's generation of the 1960s. Students today are also less violent and less likely to take their own lives, contrary to the image that is often presented in the media. Over the last twenty years crime and suicide rates, for example, are down dramatically. In fact, a report released in April 2000 by the Justice Policy Institute revealed that violence, the number of weapons, and homicides in schools were down in recent years. The chance of a student being shot in school is less that one in two million. Nevertheless, over 70 percent of parents expressed grave concern over violence in the schools. Despite the continued media focus on the "youth problem" (one bemoaned by every generation of adults in recorded history) and punctuated by recent tragic examples of violent teenage behavior, it is clear that American teachers have learned their lessons well and are doing a remarkable job.[59]

The Control
of Teachers' Destinies

During her first winter as a teacher Laura Ingalls Wilder boarded with a local family who received a portion of her pay for their services. She recalled vividly the jealousy of her "benefactor," Mrs. Brewster. One night, in a voice loud enough for Wilder to hear, she said "she'd not slave for a hoity toity snip who had nothing to do but dress up and sit in a school house all day." The following night, Wilder had frightening nightmares.[1]

Though Wilder's book was a fictional account of her teaching experiences, many teachers have had real nightmares not only about some of their students but also about those who controlled their destiny. In fact, for more than two centuries, American teachers have had to balance their teaching responsibilities with the occasional maliciousness of parents and other members of their local communities as well as the overly demanding paternalism of educational administrators and state legislators.

LOCAL COMMUNITY CONTROL OF EDUCATION

From America's colonial period through the mid-1800s, education was the province of local interests. As a result, teachers had to adjust their behavior, their disciplinary techniques and their instructional methods to the whims of the community. Local control of education often resulted in what one educator called "petty local interests and a dog in the manger spirit."[2]

Securing a teaching position in the early 1800s, for example, often depended on who you knew in the community and not necessarily your qualifications as a teacher. Warren Burton notes that his favorite teacher, Mary Smith, had received her teaching job over a local girl, Polly Patch, simply because Smith's uncle, John Carter, had recently become a member of the school board. Her candidacy was opposed not only by the Patch family but also by the influential Captain Clark who stood to lose the board money since Smith planned to stay with her uncle. This darker side of American education could make life difficult for teachers who often found themselves in a firestorm of jealousy, envy, or just plain politics.[3]

Teacher Education

Although we cannot be sure as to Mary's academic preparation, she most likely had a common-school education and perhaps a term or two at a local academy. Generally, there were few opportunities for teacher education at this time (1802). It would be another nineteen years before Emma Willard would establish her Troy Female Seminary in 1821 and thirty-four years until Mary Lyon would open Mt. Holyoke Female Seminary in 1836. In fact, it wasn't until the early 1830s that the first state normal school was established in Lexington, Massachusetts; and the first teacher institute was opened by Henry Bernard in 1839.

In short, during the summer of 1802, formal teacher training was rudimentary in the more settled areas of New England, Pennsylvania, and New York and virtually nonexistent in other areas of the country. In fact, the preparation of common-school teachers reflected the general development of the community. Ellwood Cubberly probably described it best when he said "our schools like our clothing during this early period were largely of the homespun variety."[4]

As factory-made cloth gradually replaced "homespun" fabric during these years, the nature of teacher education changed as well. By the mid-1800s there were over six thousand private academies throughout the country. Some of these institutions offered teacher training programs and some introduced the new methods of Pestalozzi and others. In New York State alone there were 887 academies in operation by 1850, many of which provided some teacher training. And as Cubberly has noted, during these years, thirty-two of these academies were established as institutions for women.[5]

Similarly, by the 1860s, thousands of copies of Samuel R. Hall's *Lectures on Schoolkeeping*, David P. Page's *Theory and Practice of Teaching*, and Alanzo Potter's *The School and the Schoolmaster* had become available to a new generation of common-school teachers. These pedagogies were read as part of a formal teacher training program in some of the premier teaching seminaries (like Troy and Mt. Holyoke), in academies and normal schools scattered throughout the country, and they were eagerly read and reread by prospective teachers before, during, and after their teaching assignments.[6]

In addition, common-school teachers might also attend a local teacher institute led by William Fowle or any number of other educational reformers of the day. In a two-, three-, or four-week workshop, experienced teachers and novices could learn about the blackboard, the basics of teaching the ABC's, the "uses and abuses of memory in education," the "opening and closing of school," the use of monitors, and the essentials of "emulation and discipline."[7]

By the mid-1800s, teachers had a number of avenues to the schoolhouse available to them. While formal teacher training was rare in the early 1800s, it had become much more common by the eve of the Civil War with the growth of academies, normal schools, and, later, high schools. In addition, both the experienced teacher and novice could receive further teacher training in some of the new ideas in curriculum and discipline at academies or teacher institutes. Supporting all of this was the publication and wide availability of a number of "modern" teaching pedagogies that revolutionized the teaching of young children.

Getting Paid

While acquiring an education and getting that first teaching position was sometimes difficult, it all seemed worth it on payday. When Laura Ingalls Wilder went home to dinner on the Friday following her last day of teaching, her father's eyes were "twinkling." He reached into his pocket and "one by one he laid in her hand four ten dollar bills." Pa explained that he had collected her pay from Mr. Brewster who said she had taught a good school. "Oh Pa! It was worth it," she said breathlessly. "Forty Dollars!" Though a fictional account based on her real life experiences, Laura revealed the excitement that most young teachers felt when they received their first pay. But not all paydays were as uneventful or as happy as Laura's.[8]

Sometimes getting paid for a semester's teaching was a Herculean task. Such was the case of Sara Ann Gue in upstate New York. When Sara Ann completed her teaching responsibilities for the winter term in April of 1848, she went with her older brother, Benjamin, to collect her pay. On Friday, April 7, 1848, Benjamin Gue recorded in his diary that he drove his sister "out to no 9 [the schoolhouse] to get her money." Though it was a "very pleasant day" it took them "5 hours going fifteen miles." First they went to the home of the school trustee, Mr. W. Durants, where they "took dinner fed [the] horses and rested."[9]

They then drove to the schoolhouse and "stopped a few minutes" while Sarah Ann took one last look at her beloved school. From there they "went to Mr. Elias Durants" where Sarah Ann had boarded, and "settled up." Next they "went to the town superintendent and got the money." Ben and Sarah Ann then picked up their friend Hul in a nearby village and at sundown they set out for the trip back home. Exhausted but excited by their journey, the three travelers "got home about ten o'clock safe and sound."[10]

For other teachers, receiving their pay was nearly impossible and took a great deal of tenacity. When he was released from his teaching duties on Saturday, January 5, 1860, Lester Ward had some difficulty receiving his pay of twenty dollars for his month in the classroom. On Tuesday, January 8, he received his check from Mr. Smith, the school commissioner, and then "went to Mr. Pierce, the President" to have it endorsed. And although he had "the majority of directors sign it . . . there was not any money in the treasury." Director Coolbaugh told him "that perhaps the collector Mr. Blobet would pay. . . ." The next morning Ward traveled to the city to cash his check but apparently he was unable to locate the collector. He then attended to some business and visited the "Susquehanna Collegiate Institute [where he] talked a little of . . . attending. . . ." Finally, on Thursday he "went to the collector's where [I] had the infinite satisfaction of getting [the] money, $20. The most money [I] ever had. *Good luck to me.*"[11]

Like young Lester Ward, Miss Augusta Hubble of North Bergan, New York also had difficulty obtaining her pay. Miss Hubble had a number of problems during her "field of labor" as a teacher. She endured jealousy from her hosts and became the brunt of rumors when she went riding with young men in the community. When she finally was relieved of her teaching responsibilities and was planning her trip back to New York State from the West (Tipton, Iowa) the school board used delaying tactics and would not pay her. Augusta wrote in a letter that "The Directors made me some trouble, by their long delay and tried to detain me as long as possible by not settling with me, until the last moment. They did not send me the money due me for teaching until the morning I left Tipton. Mr. Shaw was the collector and I have reason to believe that he was angry with me because I refused the attentions of his brother-in-law."[12]

Miss Angeline Crandell faced a similar set of problems. Crandell had attended the Troy Female Seminary in 1856 and 1857 and had received her teaching certificate. She taught for a term in Oswego, New York, but "eventually went to the Southern states in company with six other Troy pupils under the patronage of Mrs. Willard." Her destination was Henderson, North Carolina, but she and her small group were misdirected to Hendersonville "in a remote part of the state." This error cost them "eighty dollars," the equivalent of over a year's wages. Incredibly, the very next year, "these ambitious and self reliant young women who found their field of labor in the then chivalrous South" were swindled by the president of their school. Following a year of teaching they were given a note "which is still uncancelled"—their "paycheck" had bounced![13]

Unfortunately, being swindled was a common experience, especially for young, idealistic women schoolteachers. Miss Anna Howard Shaw recalled her first teaching position with both enthusiasm and shame. She arrived in her new community about a week before the beginning of the school term. She discussed her position with the school trustee, who directed her to the family where she would board. After an introduction, her prospective host requested the board money in advance so that he could go "outside" to work and provide for his family. Perhaps somewhat naively, Shaw agreed to this request. She arranged with the school commissioners to pay the board in advance and then had three dollars per week deducted from her weekly salary of five dollars. But when she returned to the "boarding place" two days later she found "the house nailed up and deserted; the man and his family had departed with [her] money."[14]

As a result of this swindle, Shaw had only two dollars per week on which to subsist and she was forced to live at home and walk four miles to school and back each day in order to make up for the "lost" board money. Frequently she had to walk through the snow or rain and would be soaking wet by the time she arrived at school. And since she had no place to change at the school, she often had to teach all day in wet clothes. Such was the life of an innocent young teacher.[15]

Loneliness, Jealousy, and "Tongues of Slander"

Beyond the shame and humiliation of slow pay, being swindled, or even having to teach in wet wool, many schoolteachers of this period (especially women) experienced an even more difficult burden: loneliness. In account after account of nineteenth-century teachers, the lament of homesickness and loneliness clearly comes through. When Caroline Seabury and her traveling companion, Miss S., arrived in Mississippi at the "Female Institute" where they were to teach, loneliness "overpowered [them] both." They "had just left school and for the first time tried a life among strangers—far from home. Both of us [were] utterly heartsick and took the usual way of making things better—sat down and cried."[16]

Less than a year after Seabury's arrival in Mississippi, and still recovering from a two-month illness, she again wrote of her isolation and loneliness: "Here I sit, weak, tired of heat, tired of my room, if I had a home on earth, how homesick I should be. . . ." The loneliness of teaching in a strange land was mediated somewhat when her sister Martha came to live and teach with her. But when she left, Seabury recorded in her diary, "How lonely it is tonight. Martha has gone to teach in the lower part of the state, I miss her everywhere. While she was here I never felt all alone, now it seems written on everything—the spring which moved me forward is gone and I can only think over and over for what am I living, to whose happiness am I contributing?" [17]

Unfortunately, loneliness was often accompanied by overt hostility from members of the community. When nineteen-year-old Augusta Hubble of Genesee County, New York, arrived in Tipton, Iowa, for her first teaching position, she was initially "warmly received by her hosts Mr. and Mrs. Goodrich" who ran a "public house . . . near the school room." Within a month, however, things had changed. Hubble's letter to a Mrs. Swift in New York, dated November 19, 1853, revealed these unfortunate circumstances. She wrote that Mr. Goodrich, her benefactor, had succumbed to a brief illness and died suddenly. From that moment on, her life at the inn became unbearable. Mrs. Goodrich, it seems, was jealous of Augusta, a situation common for educated teachers at that time. She resented the fact that her husband had "often requested [that I] join him in [singing on the] Sabbath afternoon in the Parlor. Mrs. Goodrich [alas] could not sing. . . ." Soon after Mr.Goodrich died, however, Hubble was "surprised to hear that Mrs. G. was very much displeased with [me] on that account."[18]

Mrs. Goodrich's apparent jealousy found a willing ally in her "hired girl." Hubble had always "treated the girl perfectly civil," but for a number of reasons, the girl disliked Hubble. Perhaps she felt that Hubble was a snob because she "seldom entered the kitchen and did not make [myself] intimate with her." The former teacher, Miss Fortner, it seems, "would come and kiss her every morning before she went to school. . . ." Whatever her reasons, the hired girl soon began to "carry tales" about Hubble to Mrs. G. and reported "many false stories in regard to [me]."[19]

The uneasy presence of Hubble in Mrs. Goodrich's inn eventually led to her dismissal and return to New York. Hubble had "accepted invitations a number of times to ride out Saturday afternoons [but] always returned before dark." Soon, however, "Jealous eyes were continually watching me for evil and the tongues of slander were busy against me." Then, when Hubble became ill with "Bilious and Intermittent Fever" and was unable to teach, Mrs. Goodrich and her hired girl spread a rumor that she was not really ill, but just trying to avoid work. Soon thereafter, "two of the directors" of the school came to see her and in effect terminated her employment.[20]

Laura Ingalls Wilder's fictional account of teaching during this period reflects much of what Hubble had written in her letter back home. As we have seen, Mrs. Brewster treated the character Laura miserably. When Laura returned from her first day of teaching, Mrs. Brewster was sullen and refused to talk to her the entire evening. And when Laura went to bed she could hear Mrs. Brewster speaking about her in a loud, angry voice. This kind of hostile environment made life miserable for her, and she dreaded her new life as a schoolteacher.[21]

As Laura walked home from her second day at school her mind wandered and she thought of the coming weekend: "Suddenly, Laura caught
her breath . . . two whole days in that house with Mrs. Brewster. She heard
herself say aloud 'Oh Pa, I can't.'" Clearly the presence of a young, attractive, and educated woman in a parochial community could cause jealousy
and the "tongues of slander." Teachers had to learn quickly the art of gra-
cious diplomacy in order to survive both socially and economically.
Women teachers were something very new in nineteenth-century America. They were vulnerable and often bore the brunt of rumor and slander
from men and women alike.[22]

THE SHIFT TOWARD STATE AND MUNICIPAL CONTROL

As graded elementary schools became the norm for primary education
and public high schools the standard for secondary education, school districts at the city and state levels often adopted the corporate model of
organization to deal with growing numbers of students and schools.
While this new organization promised routine pay and protected teachers from the maliciousness of the community through the administrative
structure of school boards and local school administrators, this change
came at a major social cost.

Teachers may not have had to deal, as often, with the capricious whims
of the local community, but now they were subordinated to paternalistic
principals and school boards. Gradually they were forced to give up some
of their autonomy in the classroom and found themselves as hired employees, regulated by a managerial class of school administrators.

These changes were part of an urban reform movement at the end of
the 1800s. This movement was embedded in the new ideas of "modernity" (see chapter 1) and was led by middle-class businessmen. These men
sought to apply the concepts of "social efficiency" (discussed in chapter 8)
to public education and remove the "corrupting influences" of machine
politics. In the early 1890s, this movement gained momentum in a
number of major cities and was gradually adopted in other communities
throughout the country. Three cities that were directly affected by these
changes were New York, Cleveland, and Chicago.

New York and the Butler Plan

In New York City Nicholas Murray Butler began a crusade to improve
education through administrative reorganization. He had been critical of
teachers throughout much of his career, often referring to them as mechanical and dull. He argued that the real problem with education, however
was the inefficient operation and administration of New York City's public

schools. Under the current "locally controlled" system, he noted, teachers had no incentives to teach well, and they lacked adequate supervision. Moreover, their system of promotion, based on seniority, led to mediocrity in the classroom.[23]

His proposal was to restructure the schools on the basis of the corporate model of business. At the top was the superintendent of schools who would be selected from the board of superintendents. The superintendent, in cooperation with the board, would direct policy and make final decisions regarding hiring, promotion, dismissal, and curriculum. Below the superintendent was the school board. Composed of businessmen and elected from the city at large they directed the general policy of the schools. Under the school board were the principals who were responsible for carrying out the day-to-day operations of the schools. Finally, at the bottom of the corporate model were teachers who carried out the policy directives of their "superiors."[24]

Not only did this plan place teachers at the bottom of the administrative hierarchy, it denied them traditional avenues of advancement. Under the older system, teachers who had distinguished themselves in the classroom for twenty-five to thirty years often had the chance of becoming principals of their schools. Under Butler's plan, this seniority system of promotion was abandoned in favor of one based exclusively on examinations and education. While most teachers eagerly embraced the concept of professionalism, they argued that the Butler plan was unfair and would simply lead to capriciousness on the part of school administrators. And they were right.

To complicate this situation further the Butler Plan (like those implemented in Cleveland, Chicago, and elsewhere) was opposed by teachers, who were mostly women, but appealed to both the administrators of the schools and members of the local business community, who were mostly men. Teachers argued that the new model was controlled by individuals who had little understanding of education, many of whom had never taught. Such was the case of Butler and most other educational "reformers" of the day.

Cleveland and the Draper Plan

In the next few years, other cities would adopt similar plans of school reorganization. In Cleveland, for example, educational reformers pushed through a model that created smaller boards of education appointed from the business community rather than representing local community interests. They also created a superintendent that had control over all educational affairs. Andrew Draper, the first new superintendent of the Cleveland public school system, proudly described that city's new plan to the NEA in 1895. He boasted that the new system had overcome the inefficiency of the local-board model and had eliminated corruption in the schools due to the influence of party politicians.[25]

Draper's moment of glory was checked by Albert Bushnell Hart, noted historian and member of the committee of ten who had recently presented their findings. Hart asked a simple question: What about the teachers? What role did they play in this new organizational structure? Hart argued that the Draper plan was fundamentally flawed and noted that teachers should have more control over issues of curriculum and personnel decisions. In his own Cambridge, Massachusetts, school system, Hart went on, "teacher councils" had been created to work with the administration in determining educational policy.[26]

Draper's response to Hart was typical and quite revealing. In a huff, he said, "Four or five men in the city of Cleveland who are men of affairs—not teachers but ... businessmen came together to reform this school system—and they didn't have the proceedings of the NEA either for a guide. They studied principles and I think they succeeded pretty well." In one outburst Draper admitted to the lack of credentials of the "reformers," their arrogance with regard to the work of the committee of ten (sponsored by the NEA), and their reproach for teachers.[27]

Chicago and the Harper Plan

Despite the growing objections of teachers, the corporate reform model was virtually unstoppable. By the end of the decade, it had reached Chicago. Responding to criticism of schools by a chorus of businessmen the mayor created a commission to study education in 1898. He appointed the president of the newly established University of Chicago, William Rainey Harper, as head of that commission. The final report—the Harper Plan, as it was called at the time—was virtually identical to New York's Butler Plan and Cleveland's Draper Plan. It proposed a smaller board of education, appointed on a citywide basis (rather than on the local level) and transferred real control of the schools to the superintendent, who would have the final word on curriculum and the hiring, firing, and promotions of teachers. The superintendent's term, moreover, would be extended from one to six years. The Harper Plan was also critical of teachers and recommended degree requirements, examination-based promotions and increased supervision.[28]

The plan was implemented, and in 1900 Edwin Cooley was appointed as the first superintendent of schools. Cooley acted swiftly, announcing that teacher salaries that year would not be based on experience, but on a series of examinations and very controversial supervisor ratings. This, he assured the mayor, would reduce incompetence in the classroom.[29]

TEACHERS ORGANIZE

The Harper Plan and its implementation by Cooley in 1900 mobilized the fledgling Chicago Teachers Federation (CTF). The CTF had been organized between 1895 and 1897 over the issue of protecting teachers' pensions and salaries. Under the leadership of Margaret Haley and Catherine Goggin, both elementary school teachers in the city, the CTF rejected the Harper Plan.

Interestingly, the first organized action against the Harper Plan was a series of student strikes. At the beginning of the school year in 1902, a new directive from the Cooley administration required teachers to accept new, rigidly defined standards of excellence from their students. (Yes, raising standards was a "new" reform even a century ago.) A teacher at the Clarke school on the city's west side (near the site of the University of Illinois, Chicago) demanded that her students turn in perfect papers in math or fail the test. The students revolted, arguing that no one was perfect. The principal of the Clarke School backed up the teacher's demand, and the students left the classroom *en mass*, threatening a general strike. Although the teacher and principal eventually relented and invited them back into the classroom, the students decided to have a parade before they returned. Once that little celebration was over, they went back to school, assuming that the affair had ended.[30]

Yet it was far from over; when the Cooley administration heard of the strike, William Bodine was sent to that west side neighborhood with a "squad of truant officers" and arrested over two hundred "truants." This caused a small riot when local community members (mostly mothers) taunted the truant officers and threw mud at them.[31]

Other events reflected the growing tension in the Chicago public schools. At the Andrew Jackson School, Janie McKeon, an elementary school teacher, got into trouble with the administration when she expelled a student from her classroom who had used abusive language. The new principal (who had recently replaced a popular woman principal) reinstated the boy, but McKeon refused to let him back into her large classroom of fifty-five students. As a result, McKeon was charged with insubordination and suspended by Cooley for thirty days.[32]

That event galvanized both the student body and the local community. Students at Jackson School went out on strike and marched to the home of Alderman Johnny Powers. Powers was on the reformers' "hit list" because they thought he represented everything that was wrong with the city of Chicago. As a result, Cooley's administration declared an all-out war on the alderman, the neighborhood, and the teachers.

The McKeon affair raged for the next month and generated protest, a number of other student strikes, and vigorous community action. It also provided teachers in the Chicago public schools with a lesson in city politics and set the stage for more aggressive labor organization in the next few years. While the strikes and agitation would lose their early momentum when one of the student leaders was forced to admit that he got some of his ideas from his teacher, a new era in teacher/administration relations clearly had begun in Chicago.[33]

Early Teacher Organizations: The NEA

By the early 1900s, most teachers in Chicago, Cleveland, New York, and other communities experiencing consolidation and "corporate reorganization" understood well their difficult position. The powerful reform movements associated with the Harper, Draper, and Butler Plans had begun to deprive them of their autonomy in the classroom and traditional paths to promotion. Moreover, their "own" professional organization, the National Education Association (NEA), seemed to be part of the problem and not the solution.

The National Education Association had been established in 1870 as the successor to the National Teachers Association, which had been organized in 1857. The NEA was created by ten state teacher organizations with the general goal of improving education and the teaching profession. Unfortunately for teachers however, the NEA was traditionally controlled by male administrators. In fact, during its first year of existence, the NEA actually *excluded* women from its ranks.[34]

As the NEA grew over the years, it created a number of policy-making divisions including Normal Schools, Higher Education, Superintendence, and Elementary Education. Nevertheless, administrators, working through the Superintendence Division, continued to exert extraordinary power over the entire organization and controlled it direction and agenda. That agenda typically ignored issues that were important to teachers (especially women), such as salaries, pensions, and class size.[35]

In the early 1900s however, women teachers attempted to gain more power in the organization and to redirect its policies. As expected, however, these efforts were met typically with a great deal of opposition by the leadership of the NEA. A good example of this can be seen at its 1901 meeting. At that important convention, Margaret Haley, president of the newly formed Chicago Teachers Federation (CTF), challenged the content of a speech given by the president of the NEA, William T. Harris. Harris had spoken enthusiastically about the great strides that public education had made in recent years but also reminded the assembled educators that establishing even greater connections to the business community should be their top priority. Clearly frustrated by these remarks, Haley jumped to her feet and protested that increasing the salaries of teachers should be the top priority of the NEA.[36]

Harris's response to Haley was abusive, patronizing, and revealed the low opinion that the administrative leadership typically had of elementary school teachers. Irritated by Haley's comments, he said to the assembled audience, "Pay no attention to what that teacher down there has said, for I take it she is a grade teacher, just out of her school room at the end of the year, worn out, tired and hysterical . . . and if there are any more hysterical outbursts after this I shall insist that these meetings be held at some other time of the year." Of course, Harris was suggesting that the meeting be held during the school year, when teachers would not be able to attend.[37]

Although he certainly did not know it at the time, Harris's patronizing diatribe against Haley, and by inference, *all* "grade teachers" acted as a catalyst to mobilize teachers and launch an intense period of struggle between organized "grade teachers" and the male-dominated administration of the NEA. Moreover, this struggle would eventually lead to the establishment of the American Federation of Teachers (AFT) in 1916 and a tradition of activism among teachers that continues to this day.

Gender Issues

Considering the patronizing attitude that many male administrators had toward women teachers, it is no wonder that gender politics played an important role in the early stage of the teachers union movement. The case of the Chicago Teachers Federation is a good example. From its beginnings in the late 1890s, the CTF was led by Margaret Haley and Catherine Goggin. These two women were in some ways typical of other teachers union activists during this early period in that they sought higher wages and greater autonomy for their teachers. And like many women teachers of the day they supported women's issues, especially the suffrage movement. Haley, for example, was active in the Women's Suffrage Party of Illinois, while Goggin was an outspoken activist and strong advocate of women's rights.

While the feminism of these teacher activists certainly was an asset in drawing the energy and support from the growing suffrage movement, it also was a liability. During the early years of teachers' organization, for example, the strong support teachers displayed for working women's issues tended to alienate conservative school administrators and politicians. One of the most important of these issues was the right of married women to hold teaching jobs. Traditionally, married women had been denied that right through law or custom; as late as 1914, it was illegal to hire a married women for a teaching position in 88 percent of the larger cities in this country. In rural communities this was almost universally the case; in Massachusetts, for example, there was a strict prohibition against married teachers as well as other patronizing rules. These included not leaving town without the permission of the school board, not staying out past eight in the evening, and not wearing a dress more that two inches above the ankles. The tradition of mandating dress codes continues to the present day: in Forsyth County, North Carolina, for example, the local board of education has forbidden teachers from wearing pierced jewelry on their faces (ears excluded).[38]

While members of teachers unions struggled with local administrators, school boards and politicians for these rights, they also were opposed by organized labor, especially the American Federation of Labor (AFL). The AFL was a male-dominated, craft-oriented union (i.e., organized by skilled workers) that had traditionally opposed the employment of married women. Drawing on the so-called family wage argument, their position was that since men were the primary wage earners, women (and children) workers were in direct competition with them for employment.

Samuel Gompers, president of the AFL, personally saw married women teachers as a threat because they would take jobs away from men. As such he was reluctant to support the new teachers unions at the turn of the century and simply ignored their persistent requests to affiliate at the national level. In 1902, for example, the Chicago Teachers Federation petitioned the AFL for formal membership in the union. While Margaret Haley and Catherine Goggin had managed to convince delegates at the AFL convention that year to approve their national charter, Gompers simply ignored the request and quietly blocked the CTF from officially joining.[39]

Despite opposition by reform politicians and organized labor alike, the teachers union movement continued to grow in the years prior to World War I. During this time local teachers unions were formed in New York; Gary, Indiana; Atlanta; Washington, D.C.; St. Paul; San Francisco; Cleveland; and many other communities throughout the country. Moreover, the powerful Chicago Teachers Federation added two new local chapters of high school teachers during that same period, and New York City unions also grew in membership and activities with the establishment of the *American Teacher*, an important labor publication.[40]

World War I and Teachers Unions

The early success of the teachers union movement also mobilized opposition against them, especially over the issue of war. For years, educational reformers had opposed the very idea of teachers unions and routinely attempted to have teachers unions declared illegal. Those early attempts were unsuccessful, but as the clouds of war engulfed Europe in August of 1914, the tide turned and the anti–teachers union forces once again took the offensive. Many teachers of this era, including Margaret Haley of the Chicago Teachers Federation and Henry Linville of the New York's Teachers Union, were reluctant to support America's growing involvement in the war and had opposed the use of public schools as training grounds for military preparedness. When the United States entered the war in 1917, those who opposed the conflict were seen as unpatriotic and even anti-American. This left teachers unions vulnerable to criticism and would eventually lead to the virtual end of their early labor efforts.

The Loeb Rule

The case of the Chicago Teachers Federation's struggle with the Chicago Board of Education is a good example of the great difficulties that teachers unions faced during this period. In 1916, Jacob Loeb, president of the Chicago Board of Education began a vicious attack on the CTF, especially its president, Margaret Haley. He suggested to the newspapers that Haley was a socialist, noting that she "counsels that class distinctions be brought to the attention of immature minds." He went on to say that she preached "anarchy" and would "send forward children who . . . have no regard and no respect for law and order."[41]

Influenced by this rhetoric, city officials initiated what has been called the Loeb Rule in 1916. This order made membership in teachers unions illegal. The effect of the Loeb Rule was immediate, and that year sixty-eight teachers, over half of whom were members of the Chicago Teachers Federation, were not reissued contracts. The following year the Illinois Supreme Court declared that the Loeb Rule was constitutional, and the Board of Education's war against the teachers union seemed complete. Within a year, the once powerful Chicago Federation of Teachers had been reduced to the status of a womens club and had lost much of its political power. More important, however, the Loeb Rule dramatically slowed the national momentum of the early teachers movement.

The American Federation of Teachers

In addition to destroying the Chicago Teachers Federation, the Loeb Rule crippled the fledgling American Federation of Teachers. The AFT had been created during the spring break of 1916 in the midst of the Loeb Rule controversy. This new national teachers union was organized by members of the Chicago Teachers Federation and three other local teachers organizations in and around the Chicago area, but from its very inception the AFT was plagued with problems. Because of the crisis associated with the Loeb Rule, union leaders argued that the organization needed strong *male* leadership and elected Charles Stillman, a high school teacher, as their president. This, of course, was a blow to both the female-dominated CTF and its president Margaret Haley, who had been expected to head this new national organization. Stillman's election and his eventual support of the America's entry into World War I alienated the predominantly female membership of the CTF and led to their withdrawal from the organization in 1917. Finally, the election of a high school teacher as president also defined the membership of the AFT for the next thirty years. During this period the AFT remained essentially a high school organization, and few elementary teachers joined its ranks. The result was that until after World War II the American Federation of Teachers remained a relatively small and politically weak organization.[42]

The Resurgence of the NEA

The final blow to the early organizational efforts of teachers was the resurgence of the NEA during World War I. As we have seen, the NEA traditionally had been controlled by administrators and not teachers. Nevertheless, it was the one national, professional organization that represented the entire educational community and as such it had been supported by many teachers since its inception. Moreover, during the first two decades of the 1900s, city teachers had gained considerable strength in the NEA and union activists like Margaret Haley from Chicago and Henry Linville from New York had used the organization to recruit teachers into their organizations. [43]

With the onset of World War I and the creation of the AFT, however, things began to change. During this period administrators sought to regain firm control of the NEA and weaken the AFT and local teachers unions in two ways. First they eliminated the "at-large" representative provision at national NEA conventions that had given urban teachers a foothold into the organization. Under this provision, any member of the organization who attended the convention was allowed to vote on matters of policy. This allowed local teachers from, say, Chicago or New York to attend and vote at national meetings held in their cities. The new "representative assembly" plan elected delegates from state organizations that were controlled by administrators. This seemingly innocent shift in representation policy essentially "disenfranchised" urban teachers and further slowed the momentum of the teachers union movement.[44]

The newly reconstructed NEA then began a vigorous recruitment campaign to counter the efforts of both the AFT and local unions. At its 1918 national meeting, for example, the NEA created a commission to deal with the "emergency" in education that had led to what they called the "collapse of the teaching profession." The commission recommended "compulsory Americanization," including the exclusive use of English in the classroom, and also recommended that teachers become more professional. Appalled by the poor performance of World War I soldiers on their recent induction examinations (the first standardized examinations), the commission argued that young women teachers had not done their jobs. (It appears that some things never change.) Their solution was to recruit the "girls" into the NEA and to provide them with a more professional organization. The tacit message, of course, was that membership in a local union like the CTF, much less the national AFT, was unprofessional. The strategy worked extremely well and within just three years (1917 to 1920), membership in the NEA grew tenfold from about 8,500 to over 87,000. The growing membership of the NEA and the difficulties that teachers unions were having over the issue of America's involvement in World War I further slowed the momentum of the early teachers union movement.[45]

Yet this certainly did not signal the end of teacher organizations nor the struggle of teachers to improve their material condition and professional status. Teachers adapted to these new political realities and altered their tactics and goals in order to survive. (Over the years they had plenty of occasions to do just that.) When the Loeb Rule virtually destroyed the Chicago Teachers Federation in 1916, for example, Margaret Haley simply altered the organizational structure of the group to conform to the new regulations. And although the power of the CTF had diminished, the group continued to lobby for the interests of teachers. Similarly, in New York, teachers organizations successfully dealt with setbacks in membership caused by the antiwar posture of leaders like Henry Linville. In this case they refocused their agendas and centered their attention exclusively on issues of teacher salaries rather than broader reforms. Under the leadership of Grace Strachan, for example, the Interborough Association of Women Teachers (IAWT) broke off any association from other, more radical, teacher organizations (notably New York's Teachers Union) and was able to thrive as a single-issue organization focusing exclusively on equal pay for women teachers.[46]

THE GRADUAL SHIFT TOWARD TEACHER ADVOCACY

Other activist teachers continued to work through the NEA. In fact, because of their efforts, during the 1920s the NEA gradually became more of an advocate of teachers issues, focusing on salaries and professionalism.

This was perhaps the greatest irony of the early teacher organization movement: in its attempt to undermine the growing strength of the AFT and local teachers unions, the NEA gradually become a champion of teachers. During the 1920s for example, the organization established a research division and through its *NEA Research Bulletin* began informing teachers of salary, tax, and school budget issues. The NEA also expanded its efforts to "professionalize" teaching and initiated a broad range of lobbying activities to help raise teacher salaries. Though the NEA would remain a rather conservative organization for decades to come, this step toward teacher advocacy is certainly worth noting.[47]

The gradual change in the direction of the NEA became more pronounced during the Great Depression of the 1930s. During that difficult period, the long-standing association between the business community and the educational administration became strained to the point that administrators gradually moved in solidarity with teachers in order to protect education from savage cuts in funding and support.[48]

These difficulties can clearly be seen at the national level when the United States Chamber of Commerce recommended dramatic cuts in education. In a 1932 appeal to its members, this group even suggested that schools eliminate programs like kindergarten instruction, that they shorten the school day, increase class size, and charge tuition for high school! In response to these unreasonable suggestions, the NEA established the Joint Commission on the Emergency in Education (JCEE) to fight cuts in educational programs.[49]

As relations became more strained during these years, some educators took the offensive against the business community while others openly criticized the economic system itself. Perhaps the most dramatic of these came from George Counts, a longtime critic of business and its close ties with schools. Counts was outraged at attempts to cut the funding of educational programs by the national Chamber of Commerce and hundreds of other local business groups. That outrage reached a crescendo in 1932 when he delivered a speech before the Progressive Education Association entitled "Dare the Schools Build a New Social Order?" In it he characterized capitalism as "cruel and inhuman" as well as outmoded by the emergence of new technologies. He called for a new economic system that would distribute wealth more humanely with certain forms of capital "collectively owned."[50]

While these ideas may seem a bit radical today, they were embraced by many educators at the time. The Great Depression had shaken America's confidence in its economic system. In 1932 millions of Americans (including many teachers) had lost their jobs and their homes. Moreover, the economic system was in chaos, with over 1,500 banks permanently closing their doors. As a result, many sought alternatives to the traditional "laissez faire" system of capitalism.

One indication of how frustrated American teachers had become with the socioeconomic order came at the annual meeting of the NEA in 1932. At that important convention, the NEA Committee on Social Economic Goals for America issued a report and resolution to the general membership that made reference to George Counts's recent speech. The resolution, which passed without much debate, stated that "a social order can be built in which a . . . collapse such as the present one will be impossible."[51]

By 1934, Counts's ideas had led to the creation of a small but militant group of educators sometimes called "social reconstructionists." Their journal, *Social Frontier*, routinely criticized the economic system and called for a new role of schools within society. Although social reconstruction never became a dominant theme in American education, it was clear that the NEA's long-standing ties to the business community were beginning to weaken.[52]

During World War II relations between the business community and teachers remained strained. As a result, business leaders gradually allied themselves with state legislators in order to try to direct school policy and limit school funding requests. Meanwhile, teachers gained greater power within the NEA and gradually transformed that organization into a more vocal advocate of teachers' issues including pay, autonomy, and professional status. While this transformation was a slow one it drew strength, direction, and inspiration from the success of the AFT during and immediately following World War II.[53]

In 1944, for example, the AFT successfully negotiated a labor contract with the Cicero, Illinois, school board. This was the first such collective bargaining agreements between teachers and a school board in this country. In the fall of 1946, teachers in Norwalk, Connecticut, and members of the NEA went on strike for eight days against their school system; the result of this action was a guaranteed pay raise. Two months later, in November, St. Paul teachers associated with the AFT also went on strike for higher wages. This action lasted five weeks and ended with the school board promising a tax referendum for February of 1947 (a similar referendum had failed in June of 1946). St. Paul teachers also extracted an agreement from the school board to send classes of children home from school if they could not find substitutes, which was often the case. The common practice before that was to place these children in other classes. Teachers reasoned that parents (especially those who had voted against the school bond) needed to know how crowded the schools really were. By sending children home regularly, that point would become very clear. The strategy worked, and in an April 1947 referendum (the February referendum had failed) a school funding measure was finally passed. That same year teachers in Buffalo, New York, who were affiliated with the AFT went on strike against their school system.[54]

Of course, not all teachers supported these strikes. Some questioned whether "professionals" should engage in these kinds of activities at all (which, of course, had been the traditional position of the NEA); others were simply intimidated by their administrators. Moreover, the NEA was still reluctant to publicly support any form of teachers strike. Nevertheless, the early successes of the AFT and their local union affiliates suggested a new wave of teacher activism. By the end of 1947, teachers in twelve states had gone on strike.[55]

Teachers Unions and the Red Scare

Once again, however, these successes triggered a reaction on the part of state legislators and businessmen, who began to characterize striking teachers as subversives and communists. In New York State, for example, legislators passed the Condon-Waldin Act in 1947, which made teacher strikes illegal. Then in 1949, New York passed the infamous Feinberg Law, a measure that attempted to use the growing tide of the "Red Scare" as a weapon against teachers by linking teachers organizations to communism. This law stated directly that "subversive groups . . . particularly the Communist Party and . . . its affiliated organizations have infiltrated . . . the public schools of the state."[56]

For the next ten years, these kinds of "Red Scare," McCarthy-like tactics were used again and again against teachers. As early as 1949, for example, the NEA's Tenure and Academic Freedom Committee reported that thirty-eight states had some form of "general sedition" laws, thirteen had fired teachers who they declared were "disloyal," and twenty-five had required that teachers take "loyalty oaths." Then in 1953, forty Pennsylvania teachers were called before the House Un-American Activities Committee and were later suspended. Hundreds, perhaps thousands of other similar cases went unnoticed by the press as the dark cloud of McCarthyism descended on America. One of those "unnoticed victims" was a sixth-grade teacher of writer Ellen Schrecker who suddenly disappeared in 1953. He had lost his job for political reasons and "may well have been the most typical of McCarthy era victims—someone eased out of a job quietly, with no publicity, no fuss."[57]

While we now know that the terror of McCarthyism was unjustified, illegal, and a shameful chapter in American history, it did intimidate teachers and once again slowed the momentum of teachers organizations to negotiate in good faith with their school boards. Only by the end of the 1950s and early 1960 were teachers once again able to demand higher wages and smaller class size without the fear of being labeled subversive or communist.

The real turning point came in 1962 when the NEA recognized collective bargaining and the strike as important tactics to improve the material conditions of teachers. That year the NEA began to encourage its affiliates to establish collective bargaining agreements with their local school systems. This rather stunning shift in policy reflected a new direction of the organization and signaled a more aggressive posture that attempted to match the stunning successes of the AFT. Beginning with the successful labor action of one of its locals in New York in 1960, the AFT had grown in both numbers and power. In 1960 the AFT had just under 60,000 members but within just six years it had more than doubled its membership to over 125,000. Two years later it boasted over 163,000 members, and by 1970 it had 205,000 in its ranks. During these same years, the NEA also grew in numbers, strength, and militancy. In 1970 over one million teachers were members of the NEA.[58]

The National Backlash

Yet the growing power of teachers was once again met by fierce resistance, with a backlash forming in the 1970s. As we have seen in chapter 1 this backlash suggests that we were now on the threshold of our third educational transition; but the roots of this transition are more remote and date to the 1960s and even earlier. The origin of the backlash was twofold: first was a distinctive change in federal policy toward education in the 1960s that recognized the insidious relationship between race and poverty in America; second was the growing power of teachers and their determination to help formulate national educational policy through the political process.

When Gunnar Myrdal published his now famous *An American Dilemma* in the early 1940s, he brilliantly demonstrated the insidious "cycle of poverty" among African Americans. He showed that this cycle was a product of racial discrimination that had led to a segregated system of poorer schools for blacks. This limited their access to good-paying jobs and in turn had caused a lower standard of living that eventually led to fewer educational opportunities for the next generation. This idea of a "cycle of poverty" captured the imagination of liberal-minded men and women in the 1950s and eventually made its way to the Kennedy administration in the early 1960s. President John F. Kennedy, also influenced by Michael Harrington's powerful study of poverty, *The Other America,* was determined to address these complex issues. He commissioned Walter

Heller, his foremost economic advisor, to study the problem and in January of 1964 (two months after JFK's assassination) Heller released his report, entitled "The Problem of Poverty in America."[59]

The War on Poverty

The Heller Report pointed to education as the key to solve our "American dilemma" and provided the impetus for Lyndon Johnson's famous War on Poverty. This broad-based initiative eventually led to the passage of two major pieces of legislation that would both change the direction of American education and help trigger the conservative backlash that we still see evidence of today. That legislation was the Economic Opportunity Act of 1964 (EOA) and the Elementary and Secondary Education Act of 1965 (ESEA).[60]

This legislation did a great deal. Title I of the EOA, for example, initiated the Job Corps and other work/education programs modeled after the Civil Conservation Corps of the 1930s (see chapter 10); under Title II, Head Start was begun. This important preschool educational program was initiated in the summer of 1965 and enrolled over a half million poor black children in its first year. Its stated purpose was to break the cycle of poverty by preparing "disadvantaged" students for the classroom. The ESEA was signed into law by President Lyndon Johnson in the spring of 1965. Title I of this legislation provided federal financial assistance to create educational programs for "deprived children"; title II designated federal funds for school libraries, textbooks, and other instructional materials. Finally, other components earmarked federal funds for local educational centers (Title III), educational research (Title IV), and state departments of education (Title V).[61]

But despite its support for local and state control of education through Titles III and V, the ESEA was seen by many fiscal conservatives as a thinly veiled attempt to alter the nature of school funding and shift power from the local and state government to the federal level. This fundamental fear of the growth of the federal government helped to fuel the conservative revolution that we will discuss further in chapter 10.

Teachers Unions and Presidential Politics

When teachers organizations such as the NEA and the AFT vocally supported Jimmy Carter for president in 1976, relations between the education community and conservatives reached a new low. During the election campaign in 1976, Carter had courted educators and promised them a new Education Department. He promised further that he would vigorously support the cause of education and include a secretary of education in cabinet meetings that defined national policy. Teachers responded enthusiastically, giving Carter their official endorsement and their votes. When Carter was elected, he made good on his promises, created a new U.S. Department of Education, and maintained friendly relations with educators during his four years in office. The dreams of generations of educators seemed to have come true.

Yet as with all dreams, the harsh reality of morning's light can often bring disappointment. Conservatives, already alienated from the educational establishment at the university level, now saw public schools and their teachers as a fierce political enemy as well. With the election of President Ronald Reagan in 1980 the conservative reaction reached a crescendo, and attacks on public education from a variety of quarters became commonplace.

This new conservative coalition attracted a variety of groups; most shared the idea that the federal government had gone too far in supporting the rights of minorities, women, and disadvantaged students. As a result, they argued, most schools practiced a kind of "reverse discrimination" against whites and especially white men. Others, part of the Moral Majority headed by Reverend Jerry Falwell, were outraged by Supreme Court rulings against mandatory prayers in the classroom, and routinely criticized schools as "Godless" and immoral.[62]

This was only the beginning. Making good on their promise to slow the growth of federal government and "return" power to the states, conservative legislators shifted billions of dollars to the states through block grants in order to strengthen individual states' control over education. The result of this was an unprecedented cacophony of "reforms" initiated by states to deal with the perceived crisis in the classroom. Many of these reforms directly affected teachers, especially in the area of certification and accountability.

A CACOPHONY OF REFORMS

During the 1980s and early 1990s, most states tinkered with teacher education. Many sought to limit the influence of professional schools of education by reducing the number of education courses that teachers needed to graduate while increasing the number of required "subject area" courses. Others initiated lateral entry programs allowing individuals with no teacher training to enter the nation's classrooms. Still others required that future teachers achieve higher grade point averages in college and attain higher scores on standardized teacher tests for certification. Each of these measures has had a direct effect on the training of teachers in this country.

The Texas and New Jersey Plans

A good example of these kinds of programs were in Texas and New Jersey, where state legislators allowed students to bypass professional schools of education altogether. In 1986, the Texas Legislature, unhappy with the quality of its teachers, abolished bachelor's degrees in education and actually prohibited teachers *by law* from taking more than eighteen hours of "education courses." These eighteen hours consisted of six hours of core courses, six hours of method courses, and six hours of student teaching. While exceptions were made in the case of early childhood education, reading education, special education, bilingual education, and English as a Second Language, these new restrictions had a devastating impact on the national accreditations of Texas schools of education. By the early 1990s, about a dozen schools simply lost their national accreditation through the National Council for the Accreditation of Teacher Education.[63]

New Jersey state legislators took a slightly different approach. In 1984 they initiated a program whereby individuals with bachelor's degrees could become teachers by passing a standardized examination and completing a twenty-day summer workshop in teaching methods. Then during their first year in the classroom they would be assigned a "mentor teacher." By the end of the 1990s, over 40 percent of all teachers in the state had opted for this shortcut.[64]

Perhaps the most vigorous form of state involvement in teacher education was in the area of accountability and licensure. Of course, there had been teacher licensure requirements at the local and state level since the 1800s, and since the 1940s many states had used the National Teachers Exam (NTE) as their primary measure of teacher accountability. By the late 1980s, however, with the growing demand to raise the standards of teachers, state departments of education began to mandate higher scores for licensure. At the same time, scholars criticized the old "paper and pencil" NTE as too ambiguous and inadequate to measure a teacher's ability.

Praxis

In response to this, the Educational Testing Service (ETS) introduced the Praxis series in 1992. States eagerly adopted this privately developed series, which the company billed as a "new generation of teacher assessments." It has three components; the first, Praxis I, typically given during the sophomore year, measures a student's academic skills and focuses on reading, writing, and mathematics. This component can be taken as a traditional "paper and pencil" exam or in a computer-based format. Praxis II, on the other hand, assesses the student's knowledge of the teaching field and is usually administered during or immediately following the student teaching experience. The "constructed response" component of the exam-ination places less emphasis on selecting the "right answer" from a series of multiple-choice options and more on being able to apply knowledge in a professional manner. Praxis III, the most recent component of the series, measures teaching skill through the use of interviews, tapes of class-room teaching, and other forms of evidence included in an "evaluation portfolio."[65]

The Carnegie and Holmes Plans

Meanwhile, a number of national groups including the Carnegie Forum and the Holmes Partnership, vigorously developed new approaches to teacher training and certification. Although their work is far from com-plete, they represent an important new direction in teacher empowerment. In fact, the long transformation from local to state, and now national, stan-dards for teachers is clearly an emerging reality.

Perhaps the best known of these national plans is the one developed by the Carnegie Forum in the 1980s. In 1987 the Carnegie Foundation for the Advancement of Teaching established the National Board for Pro-fessional Teaching Standards (NBPTS). Its goal was to establish "high and rigorous standards for what teachers should know and be able to do, to certify teachers who meet those standards and to advance related educa-tion reforms for the purpose of improving student learning in America." Their booklet "What Teachers Should Know and be Able to Do" has been widely distributed since its publication in 1994 and their plan has gained support of both the American Federation of Teachers and the National Education Association. The NBPTS called for teachers to have a com-mitment to students, knowledge of their subject matter, effective class-room management skills, systematic instructional practices, and direct membership in the learning community.[66]

Like the Holmes Partnership, it proposed a career ladder program that would differentiate teachers on the basis of their expertise, responsibili-ties, and pay. Very briefly the Carnegie "career ladder" consists of four levels of teachers. It begins with "licensed teachers" who are preparing for certification. The second level is that of a "certified teacher" (achieved through the approval of the NBPTS), followed by "advanced teachers" who have passed further rigorous evaluation. At the top of the ladder is the "lead teacher" who is elected by other teachers and is an instructional teacher.[67]

Although the plan has been embraced by teachers and teacher groups throughout the country, there are a number of real problems. The first has to do with money: the Carnegie assessment procedure is expensive. In 1995, when the first of eighty-one teachers received their certificates, it was shown that each application had been examined for an average of twenty-three hours at a cost of $4,000 per applicant. Of course, these costs will decline over time. Nevertheless, if the plan is implemented it will require that states and municipalities pay higher salaries to teachers who ascend the career ladder. As we know, these legislative bodies are notoriously parsimonious when it comes to raising teachers' salaries.[68]

Even if the problem of cost was resolved, however, issues of teacher autonomy would remain. The Carnegie plan presupposes greater teacher empowerment and autonomy from both school administrations and state departments of education. Breaking away from teachers' traditional status as "workers" within the state's administrative structure will be a challenge. In Nevada, for example, the state legislature passed a bill creating a teacher-controlled professional standards board. The board was overwhelmingly rejected by the state's school administration, however. Its response was simple and familiar; referring to teachers, an official of the school board stated, "These are not doctors, lawyers, accountants and engineers. These are public employees, working in the public sector and much public benefit is lost with them having total control."[69]

Despite these traditionally condescending attitudes toward teachers, and a clear lack of funding, the slow shift toward national standards of teacher accountability has begun. In Rochester, New York, for example, the local teacher's union (the Rochester Teachers Association) successfully negotiated a contract in 1987 to transform education in that city. Teachers received a significant salary increase, and a system of shared governance was established. As part of this new system, administrative review and evaluation of teachers was replaced with peer review modeled after the NBPTS plan. For their part, teachers were expected to help students significantly improve their achievement test scores.[70]

While the program has been generally successful, progress has been slow. Achievement scores have inched up, but the adversarial relationship between teachers and administrators has continued. Moreover, teachers have had difficulty adjusting to the new environment and some are reluctant to evaluate their teaching colleagues, whom they see as equals. Nevertheless, change is in the air in Rochester.[71]

Of course, teachers will continue to observe the norms of the local community in terms of dress, selection of reading materials, disciplinary methods, and interactions with parents. And they will continue to work with school administrators and boards of education. In fact, as we have seen, balancing teaching responsibilities with the expectations of the local community, school administration, and the state and city has always been a major concern of teachers.

As we move toward America's third educational transition, however, there clearly will be more available school options and greater federal control of teacher certification and student standards of achievement. As a result, teachers will gradually achieve greater autonomy. Moreover, as teachers demonstrate to skeptics (once again) that they have the knowledge, abilities, and skills to educate American children, we can expect less micromanagement of the classroom. This new "freedom," of course, will require teachers to take a much more active role in decision making and administration in their schools.

As recent educational research has demonstrated, experiments in shared governance, such as the experiment in Rochester, is time consuming, frustrating, and often bitterly opposed by administrators. Moreover, teachers unions that developed in an environment of conflict with local administrators and hostile school boards will have to adjust to the new realities of cooperation and compromise. In short, it won't be easy. Yet as teachers move from positions of hired employees to more active proprietorship of their schools, they will have a greater stake in the future of their institutions, and both the teaching environment and education in general will improve.[72]

America's Third Educational Transition

Our journey through the history of teaching in America is nearly complete. We have seen how teachers in the past have struggled through two educational transitions but have emerged from each better educated, better trained, and better able to meet the challenges of a new society. Teachers have often learned the hard way how to deal with the changing whims of parents, the local community, paternalistic administrators, and state and municipal politicians.

America's first educational transition was triggered by the forces of the American Revolution and the market revolution of the late 1700s and early 1800s. As a result of these upheavals, diverse colonial educational experiments were seen as inadequate, and eventually the common school emerged as the accepted form of universal, public education in this country. By the late 1800s however, the urban, corporate, and modern revolutions had again transformed the social, political, and economic environment of the nation and the common school came under fire. Once seen as "the greatest achievement of man" it no longer seemed to meet the needs of our growing nation. After years of conflict, the graded school and high school gradually emerged as the accepted models of public education.

And now another dramatic educational transition is imminent. The graded school, the jewel of the modern era, persisted well into the twentieth century. However, its core support gradually began to erode in the wake of three contemporary revolutions: the demographic, the communications, and the governmental. These revolutions have not only changed the way we live, but have also set into motion those forces that eventually will replace our "one best system." What form will this new system take? This is one of the questions we address in this final chapter. Before we do, however, let's examine the forces that are changing our educational system today.

THE DEMOGRAPHIC REVOLUTION

As Americans enter the twenty-first century, it has become clear that the ethnic and cultural composition of America's schools is changing rapidly, fueled by a demographic revolution that promises to transform both the classroom and the nation as a whole. Within a generation, the United States will have become a truly pluralistic nation with children once called "minorities" actually assuming the role of majority in many American schools. This fundamental shift in the structure of our population has fostered a great deal of anti-immigrant feelings. Yet as we have seen, this is not new; there has always been hostility toward newcomers to this country, usually surfacing during times of economic slowdown or rapid social change.

In 1854, for example, the Know-Nothing (American) Party was founded to protect the "vital principles of republican government" against the threat of Roman Catholicism and make certain that these strange newcomers (mostly Irish) would not take jobs from "real" Americans. Similarly, in the late 1800s, states like California prohibited the immigration of the Chinese and Japanese into this country. As we have seen, this fear and hatred of immigrants eventually resulted in America's first school schism and the creation of a separate Catholic school system.[1]

But these local nativist impulses of the mid to late 1800s paled before national immigrant restrictions of the late 1910s and 1920s. In 1917 the U.S. Congress passed its first immigration restriction bill over the veto of President Woodrow Wilson. The law required a literacy test for immigrants and prohibited "political radicals" from entering the country. Two years later, in the wake of America's first Red Scare of 1919 (the widespread fear of international communism triggered by the Russian Revolution), immigration legislation became even more restrictive. Then in 1921 and again in 1924, Congress passed immigration quota laws limiting the number of newcomers from southern and eastern Europe and banning immigration from Asia altogether. Finally, in 1927 Congress passed the National Origins Act, which limited European immigration to 150,000 people per year. Ironically these laws opened the door to Mexican immigrants and also energized the migration of African Americans from the South to the urban North; but immigration from abroad would remain at about half its 1900 level for the next forty years. The public schools of this era responded to this new wave of nativism with programs of "forced assimilation" and a stronger emphasis on patriotic nationalism in the curriculum. And as we have seen, even the NEA supported "compulsory Americanization" of immigrant children and "English only" classrooms (see chapter 9).[2]

This situation began to change in the mid-1960s with the passage of the Immigration and Naturalization Act of 1965. As part of an aggressively liberal social agenda known as the Great Society, this law swept away the archaic legislation of the 1920s. Abandoning the quota system that had been based on an individual's nationality, it opened the door to people with occupational skills needed in America. It also allowed free entry of political "refugees" (mostly from communist countries such as Cuba and later from Southeast Asia) as well as family members of U.S. citizens.[3]

The net effect of the Immigration and Naturalization Act of 1965 was dramatic. First it shifted the character of immigration from European to Hispanic and Asian people. But even more important was its effect on the numbers of immigrants arriving here. In 1965 fewer than 300,000 people entered our country each year, but by the early 1970s that number had grown to nearly 400,000. By the early 1980s it had reached about 650,000, and then, beginning in the 1990s, it more than doubled, with over 1.5 million immigrants arriving annually.[4]

Because of this demographic revolution, schools of the twenty-first century promise to be very different. The growing cultural diversity within schools has already begun to accelerate the move toward charter, corporate, and magnet schools as more and more groups (both immigrant and nonimmigrant) demand specific kinds of educational experiences and separation from certain groups of students. The growing number of private and alternative schools in recent years certainly testifies to these changes.

As we diversify our educational system, however, the need for *national* achievement standards will also be more apparent. These national standards have become necessary to ensure the quality of these diverse educational experiments, outside the administrative domain of centralized school systems. Rather than micromanaging the curriculum of schools (as state and municipalities have done in the past), these national standards will allow different kinds of educational institutions to embrace diverse forms of instructional methods and curriculums as long as academic standards are met.

Similarly, the multicultural curriculum of the public schools, so contentiously debated in our society today, will become a *fait accompli* as our classrooms begin to reflect the diverse cultures of the world at large. The need for multilingual education in the primary grades will also become more evident in this new environment. This will include the expansion of ESL and bilingual programs throughout the country.

On the other hand, as we become more diverse culturally, the public schools will embrace a moral education component of the curriculum that focuses on commonalities among cultures, appreciation of peoples with diverse backgrounds, and a greater balancing of individualism with respect for the larger community. This, of course, is already happening in public schools throughout the nation.

In short we will celebrate our ethnic diversity while maintaining our national unity. We will celebrate our individuality while recognizing the needs of our communities. We will celebrate greater standards while recognizing that there is more than one path to educational excellence. The demographic revolution and growing diversity of schools in the twenty-first century promise an exciting future for education.

THE COMMUNICATIONS REVOLUTION

The United States has experienced many periods of technological change in its two-hundred-year history. The last several decades, however, have witnessed a communications revolution the likes of which we have never experienced before. Not only have radios, televisions, cell phones, VCRs, answering, copying, and fax machines, and stereos become commonplace, but the computer has come of age as a critical instrument of communications. Its emergence has already begun to revolutionize the way we communicate and learn.

The Computer

The modern history of the computer began in 1946 when ENIAC (Electronic Numerical Integrator and Calculator), was made operational. By the early 1950s the Universal Automatic Computer (UNIVAC) had become both the industry standard and a household name by helping the U.S. Census Bureau count our growing population and by assisting political scientists to correctly predict the results of the 1952 presidential election.[5]

While hardware technology continued to improve throughout this period, there also were major breakthroughs in the development of software. In 1951, for example, Grace Hooper provided the UNIVAC computer greater utility by writing the first "assembly language" program. This program translated the instructions of the programmer directly into machine-readable language. Building on this breakthrough, John Bakus developed FORTRAN (*formula translation*), the first high-level machine-readable language for the new IBM 701. This language would revolutionize programming. With its relatively intuitive commands it allowed the development of more sophisticated (and complex) applications programs in the future like the Statistical Package for the Social Sciences (SPSS) and Statistical Analysis System (SAS).[6]

Yet the large vacuum tube computers of the 1950s ran too hot, they were unreliable, and they had limited applications; new hardware technologies clearly were needed. That need was met in 1954, when scientists at an obscure company called Texas Instruments developed the first silicon transistor. This tiny device not only replaced the vacuum tubes of earlier computers but also improved on earlier transistor technology. The silicon transistor was able to withstand the high temperatures generated by electronic equipment. And since it could be manufactured more inexpensively than its earlier counterpart, the price of transistors dropped dramatically, from about $15 to $2.50 per unit. The miniaturization revolution was under way.[7]

In the next decade, Robert Noyce would perfect the first silicon chip. By using a flat transistor to replace the connecting wires of a circuit and then printing it directly on a silicon surface, Noyce revolutionized the industry. Using his basic technology, Fairchild Semiconductor was able to put more than one thousand transistors on a single RAM (Random Access Memory) chip and thus provide the theoretical basis of microcomputer technology.[8]

It was during the 1970s, however, that these technologies were perfected. In 1971, Intel Corporation's Marcian Hoff produced the first programmable chip, with the equivalent of 2,500 transistors on a sliver of silicon. This breakthrough, in effect, launched the microcomputer revolution. Within three years, Intel's new 8080 microchip with a "64 K" memory allowed the construction of the first microcomputer.[9]

Although a number of these prototype devices had been developed in the early 1970s, the breakthrough came in 1977 when Steve Jobs and Stephen Wozniak, working initially out of Jobs's parents' garage, incorporated Apple Computer and sold the first fifty Apple microcomputers to the American people. Incredibly, that same year a Harvard freshman by the name of Bill Gates wrote Beginners All Purpose Symbolic Instructional Code (BASIC), the first programming language designed for a personal computer, and set in motion the creation of the Microsoft corporation.[10]

By 1980 many personal computers were competing for the growing educational and personal market. These included Tandy's TRS 80; Commodore's PET and 64, Texas Instrument's TI 99; and of course, the Apple II. Then on August 12, 1981, IBM introduced its first IBM PC, targeting the untapped business market. Since then, personal computers have become smaller, faster, cheaper, more powerful, and much easier to use, with graphical interface programs such as Windows allowing nonspecialists to operate them with ease. With the introduction of powerful word processing programs like Microsoft Word and WordPerfect in the 1980s, written communication has become much easier. And with innovations like "spell check," we don't embarrass ourselves as often! These programs have already transformed the way we communicate, both inside and outside the classroom.[11]

The Internet

Meanwhile, there were parallel developments in communications that would eventually intersect with the personal computer and launch the Internet revolution of the 1990s. In the early 1960s, communication engineers associated with the federal government's newly created Advanced Research Projects Division discovered that it was possible to connect computers at different locations using a common language. By the end of the decade, these engineers had created the Advanced Research Projects Agency Network (ARPANET), a system designed to link universities, defense contractors, and military installations in a communications network. The idea was simple: if the United States was attacked and conventional communication systems were destroyed, an effective network of communications would still be available. ARPANET grew rapidly over the next few years and was eventually able to handle electronic mail, transfer data, and maintain group mailing lists.[12]

By the early 1970s it was becoming clear that a uniform language (or protocol) had to be developed to allow the growing numbers of ARPANET (the present-day Internet) users to communicate effectively. By 1974, Robert Kahn and Vinton Cerf introduced the TCP/IP (transmission control protocol/internet protocol) as a common computer language for the Internet. About the same time, Robert Metcalf, working independently, developed the first local area network (LAN), which permitted computers to share software, data, and peripherals. The basic components of the Internet were now in place.[13]

During the 1970s, the U.S. government began to recognize the enormous potential of Internet communications and allowed nonmilitary users at universities and research institutions to join ARPANET. By the 1980s, commercial providers like CompuServe and America Online had been formed to provide individual access to the "Net." When the commercial possibilities of Internet communications eventually were recognized, dramatic improvements were introduced that allowed even more users to "go online."[14]

The most important of these improvements was the introduction of the World Wide Web, which allowed an Internet user to access text and graphics interactively. The Web was developed by Tim Berners-Lee of the European Laboratory for Particle Physics. Berners-Lee invented the computer language of the Internet called "hypertext." While this language was used successfully by specialists throughout the 1980s, the Web was still rather inaccessible to the average user until the development of software that could interface with it. That breakthrough came in 1991, when the University of Illinois' National Center for Supercomputing Applications introduced Mosaic, the first easy-to-use web browser. The "on ramp" to the information superhighway was now open for use.[15]

In the next few years Internet use grew dramatically with the introduction of dozens of sophisticated browsers competing with Mosaic and thousands of new local providers allowing easy access to the Internet. By 1996 it was estimated that there were more than thirty million Internet users online in the United States alone. Today, more than 100 million users are online, with that number growing every day. This is just the beginning. The prototype "optical" computers similar to the one introduced by Vincent Heuring and Harry Jordan in 1993 store information in the form of light rather than on a chip and promise to be thousands of times more powerful than today's machines. This will allow virtually instantaneous (speed of light) communication of images and will help propel us into a neural, cyberspace environment. Moreover, new object-oriented software such as Java, developed in 1996, has already allowed the delivery of working programs and digital music (through MP3 technology). The future is very exciting indeed.[16]

The Schools, the Computer, and the Internet

Advances in technology, such as the personal computer and access to the Internet, have already begun to transform our schools, the role of teachers, and student's access to information, and those changes have come in less than twenty years. In the early 1980s, less than one school in five had a computer available for instructional use. Today computers can be found in virtually every school in the nation and are routinely used in instruction. In the high-tech environment of the coming century, students will use the computer/Internet as a supplement to traditional lessons, library research, and methods of communications.

Sophisticated new educational software, as well as comprehensive educational websites, have already allowed teachers to integrate new material and techniques into their lessons. (See appendix for a list of some interesting sites.) No longer will the blackboard (an innovation of the nineteenth century) and pen and paper exercises be the primary means of learning. Teachers now have instantaneous access to new approaches, designed to appeal to young students who have grown up with the graphical imagery of television and the computer. Similarly, hard copy texts will gradually give way to "virtual texts" on all subjects, updated regularly in the face of new information and new interpretations.

In this environment, teachers will find themselves in a position of *directing* and *facilitating* learning as opposed to simply presenting it through oral lectures and written exercises. Moreover, since students will have direct and virtually unlimited access to information, teachers will be able to use student research as an integral component of learning. Rather than students spending hours, days, and weeks physically moving around a library to find information, they will use browsers and search engines to instantaneously gather and present information on a variety of subjects. This will give teachers more time to help students determine the authenticity and reliability of information rather than simply assisting them in its discovery. The focus of learning, therefore, will move from collection and description to analysis and evaluation. Finally, both students and teachers will be able to communicate more effectively through electronic mail, classroom chat rooms, parental conferencing, and electronic student advising. Clearly the nature of teaching will change in the future. That change will foster more innovative forms of learning, a shift from description to evaluation of evidence as well as more effective methods of communication between students, teachers, administrators, and parents.

GOVERNMENTAL REVOLUTION

The final element triggering America's third educational transition is the governmental revolution. While the basic structure of the federal government has been clearly defined for more than two hundred years, its size and power have grown significantly over that time and now it plays a major role in our lives. Today, the federal government provides for our national defense; protects our individual and collective rights; promotes our welfare; acts in crime prevention; regulates the excesses of industry, the stock exchanges, and commodity trading; and it serves hundreds of other important functions.

Of course, this has not always been the case. In fact, our original government, conceived under the Articles of Confederation in 1776, was a decentralized one with virtually all political power vested in the states. (Our founding fathers/mothers were fearful of central government, and that legacy has continued to this very day.) This brief experiment with the Congress of the Confederation, however, led to economic and political chaos during the 1780s and eventually gave rise, in 1789, to our current constitutional system. Here, a central government was balanced by the creation of three equal branches: the executive, legislative, and judicial. With the addition of the Bill of Rights to the U.S. Constitution in 1793, the role of federal government was proscribed. Under the Tenth

Amendment, all power not "delegated to the United States [was] reserved to the states respectively."[17]

And yet, the door had been left open "just in case." The so-called elastic clause of the Constitution (Article I, Section 8) stated that Congress had the authority to "make all laws . . . necessary and proper for carrying into execution . . . all . . . powers vested . . . in the government of the United States." Similarly, Article VI of the Constitution clearly stated that all "laws of the United States" were the "supreme law of the land." In short, while the founding fathers wanted to limit the power of the federal government, they also understood that stronger central authority might be necessary in the future.[18]

Much of the history of the early republic was a power struggle between the federal government and the states. For example, while the American Civil War clearly was fought over the issue of slavery and its extension, the underlying constitutional issue was one of states' rights. Did the states in the Confederacy have the right to maintain and expand the system of slavery? And did they have the right to secede from the Union? These questions were clarified in 1865, but only after the nation had been torn apart and over a half million young American soldiers throughout the country had given their lives. As a result, the Civil War has been described by some historians as America's "second revolution" because it settled once and for all the issue of state versus federal power. Or did it?

The Regulating Role of the Federal Government

In the years following the Civil War, the power of federal government grew dramatically by assuming a new and unaccustomed role: regulating big business and limiting the growth of monopolies. When Congress created the Interstate Commerce Commission (ICC) in 1887, the federal government moved beyond its traditional role of stimulating and supporting business. It now began to regulate the excesses of industries deemed "out of control." The passage of the Sherman Anti-Trust Act three years later in 1890 was further evidence of the growing regulatory role of the federal government.

Of course, the federal government had always played an important role in the development of the U.S. economy. From its early support of business community through patent law and legal concepts of eminent domain (the use of private property for the common good) to its enormous land grants for railroads in the nineteenth century, the federal government had always acted as the "silent partner" of business. In fact, at the time, many Americans saw the ICC and the Sherman Anti-Trust Act as additional services to the business community, namely guaranteeing economic democracy for all companies, small and large.

The federal government's direct role in the economy continued to grow during the 1900s. Its support of labor organization beginning in the 1930s through the creation of the National Labor Relations Board and the Occupational Safety and Health Administration in the 1970s; its continuing support of agriculture, its financing of airports, its development of the interstate road system and, of course, its role in human capital development through educational grants and research assistance are just a few examples of its ongoing involvement in the American economy.

Stimulating the American Economy

But perhaps even more important has been the federal government's role in stimulating the American economy through various forms of "counter-cyclical economic policies." For years economists have understood that the mixed economy of the United States was cyclical in nature. However, most felt that the federal government should not interfere in those "normal" business cycles. The depressions of 1837, 1857, 1873, 1893, and 1907 all testified to a persistent problem. When the stock market crashed in 1929, the banks failed in the early 1930s, and the nation was plunged into the Great Depression, Americans demanded that the government do something.

For years a number of economists, led by John Maynard Keynes, had rejected our traditional laissez faire approach to the economy, which held that the best policy was to allow the business cycle to "self-correct." Keynes argued that the real cause of economic depression was a decline in the "aggregate demand" of goods and services. In other words, for a variety of reasons, people were not buying enough. As a result, he argued, the most effective policy of the federal government during periods of economic slowdown was not to pull back, limit credit, and spend less, but to open lines of credit and spend more—*much* more—especially in job creation. If people had jobs, he argued, they would naturally stimulate economic growth by purchasing goods and services.[19]

What Keynes was arguing for was a countercyclical economic policy. He felt that the federal government could reinflate a deflated economy to get it "back on track." By lowering the interest rates at the Federal Reserve, for example, Americans would then be in a better position to borrow money to purchase automobiles and homes and other "big ticket items." This in turn would stimulate job growth and general economic expansion. Similarly, if the federal government were to create jobs, provide pensions, and raise the minimum wage of workers through legislation, Americans could purchase more and thus stimulate normal economic growth. Once again, the idea was for the federal government to do whatever it could to increase aggregate demand for goods and services, which in turn would create jobs and stimulate further demand.

Of course, the New Deal (the job-creation program initiated under President Franklin D. Roosevelt) did not, by itself, end the depression, but it did help considerably. Moreover it was difficult to ignore the fact that the government's massive "job creation" during World War II (commonly known as the draft) had dramatically stimulated the U.S. economy. In short, the era of Keynesian countercyclical policy was launched in the 1930s came of age during World War II, and became an accepted economic policy in the heady postwar years.[20]

Americans had discovered a kind of economic panacea. By lowering interest rates during periods of economic slowdown, the government could bring the economy back on course. And with limited welfare and pension programs in place, it could literally control the demand for goods and services and at the same time allow market forces to operate freely. No longer would the American people have to endure the pain of a protracted depression and high unemployment. We now had a solution, and it worked well—at least most of the time.

Welfare

The final component of growth in the federal government involved the creation of individual "welfare" programs. From the opening sentence of the Preamble to the Constitution, which recognized a need to "promote the general welfare," to today's Social Security, Medicare, and Medicaid programs, the federal government has gradually expanded its role in providing a safety net for the American people. The social and intellectual roots of individual welfare programs date to the late 1800s, when the Progressive Reform Party developed a platform calling for federal insurance for accidents, old age, and unemployment. Then, when the American people ratified the Sixteenth Amendment to the Constitution (1913) and gave the federal government the right to collect a progressive tax on incomes, we had an enormous source of revenue with which to fund these sorts of programs. Prior to 1913 most taxes were "regressive" in nature, like a sales tax, and the greatest burden fell on the poor. The progressive income tax was designed so that individuals were taxed on the basis of their ability to pay.[21]

The real turning point, however, came during Roosevelt's "New Deal." As we have seen, the Great Depression of the 1930s devastated the American people. In 1933, for example, over a million and a half people were homeless with millions more unemployed. Roosevelt and Congress responded to this crisis by providing direct grants to cities and by creating jobs for over four million Americans through the Civil Works Administration (CWA). The CWA built 40,000 schools and 1,000 airports, and built or repaired over 500,000 miles of roads. Other jobs programs, like the Works Projects Administration (WPA) and the Civilian Conservation Corps (CCC), created over three million additional jobs.[22]

The centerpiece of these "welfare programs," however, was the Social Security Act of 1935. This law not only provided small pensions for the nation's poorest citizens—the elderly—but established a cooperative state/federal system of unemployment insurance and provided funds for the disabled and blind. A safety net for Americans was being created.[23]

Roosevelt's successor, Harry Truman, shared Roosevelt's vision of federal government ensuring the social welfare of all Americans. Within days of the conclusion of World War II, Truman submitted to Congress an ambitious twenty-one point social program. This program, based in part on the ideas of Keynes, included provisions for full employment, minimum wage, and greater unemployment benefits. While liberals supported his proposals, Truman was opposed by a growing presence of conservatives in Congress. And when his political support plummeted to 32 percent in 1947, he was forced to retrench. Meanwhile, a worldwide diplomatic crisis had begun to dominate his attention (the beginning of the Cold War), and he all but abandoned his ambitious social programs.[24]

It wasn't until the 1960s that the commitment to individual welfare again resurfaced in this country, this time by presidents John F. Kennedy and Lyndon B. Johnson. While many of the ideas of the Great Society's programs of the 1960s were envisioned during the Kennedy administration, it took the pragmatic political savvy of Johnson to turn these ideas into reality. There were many important pieces of legislation passed in the years 1964 and 1965 including the Civil Rights Act, the Voting Rights Act, the Elementary and Secondary Education Act, the Wilderness Protection Act, and the Clean Air Act, to name just a few. The era also saw the creation of the National Endowment for the Humanities and Arts as well as the Department of Housing and Urban Development.[25]

Three laws, however, completed the work of FDR and firmly established the concept of individual welfare in this country. The first was the Economic Opportunity Act, which created ten distinct job programs including Volunteers in Service to America (VISTA) and the Job Corps. The second was the creation of Medicare and Medicaid in 1965. These provisions made medical care accessible to those on Social Security as well as to the very poor. Finally, the Omnibus Housing Act provided rent subsidies to poor families and also earmarked federal funds to place low-income Americans in private housing. The welfare safety net, envisioned by the progressives at the turn of the century and put in motion by the New Deal programs of Franklin D. Roosevelt, was nearly complete.[26]

The Federal Government and Education

As the influence of the federal government expanded over time, so did its role in education. The federal government, of course, has always been involved with the education of the American people, at least indirectly. Even before the ratification of the U.S. Constitution in 1789, it actively supported education. Beginning with the Congress of the Confederation's Survey Ordinance of 1785 through the Northwest Ordinance of 1787, for example, the federal government awarded states enormous land grants to be used to support education. In fact, nearly one hundred million acres of land were directly deeded to the states for that purpose. That land would then be sold by the states to finance the construction and maintenance of schools (see chapter 1).

With the ratification of the U.S. Constitution in 1789 and the adoption of the Tenth Amendment in 1793, however, the federal government's support of education became more symbolic and indirect. The Tenth Amendment, as you recall, stated that all powers not directly given to the federal government were to be held by the states. As a result, for the next seventy years the federal government played virtually no direct role in American education with states and local communities controlling its direction and providing its funding.

That situation gradually began to change during and immediately following the Civil War. Early in the war, reformers pushed the Morrill Act (1862) through Congress and it was signed into law by President Abraham Lincoln. This important law established the first land grant colleges in the country to promote agriculture and the mechanical arts. The Morrill Act was expanded and reinforced in 1890 through the "Second Morrill Act" in 1914 as the Smith-Lever Act, and in 1917 as the Smith-Hughes Act.[27]

Paralleling these important provisions for postsecondary education, the federal government also established the U.S. Office of Education (USOE) in March of 1867. This agency was created to "promote the cause of education throughout the country." While its purpose was idealistic, its long-term effectiveness was limited by partisan politics (infighting between the Democrats and Republicans), lack of funding, and jealousy within the federal bureaucracy. Within a decade the USOE was quietly pushed into obscurity and remained there for over a century.[28]

During World War II and the Cold War, however, the federal government once again became active in the area of education. With the passage of the GI Bill in 1944, the face of higher education was forever changed. Hundreds of thousands of veterans were given the opportunity to go to college through direct funding from the U.S. government. These veterans benefits continue to the present day.

The turning point for elementary and secondary education, however, came in 1958 with the passage of the National Defense Education Act (NDEA). As its name implied, the primary purpose of the NDEA was national defense. When the Soviet Union launched the first manmade satellite, Sputnik, politicians in this country felt that we had somehow fallen behind the "evil empire" with regard to technological expertise. The "space race," as it was called at the time, was *on*, and the resulting panic led to the passage of the NDEA. This important federal program provided funding for educational programs in math, science, engineering, and foreign languages.[29]

The National Defense Education Act proved to be very successful and popular. These funds, however, were earmarked for specific programs deemed important for national defense and were not designed for general educational use. That situation changed in mid-1960s under President Lyndon Johnson. As we have seen, the Elementary and Secondary Education Act (ESEA) provided federal funds for a variety of important educational programs. In fact, during the 1960s the federal government increased its funding of schools by a factor of seven, from about one-half billion to over 3.5 billion dollars.[30]

These programs were important, and clearly had an impact on the education of the children of this country. Despite their early success, however, their effectiveness was undermined by partisan politics and a lack of coordination. Just as the ill-fated U.S. Office of Education was quietly stripped of its power by political infighting, the idealistic educational programs associated with the ESEA were routinely ridiculed and underfunded by politicians in the 1970s and 1980s. As a result, many of the programs associated with the ESEA simply collapsed. Similarly, because there was no effective educational agency to coordinate these programs (the U.S. Department of Education was not created until 1979), the control and direction of the 130 distinct programs associated with the law were distributed among various offices and departments of the government ranging from Housing to Agriculture. As politicians searched for ways to cut the budget during this period they often found these "orphaned" programs vulnerable and easy prey. One can only wonder how effective these programs might have been if funding had been maintained and if they had been effectively coordinated through a central U.S. Department of Education.[31]

Recent research also has demonstrated that many of these programs were not adequately evaluated as to their effectiveness. Part of the problem here was the lack of research and evaluation expertise, but an even more important problem was politics. Because of the partisan nature of educational funding, supporters of programs such as Head Start were often reluctant to critically evaluate whether the program was accomplishing what it was intended to do. On the other hand, those politicians opposed to Head Start were eager to demonstrate that it was not effective. What resulted was a political environment of grandstanding where each political coalition either unflinchingly supported or rejected the program. What seemed to be lost in the shouting was what was best for American children.[32]

In short, the success of the federal government's involvement in education was mixed. Through vigorous executive initiatives, court action, and legislation, it helped to force open the doors of education, to admit people of color and individuals with disabilities. Moreover, the federal government has played a major role in establishing and maintaining schools, providing scholarships and grants for students and in more recent years providing general funds for a wide range of educational programs. Due to partisan politics leading to funding cuts, a lack of coordinated administration of these educational programs, and a failure to evaluate their effectiveness, the overall success of the federal government in this area has been limited.

Over the years we have learned that the federal government works best when its power is balanced and controlled. In the area of education it works best as a *benefactor* and a *facilitator*. As a benefactor it can provide needed funding for specific educational programs. As a facilitator it can promote equality, demand equal access to educational facilities, and create independent agencies to study and evaluate educational programs. Removed from the firestorm of partisan politics and the jealousy of local communities and states, the federal government can expand the role of the Department of Education and establish fair academic standards for American children, teachers, and the schools.

On the other hand, the federal government cannot and should not be allowed to control the content of the curriculum, methods of instruction, or administration of the schools. In these areas it must share responsibility with the local community, states, and especially teachers themselves. In short, as we enter the next century, the role of the federal government should be one of establishing standards with states and local communities acting in a capacity of advocacy and balance. In this context teachers will be able to assume greater proprietorship of the schools and a more active participation in the administration of the schools themselves.

POSTMODERNISM

The demographic, communication, and governmental revolutions of recent years have fundamentally changed America. But these three revolutions have been *so* dramatic and *so* sudden that they have helped catapult Americans into an environment of collective malaise what historians have called postmodernism. In education, postmodernism has already begun to transform education and replace our "one best system" of graded schools. So just *what is* this thing called postmodernism?

If modernism was characterized by an unbridled confidence in science, technology, and government (see chapter 1), postmodernism is a collective disillusionment with this "modern trinity." This is not to say that Americans have completely lost their faith in science, technology, and government but rather that this early optimism, characteristic of modernism, has faded and now we often understand the "darker" side of each. We have begun to recognize that there is no panacea for our social and political problems, no cure-all for the diseases that plague us, and that while government can help solve some of our problems, it cannot do everything, and certainly needs to be carefully controlled.[33]

The Liberal Phase

Postmodernism emerged in this country not as a particular partisan reform effort but as a result of the changing perceptions and attitudes of very different groups in American society, for very different reasons. The early liberal phase of postmodernism began with the first use of nuclear weapons by the United States against Japan in August of 1945. While dropping atomic bombs on Hiroshima and Nagasaki effectively ended World War II, the awesome power of nuclear technology was now revealed to a stunned world. In addition, the key role played by scientists in developing these destructive weapons had also become clear to many Americans.

From that point on, the scientist, once the proud purveyor of material progress, would now be linked with the potential mass destruction of the entire world. Although the ominous image of the mad scientist in movies and on television had been around for some time, it grew dramatically during the 1950s and 1960s, as did apocalyptic films featuring mutated ants, spiders and even rabbits! This trend continues to this day, with "end of the world" movies released virtually every summer. Of course, not everyone shared these views, but gradually our unflinching embrace of "progress" was questioned by a growing number of Americans.

The real turning point for this phase of postmodernism came with the publication of Rachel Carson's *Silent Spring* in 1962. In this unassuming book, Americans for the first time read of the dangers of one of science's most celebrated victories, DDT. This insecticide, hailed as one of the great achievements of humankind, now was linked to the pollution of our environment. More disturbingly, its widespread use had led to the near extinction of a number of species of plant and animal life—most notably, our national bird, the bald eagle. Americans, grudgingly at first, began to accept the fact that there often was a high price pay for "progress." For some, that price was too high.[34]

Similarly, Americans became more concerned about the potential dangers of nuclear power. While the early antinuclear movement began in the 1950s in response to unlimited nuclear weapons testing, Americans gradually came to see that even the peaceful use of nuclear power was just too dangerous. The Harrisburg, Pennsylvania, Three Mile Island nuclear plant shutdown in 1979, followed by the devastating "meltdown" at Chernoble in the Ukraine a few years later, led to an unprecedented antinuclear backlash in this country and further strengthened our postmodernism. Nuclear power, once seen as the answer to all our energy problems, was now just seen as dangerous.[35]

Finally, there was a growing uneasiness concerning the role of the computer in our lives, the fear that we were losing our individuality and becoming "just a number." By the 1960s, novels and films told a dark tale of the threat of computers. In John Barth's *Giles the Goat Boy*, computers take over the world and in Stanley Kubrick's film *2001: A Space Odyssey*, HAL, the master computer, tries to take over the space ship. HAL is foiled by a clear-thinking human who disconnects the machine, often to the cheers of theater audiences. In the late 1980s and early 1990s, two *Terminator* films offered a dark perspective on computers that seize control of our defense systems and ultimately lead the world to thermonuclear disaster. Since then there have been other such films.

Tom Wicker of the *New York Times* was one of the first to articulate this cyberphobia (fear of computers) when he wrote in the late 1960s, "Man is being dwarfed by his own handiwork . . . hapless and driven . . . among his reactors and data banks." Mario Savio of the Berkeley Free Speech movement had a remedy that appealed to many Americans at the time: "We must put our bodies against the gears . . . and make the machine stop." Today, millions of Americans have made their peace with the computer, and routinely "go online" for research and fun. Moreover most young people who have grown up with computers find this cyberphobia difficult to understand. Yet the anxiety over the "cyberrevolution" (and the potential for misuse by the federal government) is real, and has been a driving force in defining our postmodernism.[36]

The other major dimension of our contemporary postmodernism (the first two being science and technology) is a reaction against the growing power of government. This impulse began during the 1960s in response to our involvement in the Vietnam War and our recognition of the central role that America's national security agencies were playing in foreign policy. Their covert activities (often illegal, sometimes immoral) simply reinforced our skeptical attitudes toward government. The capstone of this phase of postmodernism, however, was the Watergate scandal. The illegal action of aides to President Richard Nixon (the break-in at the Democratic Party's headquarters), his coverup of the affair, and the impeachment hearings that followed reinforced our growing distrust of government. Could we ever trust our government again? The answer for many people—especially young people—was no.

The Conservative Phase

The critical link between the early, liberal phase of postmodernism and its more conservative phase was the reaction to the growth of government. Though it centered on very different issues, this phase began in the 1970s and was embraced by older and more established Americans. It began slowly, as a reaction to the liberal legislation and judicial decisions of the 1960s, but there was a distinct shift in its momentum beginning with the Supreme Court's landmark *Roe v. Wade* decision in 1973, guaranteeing women their reproductive rights. It was further reinforced by the perception that Americans had become weak and immoral resulting in our "defeat" in Vietnam.

By the early 1980s, the movement had gained momentum in the wake of a sluggish economy, growing unemployment, and high interest rates (sometimes referred to as "stagflation"). These attitudes were reinforced by our collective anxiety over a "hostage crisis" in Iran that had been triggered by the fundamentalist Islamic revolution in that nation and our continued support of the unpopular shah of Iran. Again, conservative Americans blamed the federal government for our problems.

The new, conservative postmodernists whisked Ronald Reagan and later George Bush into the White House, shifted political power in the South from the Democrats to the Republicans and eventually altered the balance of power of Congress. In addition, its more radical wing, the militia movement, gave impetus to the growing antigovernment impulse. Scattered militia groups throughout the nation were led by a handful of disillusioned antigovernment radicals. These groups reflected a widespread despair of many Americans who felt that their values and status were being challenged by a rapidly changing society. The conservative turn of the country emboldened them, and by the early 1990s the events at Waco, Texas, where armed militant Christian fundamentalists clashed with federal agents, mobilized them toward action. On the anniversary of the Waco tragedy, a federal office building in Oklahoma City was bombed by members of one militia movement, killing 169 men, women, and children in the building.

Thus, by the mid-1990s, a growing number of both liberal and conservative Americans had become postmodernists. More recently the impeachment trial of president Clinton, the growing outcry against those proceedings, and the polarization of politics resulting from the 2000 election has served only to intensify this postmodernism.

Postmodernism and the Schools

In the wake of this growing postmodernism, the image of the public school—both the accepted hallmark of progress and the crown jewel of government—had been tarnished. By the late 1970s and early 1980s Americans had begun to closely examine our schools, our students, and our teachers and often found them to be deficient. There were a number of direct causes of this criticism. The innovative curricular programs of the 1960s and 1970s, such as "the new math," the "open classroom," and new forms of classroom discipline, for example, were seen as the root causes of declining test scores, school violence, drug use, and even immorality in schools.

By the 1980s the rising costs of education estranged many Americans who saw few improvements in the quality of education or the academic achievement of students. With the publication of *A Nation at Risk* in 1983, these general feelings were given the credence of a presidential commission, the National Commission on Excellence in Education. If "reformers" had bothered to read the report, however, they would have recognized that it was not an indictment of American education but an "invocation of collective action . . . inspiring . . . a feeling of common cause rather than one of division and blame." Nevertheless, with unopened copies of the report in hand, state legislators and local school boards throughout the country soon clamored for some kind of educational reform. They often embraced (among other things) standardized exams for students and an end to so-called social promotions. The call for school "accountability" also became stronger throughout the conservative 1980s and by the 1990s that call had been extended toward teachers as well as students.[37]

In this chaotic environment, moreover, schools of education were also routinely criticized for not providing adequate training for teachers. The so-called Massachusetts embarrassment, when large numbers of future teachers failed that state's proficiency exam in 1998, simply added fuel to the growing fire and seemed to demonstrate that *something* needed to be done. As a result, state legislators and municipal officials throughout the country have become much more intrusive in recent years, routinely mandating specific curricular programs and defining standards. The new Praxis series of teacher exams, for example, has been almost universally adopted as a standard credentialing measure. Other legislatures have recommended a potpourri of reforms ranging from school uniforms, vouchers for private schools, corporate sponsorship of schools, to the creation of charter schools.

Yes, we are in the midst of yet another educational transition. This transition has been shaped by our rapid shift toward a more culturally diverse society, by a dramatic communications revolution, and by the expansion of the federal government. Moreover, this transition has been energized by a deep cultural malaise associated with postmodernism. The third educational transition, like the two others that preceded it, has challenged our existing educational system and will eventually alter it significantly. Changes are ahead.

By using history as our guide, however, we can expect that the new model will be a diverse set of competing education experiments like charter schools, corporate schools, magnet schools, and a core of more traditional public schools, each reflecting the growing diversity of the American population. In this new environment, teachers will certainly gain greater autonomy through proprietorship of their schools, and the curriculum will be energized as teachers embrace the cyber classroom environment, linked to resources that are beyond our imagination today. In addition to this growing diversity, new instructional methods, and increased autonomy of teachers, national standards of excellence will help define the curriculum. The two-hundred-year-long shift from local to state to national control of the schools will be complete. The future of teaching in America is a little frightening but very exciting.

As teachers move into the uncharted territory of the twenty-first century they will have few road signs to direct them. Only by understanding the history of teaching will they be able to anticipate what is to come. Moreover, only by appreciating the struggles of generations of teachers in the past will they be prepared for what lies ahead. One thing is sure, however: teachers have a rich and proud historical heritage. And like generations of young men and women who came before, they *will* survive and they *will* change the world!

Appendix I: Research Note

Although this book is primarily a work of synthesis, it has benefited from an examination of a number of primary historical documents, both published and unpublished. These include teachers' letters and diaries, personal journals, pedagogies, school primers and readers, alumnae directories, official proceedings of professional associations, and reports of presidential commissions on education.

In addition, the authors conducted classroom observations and interviewed dozens of teachers and principals for this book. These "oral histories" and classroom observations took place from 1997 to 1999. Ten public elementary schools from two different school districts were examined. The first was a large metropolitan school district where a great number of the students were from racial minorities; the second was a rural district where minorities represented about 25 percent of the student population. Excerpts from these interviews and classroom observations were used to illustrate ideas developed in the book.

To assure the confidentiality of the teachers and principals interviewed, the names were changed. Likewise, the names of schools and districts were omitted to assure privacy.

INTERVIEWS AND CLASSROOM OBSERVATIONS

Preface

Mary Cunningham, former elementary school teacher, interview by authors, North Carolina.

Chapter 6

Dennis Jenkins, fifth-grade teacher, interview and classroom observation by authors, North Carolina.

Debbie White, fifth-grade teacher, classroom observation by authors, North Carolina.

Diane Baker, first-grade teacher, interview and classroom observation by authors, North Carolina.

Mary Lane, second-grade teacher, classroom observation by authors, North Carolina.

Richard Woody, elementary school principal, interview by authors, North Carolina.

Chapter 7

Sara Whitfield, eighth-grade teacher, interview by authors, North Carolina.

Chapter 8

Lou Ann Ryan, third-grade teacher, interview and classroom observation by authors, North Carolina.

Barbara Taylor, fourth-grade teacher, interview and classroom observation by authors, North Carolina.

Cathy Lee Gates, fifth-grade teacher, interview and classroom observation by authors, North Carolina.

Amy Prescott, sixth-grade teacher, interview and classroom observation by authors, North Carolina.

Appendix II:
Selected Internet Sites
for Teachers

MARY LYON AND MOUNT HOLYOKE COLLEGE

http://www.mtholyoke.edu/marylyon
This is an excellent site describing the background and early days of Mount Holyoke College. It includes pictures and discussion questions that could be used in the classroom.

HISTORY OF EDUCATION

http://www.cedu.niu.edu/blackwell
The Blackwell History of Education Museum and Research Collection has a wealth of information regarding the history of education. It also contains a variety of instructional materials.

http://www.msc.cornell.edu/~weeds/School Pages/welcome.html
This site has examples of old one-room country schools.

http://www.history.cc.ukans.edu/heritage/orsh/Library/orsh_Lib.html
This site contains examples of one-room schools in its graphics section.

BLACK HISTORY

http://www.blackhistory.com
At this site users can learn about and participate in black history. It has areas designed for students and teachers. Teachers can find and download materials for class use and share lesson plans with other teachers. Students can contribute stories and pictures about black history.

http://www.blackhistory.eb.com
The Encyclopaedia Britannica maintains this site, which has a great deal of information about African-American history.

CHILDRENS BOOKS

http://www.harperchildrens.com
Harper's Children's Division highlights recent books, interviews authors, and provides children the opportunity to communicate with authors by e-mail.

TEACHER RESOURCES

http:/members.aol.com/_ht_a/historiography/
Scholars Guide to the WWW, by Richard Jensen, has links to history, education, political science, economics, and humanities as well as maps, museums, and more.

http://pacificnet.net/~mandel
Teachers Helping Teachers provides assistance and tips for teachers.

http://www.teachervision.com
This site has lesson plans and links to other resources.

http://www.lessonplansearch.com
Another site that contains lesson plans for a variety of subjects.

http:www.education-world.com
This site has links to education news, lessons, and teacher resource websites for K–12 schools.

http://Web66.coled.umn.edu
The University of Minnesota maintains this website for K–12 schools.

http://www.onr.com/schoolhouse
Award winning Internet Schoolhouse.

http://www.si.edu
This site provides links to each of the museums of the Smithsonian Institute.

HISTORY

http://www.nara.gov/education
The National Archives and Records Administration has a Digital Classroom. Teachers can access documents for teaching history and social studies and get suggestions for lesson plans.

http://www.nytimes.com/learning
This site is a learning network developed by the *New York Times.*

ENCYCLOPEDIA

http://www.britannica.com
Free Internet access to the *Encyclopaedia Britannica.*

RESEARCH ON EDUCATION, TEACHING, STUDENTS, ETC.

http://www.accesseric.org
This is an online source of educational research that contains abstracts and text of some articles (ERIC).

http://www.ed.gov/pubs/SER
This site contains reports on educational reform (Office of Educational Research).

LITERATURE AVAILABLE AS E-TEXT

http://www.gutenberg.net
The Gutenberg Project provides free access to literature for teachers.

http://www.promo.net/pg
This section of the Gutenberg Project provides online text for many classics in educational history and philosophy including John Dewey's *Democracy and Education*.

http://etext.virginia.edu
The University of Virginia has an extensive collection of literature that can be downloaded and printed by teachers.

TEACHER UNIONS

http://www.nea.org
This is the site for the National Education Association.

http://www.aft.org
This is the site for the American Federation of Teachers.

U.S. DEPARTMENT OF EDUCATION

http://www.ed.gov
This is the website for the U.S. Department of Education, and it has an abundance of data and information on schools.

NATIONAL COUNCIL FOR THE ACCREDITATION OF TEACHER EDUCATION (NCATE)

http://www.ncate.org
This site lists colleges and universities with accredited Teacher Education programs and contains standards and updates on policy issues.

EDUCATION WEEK

http://www.edweek.org
The K–12 journal *Education Week* maintains this site.

READING

http://reading.org
A site of the International Reading Association, that contains lists of children's and young people's reading choices, and teachers' choices.

http://readingonline.org
Another International Reading Association site, this online journal focuses on reading and children's literature.

SPECIAL EDUCATION

http://www.cec.sped.org

The Council for Exceptional Children home page has information regarding special education.

http://www.cet.fsu.edu/tree

Through this site you can access teaching tips for working with main-streamed/inclusive classes.

BANNED BOOKS

http://www.ala.org

The American Library Association site has a page for the Office for Intellectual Freedom that contains information on banned books. (Click "Search the website", then type banned books.)

Notes

Preface

1. Mary Cunningham, former elementary school teacher, North Carolina (see appendix 1).
2. M. Scott Norton, "Teacher Retention: Reducing Costly Teacher Turnover," *Contemporary Education* 70, no. 3 (spring 1999): 52–55; L. C. Lemke, "Attracting and Retaining Special Educators in Rural and Small Schools: Issues and Solutions," *Rural and Special Education Quarterly* 14, no. 20 (1995): 25–30; J. Ponessa, "High Teacher Attrition Grabs Attention in North Carolina," *Education Week* 15, no. 39 (June 1996): 3.

Chapter 1: The Cycles of Educational Change

1. Benjamin Franklin, *The Autobiography of Benjamin Franklin*, ed. Leonard W. Labaree (New Haven, Conn.: Yale University Press, 1964).
2. John Locke, *An Essay Concerning Human Understanding*, ed. Peter N. Nidditch (Oxford: Clarendon Press, 1979); Voltaire, *Philosophical Dictionary*, ed. and with an introduction and glossary by Peter Gay (New York: Harcourt, Brace & World, 1962); Denis Diderot and Jean le Rond d'Alembert, *Encyclopedia*, trans. with an introduction and notes by Nelly S. Hoyt and Thomas Cassirer (Indianapolis: Bobbs-Merrill, 1965).
3. James Henretta, *The Evolution of American Society, 1700–1815: An Interdisciplinary Analysis* (Lexington, Mass.: D.C. Heath, 1973).
4. David M. Ellis et al., *A Short History of New York State* (Ithaca, N.Y.: Cornell University Press, 1957).
5. Thomas Paine, *Common Sense*, ed. and introduced by Isaac Krammick (New York: Penguin Classic); Thomas Jefferson, Declaration of Independence, in Gary B. Nash et al., *The American People: Creating a Nation and a Society*, 4th ed. (New York: Longman, 1998), A-1.
6. Donald H. Parkerson and Jo Ann Parkerson, *The Emergence of the Common School in the U.S. Countryside* (Lewiston, N.Y.: Edwin Mellen Press, 1998), chapter 1.
7. Thomas Jefferson, "For the More General Diffusion of Knowledge," in *American Education*, ed. Tyrus Hillway (Boston: Houghton Mifflin, 1964 [1779]), 27–33; Thomas Jefferson, "Letter to Joseph Cabell, 1816," in *American Writings on Popular Education: The Nineteenth Century*, ed. Rush Welter (New York: Bobbs-Merrill, 1971), 9–13; Thomas Jefferson, "Notes on the State of Virginia," in *Crusade Against Ignorance*, ed. Gordon C. Lee (New York: Teachers College, Columbia University, 1961), 96–97.

8. Benjamin Rush, "A Plan for the Establishment of Public Schools and the Diffusion of Knowledge in Philadelphia, Pennsylvania, 1786," in *Essays on Education in the Early Republic*, ed. Frederick Rudolph (Cambridge: Belknap Press of Harvard University Press, 1965), 14, 10.

9. Rush, "A Plan for the Establishment of Public Schools," 14, 10. A generation later, Horace Mann, in his *Twelfth Annual Report on Education*, would use a similar argument to convince Massachusetts legislators of the need for common schools. Citizens were taxed, he argued, to support the common school: "As a *preventative* means against dishonesty, against fraud and against violence; on the same principle that he is taxed to support Criminal courts as a *punitive* measure against the same offenses. " Horace Mann, "Twelfth Annual Report on Education—1848," in *The Republic and the School: Horace Mann on the Education of Free Man*, ed. Lawrence A. Cremin (New York: Teachers College Press, 1957), 103.

10. Ellwood P. Cubberley, *Public Education in the United States* (Boston: Houghton Mifflin, 1919), 59.

11. U.S. Constitution, Tenth Amendment, in Gary B. Nash et al., *The American People: Creating a Nation and a Society*, 4th Ed. (New York: Longman, 1998): A–8.

12. Nicholas Biddle, "Report on Education," *Journal of the Twenty First House of Representatives of the Commonwealth of Pennsylvania* (1810), 108–14.

13. Noah Webster, "On the Education of Youth in America," in *Essays on Education in the Early Republic*, ed. Frederick Rudolph (Cambridge: Belknap Press of Harvard University Press, 1965), 65, 66.

14. Cubberley, *Public Education in the United States*, 112.

15. Ibid., 111–12.

16. Michael Katz, "The Origins of Public Education," in B. Edward McClellan and William J. Reese, eds., *The Social History of American Education* (Urbana: University of Illinois Press, 1988), 107.

17. For an excellent discussion of the decline of the artisan, see Sean Wilentz, *Chantz Democratic: New York City and the Rise of the American Working Class, 1788–1850* (New York: Oxford University Press, 1994).

18. Stuart Noble, *A History of Education* (New York: Rinehart & Co., 1955), 170.

19. Seth Luther, *An Address to the Workingmen of New England on the State of Education* (Boston: author, 1836), 6; emphasis in the original.

20. E. P. Thompson, "Time, Work, Discipline and the Industrial Capitalism," *Past and Present* 38 (December 1967): 56–97.

21. Donald H. Parkerson, *The Agricultural Transition in New York State: Markets and Migration in Mid-Nineteenth Century America* (Ames: Iowa State University Press, 1995).

22. Luther Tucker, *The Cultivator* 8, no. 12 (December 1851): 358.

23. Percy Wells Bidwell and John I. Falconer, *History of Agriculture in the Northern United States, 1620–1860* (New York: Peter Smith, 1941), 206.

24. Parkerson and Parkerson, *The Emergence of the Common School in the U.S. Countryside*, chapter 6.

25. Ibid.

26. Ibid.

27. Parkerson and Parkerson, *The Emergence of the Common School in the U.S. Countryside*, see chapter 1.

28. Alfred Chandler, *The Visible Hand: The Managerial Revolution in American Business* (Cambridge: Belknap Press of Harvard University Press, 1977).

29. Ibid.

30. Ibid.

31. Richard Hofstadter, *The Age of Reform: From Bryan to F. D. R.* (New York: Harper & Row, 1955).

32. Ibid.

33. Ibid.

34. William J. Reese, *The Origins of the American High School* (New Haven, Conn.: Yale University Press, 1995); The Carnegie Foundation for the Advancement of Teaching, *First Annual Report of the President and Treasurer* (New York: Carnegie Foundation for the Advancement of Teaching, 1906).

35. Gerald Grant and Christine E. Murray, *Teaching in America: The Slow Revolution* (Cambridge, Mass.: Harvard University Press, 1999), 13.

Chapter 2: Our Diverse Cultural History

1. Virginia D. Anderson, *New England's Generation: The Great Migration and the Formation of Society and Culture in the Seventeenth Century* (Cambridge: Cambridge University Press, 1991).

2. Ibid.

3. James Axtell, *The School Upon a Hill: Education and Society in Colonial New England* (New Haven, Conn.: Yale University Press, 1974).

4. For a discussion of these early laws, see Jon Teaford, "The Transformation of Massachusetts Education, 1670–1780," in *The Social History of American Education*, ed. B. Edward McClellan and William J. Reese (Urbana: University of Illinois Press, 1988), 23–38; For the text, see "The Old Deluder Law of 1647," in *American Education*, ed. Tyrus Hillway (Boston: Houghton Mifflin, 1964).

5. Sheldon S. Cohen, *A History of Colonial Education; 1607–1776* (New York: John Wiley, 1974); James Axtell, *The Invasion Within: The Contest of Cultures in Colonial North America* (New York: Oxford University Press, 1985); David M. Ellis et al., *A Short History of New York State* (Ithaca, N.Y.: Cornell University Press, 1957).

6. Cohen, *A History of Colonial Education;* Axtell, *The Invasion Within;* Ellis et al. *A Short History of New York State.*

7. Axtell, *The Invasion Within.*

8. Gary B. Nash, *Quakers and Politics: Pennsylvania, 1681–1726* (Princeton, N.J.: Princeton University Press, 1968).

9. Edwin Bronner, *William Penn's "Holy Experiment"* (New York: Temple University Publications [Distributed by Columbia University Press], 1962).

10. Sally Schwartz, *A Mixed Multitude: The Struggle for Toleration in Colonial Pennsylvania* (New York: New York University Press, 1987).

11. Ibid.

12. Cohen, *A History of Colonial Education;* Ellis et al., *A Short History of New York State.*

13. Charles L. Maurer, *Early Lutheran Education in Pennsylvania* (Philadelphia: Dorrance, 1932).

14. Lawrence Cremin, *American Education: The Colonial Experience, 1607–1783* (New York: Harper & Row, 1971); Cohen, *A History of Colonial Education;* James A. Burns, *The Principles, Origin and Establishment of the Catholic School System in the United States* (New York: Arno Press, 1969).

15. Cremin, *American Education: The Colonial Experience, 1607–1783;* Cohen, *A History of Colonial Education; 1607–1776.*

16. Wesley Craven, *The Southern Colonies in the Seventeenth Century, 1607–1689* (Baton Rouge: Louisiana State University Press, 1949).

17. Craven, *The Southern Colonies in the Seventeenth Century.*

18. Edgar W. Knight, *A Documentary History of Education in the South before 1860* (Chapel Hill: University of North Carolina Press, 1949); Cohen, *A History of Colonial Education; 1607–1776.*

19. Knight, *A Documentary History of Education in the South before 1860*; Cohen, *A History of Colonial Education.*

20. Knight, *A Documentary History.*

21. Ibid.

22. Harry Morgan, *Historical Perspectives on the Education of Black Children* (Westport, Conn.: Praeger, 1995).

23. Morgan, *Historical Perspectives on the Education of Black Children*; Frederick Douglass, *My Bondage and My Freedom* (New York: Miller, Orton & Mulligan, 1855); Frederick Douglass, *Narrative of the Life of Frederick Douglass*, ed. Benjamin Quarles (Cambridge: Belknap Press, 1960 [1845]); George Rawick, *From Sundown to Sunup: The Making of a Black Community* (Westport, Conn.: Greenwood, 1972); John Blassingame, *The Slave Community*, rev. ed. (New York: Oxford University Press, 1979); Jacqueline Jones, *Labor of Love, Labor of Sorrow: Black Women, Work, and the Family from Slavery to the Present* (New York: Basic Books, 1985).

24. Benjamin Rush, "Plan for the Establishment of Public Schools and the Diffusion of Knowledge in Philadelphia, Pennsylvania, 1786," in *Essays on Education in the Early Republic*, ed. Frederick Rudolph (Cambridge: Belknap Press of Harvard University Press, 1965), 14, 10.

25. Thomas Jefferson, "Notes on the State of Virginia," in *Crusade against Ignorance*, ed. Gordon C. Lee (New York: Teachers College, Columbia University, 1961), 96–97.

26. Noah Webster, "On the Education of Youth in America," in *Essays on Education in the Early Republic*, ed. Frederick Rudolph, 1965 (Cambridge: Belknap Press of Harvard University Press, 1790), 65.

27. Webster, "On the Education of Youth in America"; William McGuffey, *McGuffey's Eclectic Readers, First–Fourth Readers* (Cincinnati: Truman and Smith, 1836–1837).

28. Charles Sellers, *The Market Revolution* (Oxford: Oxford University Press, 1991); Donald H. Parkerson and Jo Ann Parkerson, *The Emergence of the Common School in the U.S. Countryside* (Lewiston, N.Y.: Edwin Mellen Press, 1998).

29. Horace Mann, "Twelfth Annual Report," in *The Republic and the School: Horace Mann on the Education of Free Men*, ed. Lawrence A. Cremin (New York: Teachers College Press, 1957 [1848]), 79–112.

30. Parkerson and Parkerson, *The Emergence of the Common School.*

31. Calvin Cotton, *A Voice from America* (London, 1839), 60.

32. David P. Page, *Theory and Practice of Teaching* (New York: American Book Company, 1867), 30.

33. See Parkerson and Parkerson, *The Emergence of the Common School*, 82–83, for a discussion of the content of the McGuffey Readers. For the stories, see McGuffey, *First Eclectic Reader.*

34. McGuffey, *First Eclectic Reader.*

Chapter 3: The Struggle for Diversity

1. John Higham, *Strangers in the Land: Patterns of American Nativism, 1860–1925* (New Brunswick, N.J.: Rutgers University Press, 1988 [1963]); Carl Kaestle, *Pillars of the Republic: Common Schools and American Society, 1780–1860* (New York: Hill and Wang, 1983).

2. Higham, *Strangers in the Land.*

3. Lyman Beecher, *A Plea for the West*, 2d ed. (Cincinnati, 1835).

4. "To the Honorable Board of Aldermen of the City of New York," in *Catholic Education in America: A Documentary History*, ed. Neil McCluskey (New York: Teachers College Press, 1964), 66–77.

5. McCluskey, ed., *Catholic Education in America.*

6. William McGuffey, *McGuffey's Eclectic Readers, First–Fourth Readers* (Cincinnati: Truman and Smith, 1836–1837).

7. Lindley S. Butler and Alan D. Watson, eds., *The North Carolina Experience* (Chapel Hill: University of North Carolina Press, 1984), 209–10; Herbert Aptheker, *Nat Turner's Slave Rebellion* (New York: Humanities Press, 1966); John Lofton, *Denmark Vesey's Plot: The Slave Plot That Lit a Fuse to Fort Sumter* (Kent: Kent State University Press, 1983); For the text of laws forbidding the education and teaching of slaves in Mississippi (1823), Louisiana (1830), North Carolina (1830, 1831), Virginia (1831), Alabama (1832), and South Carolina (1834), see Sol Cohen, ed., *Education in the United States: A Documentary History, Volume 3* (New York: Random House, 1974), 1621–24.

8. Harry Morgan, *Historical Perspectives on the Education of Black Children* (Westport, Conn.: Praeger, 1995).

9. Morgan, *Historical Perspectives on the Education of Black Children*; Thomas L Webber, *Deep Likes Rivers: Education in the Slave Quarters, 1831–1865* (New York: Norton, 1978).

10. Morgan, *Historical Perspectives on the Education of Black Children;* William E. Montgomery, *Under Their Own Vine and Fig Tree: The African-American Church in the South, 1865–1900* (Baton Rouge: Louisiana State University Press, 1993).

11. Lawrence Cremin, *American Education: The National Experience; 1783–1876* (New York: Harper & Row, 1980), 242; Montgomery, *Under Their Own Vine and Fig Tree;* For the text of the law creating the Freedmen's Bureau and a selection of letters from Port Royal, see Cohen, ed., *Education in the United States*, vol. 3, 1635, 1632.

12. Morgan, *Historical Perspectives on the Education of Black Children*; Michael Perman, *Reunion Without Compromise: The South and Reconstruction, 1865–1868* (Cambridge: Cambridge University Press, 1973).

13. Eric Foner, *Reconstruction: America's Unfinished Revolution, 1863–1877* (New York: Harper & Row, 1988); Neil McMillen, *Dark Journey: Black Mississippians in the Age of Jim Crow* (Urbana: University of Illinois Press, 1989); Butler and Watson, eds., *The North Carolina Experience.*

14. Foner, *Reconstruction.*

15. Michael Perman, *The Road to Redemption: Southern Politics, 1869–1879* (Chapel Hill: University of North Carolina Press, 1984); Sarah Jane Foster, *Teacher of the Freedmen: A Diary and Letters*, ed. Wayne E. Reilly (Charlottesville: University Press of Virginia, 1990), 52–53.

16. Butler and Watson, eds., *The North Carolina Experience*; C. Vann Woodward, *Origins of the New South, 1877–1913* (Baton Rouge: Louisiana State University Press, 1951).

17. C. Vann Woodward, *The Strange Career of Jim Crow*, 3d rev. ed. (New York: Oxford University Press, 1974).

18. Butler and Watson, eds., *The North Carolina Experience*; Morgan, *Historical Perspectives on the Education of Black Children.*

19. Butler and Watson, eds., *The North Carolina Experience.*

20. Woodward, *Origins of the New South, 1877–1913.*

21. Morgan, *Historical Perspectives on the Education of Black Children*; Allen Trelease, *White Terror: The Ku Klux Klan Conspiracy and Southern Reconstruction: War, Radicalism, and Race in Louisiana, 1862–1877* (New York: Harper & Row, 1971); W. Fitzhugh Brundage, *Lynching in the New South: Georgia and Virginia, 1880–1930* (Urbana: University of Illinois Press, 1993); for a powerful visual interpretation of lynching in the South during this period, see Jim Allen, *Without Sanctuary: Lynching Photography in America* (Santa Fe, N.M.: Twin Palms Press, 1999).

22. Allan H. Spear, *Black Chicago: The Making of a Negro Ghetto, 1890–1920* (Chicago: University of Chicago Press, 1967); Nathan Huggins, *Harlem Renaissance* (New York: Oxford University Press, 1971).

23. Zane L. Miller, *The Urbanization of Modern America* (New York: Harcourt Brace Jovanovich, 1973); Charles N. Glaab and A. Theodore Brown, *A History of Urban America*, 3d ed. (New York: Macmillan, 1983).

24. Miller, *The Urbanization of Modern America*.

25. William M. Tuttle Jr., *Race Riot: Chicago in the Red Summer of 1919* (New York: Atheneum, 1980); Elliot Rudwick, *Race Riot at East St. Louis, July 2, 1917* (Carbondale: Southern Illinois University Press, 1964); Robert Weaver, *The Negro Ghetto* (New York: Russell and Russell [1948], 1967).

26. Emma Lou Thornbrough, "Segregation in Indiana during the Klan Era of the 1920's," *Mississippi Valley Historical Review* 47 (March 1961): 594–618.

27. Ibid.

28. Morgan, *Historical Perspectives on the Education of Black Children;* Elliott Rudwick, "The Niagara Movement," *Journal of Negro History* 42, no. 3 (July 1957): 177–200.

29. Morgan, *Historical Perspectives on the Education of Black Children;* Charles C. Moskos Jr., "Racial Integration in the Armed Forces," *American Journal of Sociology* 72 (September 1966): 132–48.

30. Moskos, "Racial Integration in the Armed Forces. "

31. Richard Kluger, *Simple Justice: The History of Brown v. Board of Education and Black America's Struggle for Equality* (New York: Knopf, 1975).

32. Harvard Sitkoff, *The Struggle for Black Equality, 1954–1992*, rev. ed. (New York: Hill & Wang, 1993).

33. David Cecelski, *Along Freedom Road: Hyde County, North Carolina and the Fate of Black Schools in the South* (Chapel Hill: University of North Carolina Press, 1994); for a sobering examination of the education of black children, see Carl Husemoller Nightengale, *On the Edge: A History of Poor Black Children and Their American Dreams* (New York: Basic Books, 1993); for a classic study of black education during the Civil Rights era, see Herbert Kohl, *36 Children* (New York: New American Library, 1967).

34. Ronald Takaki, *A Different Mirror: A History of Multicultural America* (Boston: Little, Brown, 1993).

35. Takaki, *A Different Mirror*.

36. Michi Weglyn, *Years of Infamy: The Untold Story of America's Concentration Camps* (Seattle: University of Washington Press, 1996).

37. Charlotte Brooks, "In the Twilight Zone Between Black and White: Japanese American Resettlement and Community in Chicago, 1942–1945," *Journal of American History* 86, no. 4 (March 2000): 1655–87.

38. Hilary Conroy, *The Japanese Frontier in Hawaii, 1868–1898* (New York: Arno Press, 1978); Andrew W. Lind, *Hawaii's Japanese* (Princeton, N.J.: Princeton University Press, 1946).

39. Alejandro Portes and Ruben G. Rumbaut, *Immigrant America: A Portrait, 2d ed.* (Berkeley and Los Angeles: University of California Press, 1996).

40. Portes and Rumbaut, *Immigrant America.*

41. Rodolfo Acuña, *Occupied America: A History of Chicanos*, 3d ed. (New York: Longman, 1988).

42. Acuña, *Occupied America: A History of Chicanos.*

43. Acuña, *Occupied America: A History of Chicanos*; Peter Skerry, *Mexican Americans: The Ambivalent Minority* (New York: Free Press, 1993).

44. Eleanor Meyer Rogg, *The Assimilation of Cuban Exiles: The Role of Community and Class* (New York, 1974).

45. Rogg, *The Assimilation of Cuban Exiles;* Benigno Aguirre, "Differential Migration of Cuban Social Races," *Latin American Research Review* 11 (1976): 103–24.

46. Aguirre, "Differential Migration of Cuban Social Races."

47. Ibid.

48. Rogg, *The Assimilation of Cuban Exiles.*

49. U.S. Senate Committee on Labor and Public Welfare, 91st Congress, *Indian Education: A National Tragedy—A National Challenge, 1969 Report* (Washington D.C.: U.S. Government Printing Office, 1969); Although Spring focuses his attention on the plight of the Choctaw Nation, he provides insight into the effect of federal policies upon the education of Native Americans, see Joel Spring, *The Cultural Transformation of a Native American Family and Its Tribe, 1763–1995: A Basket of Apples* (Mahwah, N.J.: Lawrence Erlbaum Associates, 1996).

50. Roger Daniels, *Coming to America: A History of Immigration and Ethnicity in American Life* (New York: HarperCollins, 1990); Reed Ueda, *Postwar Immigrant America: A Social History* (Boston: Bedford Books of St. Martin's Press, 1994).

51. This incident was witnessed firsthand by coauthor Jo Ann Parkerson.

52. Joan McCarty and John Carrera Willshire, *New Voices: Immigrant Students in U.S. Public Schools* (Boston: National Coalition of Advocates for Students, 1988); Jim Cummins, *Bilingualism and Special Education: Issues in Assessment and Pedagogy* (San Diego: College-Hill Press, 1984). For an excellent introduction to preparing teachers in this area, see Carmen Zuniga-Hill and Carol Barnes, "Effective Teacher Preparation for Diverse Student Populations: What Works Best?" in *Class, Culture, and Race in American Schools*, ed. Stanley William Rothstein (Westport, Conn.: Greenwood, 1995).

Chapter 4: Women Enter Teaching

1. James Axtell, *The School Upon a Hill: Education and Society in Colonial New England* (New Haven, Conn.: Yale University Press, 1974); Walter Herbert Small, *Early New England Schools* (New York: Arno Press & the *New York Times*, 1969).

2. Ibid.

3. Axtell, *The School Upon a Hill.*

4. Ibid.

5. Ibid.

6. Cornelius J. Heatwole, *A History of Education in Virginia* (New York: Macmillan Company, 1916).

7. Small, *Early New England Schools*, 163.

8. Ibid., 162–65.

9. Thomas Woody, *Early Quaker Education in Pennsylvania* (New York: Arno Press & the *New York Times*, 1969), 54, 208–14.

10. Kenneth Lockridge, *Literacy in Colonial New England* (New York: Norton, 1974), 4.

11. Small, *Early New England Schools*, 277.

12. Ibid., 275.

13. Ibid., 280, 279.

14. Woody, *Early Quaker Education in Pennsylvania*, 36–37.

15. Geraldine Joncich Clifford, "Man/Woman/Teacher: Gender, Family, and Career in American Educational History," in *American Teachers: Histories of a Profession at Work*, ed. Donald Warren (New York: Macmillan, 1989), 293–343.

16. Jacqueline Reinier, "The Republican Child: Attitudes and Practices in Post-Revolutionary Philadelphia," *William & Mary Quarterly* 39, 3 (1982): 150–63.

17. Thomas Woody, *A History of Women's Education in the United States,* vol. 1 (New York: The Science Press, 1929); Gerda Lerner, *The Female Experience: An American Documentary* (Oxford: Oxford University Press, 1977), 209.

18. Mrs. A. W. Fairbanks, *Emma Willard and Her Pupils: Or 50 Years of Troy Female Seminary, 1822–1872* (New York: Mrs. R. Sage, 1898); Mrs. Mary C. J. Higley, ed., *One Hundred Year Biographical Directory of Mount Holyoke College, 1837–1937* (South Hadley, Mass.: Alumnae Association of Mount Holyoke College, 1937); Anne Firor Scott, "The Ever Widening Circle: The Diffusion of Feminist Values from the Troy Female Seminary," *History of Education Quarterly*, spring 1979, 3–25.

19. Sarah D. Locke Stowe, *History of Mount Holyoke Seminary, South Hadley, Massachusetts, During the First Half-Century* (South Hadley, Mass.; 1887); Higley, *One Hundred Year Biographical Directory of Mount Holyoke College.*

20. Richard M. Bernard and Maris A. Vinovskis, "Beyond Catherine Beecher: Female Education in the Antebellum Period," *Signs* 3 (summer 1978): 856–69; Donald H. Parkerson and Jo Ann Parkerson, *The Emergence of the Common School in the U.S. Countryside* (Lewiston, N.Y.: Edwin Mellen Press, 1998), 49–50; Woody, *A History of Women's Education in the United States*, vol 1. For a good introduction to female education during this period see Geraldine Joncich Clifford, "Eve: Redeemed by Education and Teaching School," *History of Education Quarterly*, winter 1981, 479–91.

21. Alanzo Potter, *The School and the Schoolmaster: A Manual for the Use of Teachers, Employers, Trustees, Inspectors, Etc., of Common Schools*, pt. 1 (New York: Harper & Brothers, 1842), 198; Warren Burton, *The District School as It Was* (Boston: T. R. Marvin, 1852). When district school teacher Benjamin Gue found a higher-paying job, he simply "closed the school" in midsemester, Benjamin F. Gue, *Diary of Benjamin F. Gue in Rural New York and Pioneer Iowa, 1847–1856*, ed. Earle D. Ross (Ames: Iowa State University Press, 1962).

22. Potter, *The School and the Schoolmaster*, 204–5.

23. Randolph W. Burgess, "Four Censuses of Teacher's Salaries," *American School Board Journal* 61 (September 1920): 27–28.

24. Potter, *The School and the Schoolmaster*, 205; John Locke, "Some Thoughts Concerning Education," in *The Educational Writings of John Locke*, ed. James L Axtell (New York: Cambridge University Press, 1968), 238.

25. Reinier, "The Republican Child: Attitudes and Practices in Post-Revolutionary Philadelphia"; Carl Kaestle, ed., *Joseph Lancaster and the Monitorial School Movement: A Documentary History* (New York: Teachers College Press, 1973); David Hogan, "The Market Revolution and Disciplinary Power: Joseph Lancaster and the Psychology of the Early Classroom System," *History of Education Quarterly* 29, 3 (1989): 381–417.

26. Locke, "Some Thoughts Concerning Education," 211.

27. Potter, *The School and the Schoolmaster*, 205.
28. Myra H. Strober and David Tyack, "Why Do Women Teach and Men Manage? A Report on Research on Schools," *Signs* 5, no. 3 (spring 1980): 497; Myra Strober and Audri Gordon Langford, "The Feminization of Teaching: A Cross-Sectional Analysis," *Signs* 11, no. 2 (1986): 217.
29. Strober and Gordon Langford, "The Feminization of Teaching," 217, 219.
30. Thomas Morain, "The Departure of Males from the Teaching Profession in Nineteenth Century Iowa," *Civil War History* 26, no. 2 (June 1980): 164.
31. Donald H. Parkerson, *The Agricultural Transition in New York State: Markets and Migration in Mid-Nineteenth Century America* (Ames: Iowa State University Press, 1995), see chapter 1, note 7.
32. Parkerson, *The Agricultural Transition in New York State*, see chapter 1, note 10; Percy Wells Bidwell and John I. Falconer, *History of Agriculture in the Northern United States, 1620–1860* (New York: Peter Smith, 1941), 504.
33. Alexis de Tocqueville, *Democracy in America* (New York: Vintage Books, 1945), 212.
34. Gue, *Diary of Benjamin F. Gue in Rural New York and Pioneer Iowa*, 30–31.
35. Social and occupational mobility were also core values of the common school education, see Donald H. Parkerson and Jo Ann Parkerson, *The Emergence of the Common School in the U.S. Countryside* (Lewiston, N.Y.: Edwin Mellen Press, 1998).

Chapter 5: Race and Ethnicity in the Teaching Profession

1. Horace Mann Bond, *The Education of the Negro in the American Social Order* (New York: Octagon Books, 1966); Harry Morgan, *Historical Perspectives on the Education of Black Children* (Westport, Conn.: Praeger, 1995); Sheldon S. Cohen, *A History of Colonial Education; 1607–1776* (New York: John Wiley, 1974).
2. Cohen, *A History of Colonial Education;* Morgan, *Historical Perspectives on the Education of Black Children*.
3. Thomas Woody, *Early Quaker Education in Pennsylvania* (New York: Arno Press & the New York Times, 1969); Morgan, *Historical Perspectives on the Education of Black Children*.
4. Edmund Fuller, *Prudence Crandall* (Middletown, Conn.: Wesleyan University Press, 1971).
5. Herbert Aptheker, *Nat Turner's Slave Rebellion* (New York: Humanities Press, 1966); John Lofton, *Denmark Vesey's Plot: The Slave Plot That Lit a Fuse to Fort Sumter* (Kent, Ohio: Kent State University Press, 1983); For a text of laws forbidding slave education in the South, see Sol Cohen, ed., *Education in the United States: A Documentary History* (New York: Random House, 1974), 1621–24.
6. Carter G. Woodson, *The African Background Outlined: Or Handbook for the Study of the Negro* (New York: Negro Universities Press, 1968); Linda M. Perkins, "The History of Blacks in Teaching: Growth and Decline within the Profession," in *American Teachers: Histories of a Profession at Work*, ed. Donald Warren (New York: Macmillan, 1989), 344–69.
7. Bond, *The Education of the Negro in the American Social Order;* H. A. Bullock, *A History of Negro Education in the South: From 1619 to Present* (Cambridge, Mass.: Harvard University Press, 1967); Morgan, *Historical Perspectives on the Education of Black Children*.
8. Bond, *The Education of the Negro in the American Social Order;* Morgan, *Historical Perspectives on the Education of Black Children*.

9.   Ray Allen Billington, ed., *The Journal of Charlotte L. Forten: A Free Negro in the Slave Era* (New York: W. W. Norton, 1953).

10. Perkins, "The History of Blacks in Teaching: Growth and Decline within the Profession," 344–69.

11. Morgan, *Historical Perspectives on the Education of Black Children*; E. A. Toppin, *A Biographical History of Blacks and America Since 1528* (New York: David McKay, 1971).

12. Olive W. Burt, *Mary McLeod Bethune* (Indianapolis: Bobbs-Merrill, 1970); Toppin, *A Biographical History of Blacks and America Since 1528.*

13. Ibid.

14. *120 Years of American Education: A Statistical Portrait*, ed. Thomas D. Snyder (Washington, D.C.: U.S. Department of Education, 1993).

15. Morgan, *Historical Perspectives on the Education of Black Children*; Atticus G. Haygood, *A Report to the Board of Trustees of the Stater Fund (1885)*, vol. 3 of *Education in the United States: A Documentary History*, ed. Sol Cohen (New York: Random House, 1974), 1680–81; George A. Dillingham, *The Foundation of the Peabody Tradition* (Lanham, Md.: University Press of America, 1989).

16. Morgan, *Historical Perspectives on the Education of Black Children*; Bond, *The Education of the Negro.*

17. Morgan, *Historical Perspectives on the Education of Black Children*; Louis R. Harlan, *Separate and Unequal: Public School Campaigns and Racism in the Southern Seaboard States, 1901–1915* (Chapel Hill: University of North Carolina Press, 1958).

18. James D. Anderson, "Northern Foundations and the Shaping of Southern Black Rural Education, 1902–1935," in *The Social History of American Education*, ed. B. Edward McClellan and William J. Reese (Urbana: University of Illinois Press, 1988), 287–312; Harlan, *Separate and Unequal.*

19. Harlan, *Separate and Unequal*; Anderson, "Northern Foundations and the Shaping of Southern Black Rural Education, 1902–1935," 287–312.

20. Anderson, "Northern Foundations and the Shaping of Southern Black Rural Education, 1902–1935;" Harlan, *Separate and Unequal.*

21. Booker T. Washington, "Up From Slavery," in *Three Negro Classics*, ed. John Hope Franklin (New York: Avon Books, 1965), 77, 94; Booker T. Washington, "Atlanta Exposition Address," in *Education in the United States: A Documentary History*, vol. 3, ed. Sol Cohen (New York: Random House, 1974), 1672–75.

22. W. E. B. DuBois, *The College-Bred Negro American* (Atlanta: Atlanta University Press, 1900).

23. DuBois, *The College-Bred Negro American.*

24. Perkins, "The History of Blacks in Teaching"; Anderson, "Northern Foundations and the Shaping of Southern Black Rural Education. "

25. Linda M. Perkins, *Fanny Jackson Coppin and the Institute for Colored Youth, 1865–1902* (New York: Garland, 1987), 136.

26. Sheldon S. Cohen, *A History of Colonial Education.*

27. Woody, *Early Quaker Education in Pennsylvania.*

28. Ibid.

29. Woody, *Early Quaker Education in Pennsylvania*; Donald H. Parkerson and Jo Ann Parkerson, *The Emergence of the Common School in the U.S. Countryside* (Lewiston, N.Y.: Edwin Mellen Press, 1998).

30. Neil G. McCluskey, ed., *Catholic Education in America: A Documentary History* (New York: Bureau of Publications, Teachers College, Columbia University, 1964);

James A. Burns, *The Principles, Origin and Establishment of the Catholic School System in the United States* (New York: Arno Press & the *New York Times*, 1969).

31. McCluskey, ed., *Catholic Education in America*; Burns, *The Principles, Origin and Establishment of the Catholic School System*.

32. McCluskey, ed., *Catholic Education in America*; Burns, *The Principles, Origin and Establishment of the Catholic School System*.

33. Paul Monroe, *Source Book of the History of Education* (New York: Macmillan, 1901). For a discussion of Commenius, see William H. Schubert, *Curriculum: Perspective, Paradigm, and Possibility* (New York: Macmillian, 1986), 65, 85, 129.

34. Monroe, *Source Book of the History of Education*; Thomas Kessner, *The Golden Door: Italian and Jewish Immigrant Mobility in New York City, 1880–1915* (New York: Oxford University Press, 1977).

35. Carl F. Kaestle, *Pillars of the Republic: Common Schools and American Society, 1780–1860* (New York: Hill and Wang, 1983). For Seward's comments see Burns, *The Principles, Origin and Establishment of the Catholic School System, 362.*

36. David M. Kennedy, *Over Here: The First World War in American Society* (New York: Oxford University Press, 1980).

37. Kennedy, *Over Here: The First World War.*

38. Ronald Takaki, *A Different Mirror: A History of Multicultural America* (Boston: Little, Brown, 1993).

39. Ibid.

40. Takaki, *A Different Mirror: A History of Multicultural America*; Joan McCarty and John Carrera Willshire, *New Voices: Immigrant Students in U.S. Public Schools* (Boston: National Coalition of Advocates for Students, 1988).

41. McCarty and Willshire, *New Voices: Immigrant Students in U.S. Public Schools,* Appendix D.

42. Ibid., 127–28.

Chapter 6: The Struggle for Control of Instruction and Curriculum

1. Warren Burton, *The District School as It Was* (Boston: T. R. Marvin, 1852).

2. Paul Leicester Ford, ed., *The New England Primer: A History of Its Origin and Development* (New York: Teachers College, Reprinted, 1962).

3. Ibid.

4. Ibid.

5. Ibid.

6. Ibid.

7. Donald H. Parkerson and Jo Ann Parkerson, *The Emergence of the Common School in the U.S. Countryside* (Lewiston, N.Y.: Edwin Mellen Press, 1998), 82.

8. Parkerson and Parkerson, *The Emergence of the Common School*, 84–85; William H. McGuffey, *The Eclectic First Reader, for Young Children* (Milford, Mich.: Mott Media, 1982 [1836]).

9. Ruth Miller Elson, *Guardians of Tradition* (Lincoln: University of Nebraska Press, 1964).

10. John S. L. Abbott, "George Washington," *Harpers New Monthly Magazine* 12, no. 69 (February 1856): 291.

11. William McGuffey, *McGuffey's Fifth Eclectic Reader* (New York: New American Library, 1962 [1879]); emphasis in the original.

12. Burton, *The District School as It Was*; see chapter 12.

13. David Hogan, "The Market Revolution and Disciplinary Power: Joseph Lancaster

and the Psychology of the Early Classroom System," *History of Education Quarterly* 29:3 (1989): 381–417.

14. Edwin C. Hewett, *A Treatise on Pedagogy for Young Teachers* (Cincinnati: Van Antwerp, Bragg, 1884); Charles Northend, *The Teacher and the Parent: Treatise Upon Common School Education, Containing Practical Suggestions to Teachers and Parents* (Boston: Jenks, Hickling and Swan, 1853).

15. Hewett, *A Treatise on Pedagogy for Young Teachers*, 214; Northend, *The Teacher and the Parent*, 114.

16. Burton, *The District School as It Was*, 65.

17. For an example of these "vowel and consonant sounds" see Samuel Kirkham, *English Grammar in Familiar Lectures* (New London: Bolles & Williams, 1847).

18. Burton, *The District School as It Was*, 65.

19. Isaac Phillips Roberts, *Autobiography of a Farm Boy* (Ithaca, N.Y.: Cornell University Press, 1946, [1916]), 36.

20. Laura Ingalls Wilder, *These Happy Golden Years* (New York: Harper/Trophy, 1971 [1941], 59.

21. Roberts, *Autobiography of a Farm Boy,* 34.

22. Burton, *The District School as It Was*, 61.

23. Ibid., 66–67.

24. Ibid., 71.

25. Ibid., 64.

26. Wilder, *These Happy Golden Years,* 48.

27. Parkerson and Parkerson, *The Emergence of the Common School.*

28. William H. McGuffey, *The Eclectic Second Reader, for Young Children* (Milford, Mich.: Mott Media, 1982 [1936]), Suggestions to Teachers.

29. Ibid.

30. Jean-Jacques Rousseau, *Emile*, trans. Barbara Foxley (London: Everyman's Library, 1974).

31. Johann Heinrich Pestalozzi, *Leonard and Gertrude*, ed., trans. Eva Channing (Lexington, Mass.: Heath, 1901 [1781]), 130–31.

32. Pestalozzi, *Leonard and Gertrude*; Johann Heinrich Pestalozzi, *How Gertrude Teaches Her Children*, ed. Ebenezer Cooke, trans. Lucy E. Holland and Francis C. Turner (London, 1894).

33. Edgar Knight, ed., *Reports on European Education* (New York: McGraw Hill, 1930), 60.

34. Kate Silber, *Pestalozzi: The Man and His Work* (London: Routledge and Kegan Paul, 1960).

35. Lester Frank Ward, *Young Ward's Diary*, ed. Vernhard J. Stern (New York: G. P. Putnam's Sons, 1935), January 24, 1860; Larry Cuban, *How Teachers Taught: Constancy and Change in American Classrooms, 1890–1980* (New York: Longman, 1984).

36. Burton, *The District School as It Was,* 103.

37. Roberts, *Autobiography of a Farm Boy*, 33.

38. Charles DeGarmo, *Herbart and the Herbartians* (New York: Scribner, 1895).

39. William H. Kilpatrick, ed., *The Educational Frontier* (New York: D. Appleton-Century Company, 1933).

40. William James, *Principles of Psychology* (New York: Dover, 1950 [1890]).

41. Edward Thorndike, *Educational Psychology* (New York: Teachers College Columbia University, 1913).

42. Thorndike, *Educational Psychology*; Richard Herrnstein and Charles Murray, *The Bell Curve: Intelligence and Class Structure in American Life* (New York: Free Press, 1994).

43. John B. Watson, *Behaviorism* (New York: W. W. Norton, 1924); B. F. Skinner, *Science and Human Behavior* (Boston: Houghton Mifflin, 1951).

44. William S. Gray et al., *The New Fun with Dick and Jane* (Glenview, Ill.: Scott Foresman, 1951); William S. Gray et al., *The New We Look and See* (Glenview, Ill.: Scott Foresman, 1951); William S. Gray et al., *The New We Come and Go* (Glenview, Ill.: Scott Foresman, 1951).

45. Parkerson and Parkerson, *The Emergence of the Common School;* Gray et al., *Dick and Jane.*

46. Gray et al., *Dick and Jane, Teachers Editions.*

47. R. C. Anderson et al., *Becoming a Nation of Readers: The Report of the Commission on Reading* (Washington, D.C.: National Institute of Education, 1985).

48. Gray et al., *Dick and Jane*; *Scope and Sequence Charts.*

49. Larry A. Hickman, "Dewey, John (1959–1952)," in *Philosophy of Education: An Encyclopedia*, ed. J. J. Chambliss (New York: Garland, 1996), 146–53.

50. John Dewey, *The School and Society* (Chicago: University of Chicago Press, 1965 [1899]).

51. John Dewey, *Democracy and Education: An Introduction to the Philosophy of Education* (New York: Macmillan, 1916).

52. Ibid.

53. Ibid.

54. Ibid.

55. Maria Montessori, *The Montessori Method* (New York: Schocken Books, 1964); Rita Kramer, *Maria Montessori* (New York: G. P. Putnam's Sons, 1976); Elizabeth Hainstock, *The Essential Montessori* (New York: Plume, 1986).

56. John D. Pulliam and James Van Patten, *History of Education in America*, 6th ed. (Englewood Cliffs, N.J.: Merrill, 1995); Judith Ford, "Innovative Methods in Elementary Education," unpublished dissertation (School of Education: University of Oklahoma, 1977); Dennis Jenkins, interview and classroom observation by authors, North Carolina; Debbie White, classroom observation by authors, North Carolina.

57. Charles E. Silberman, *Crisis in the Classroom: The Remaking of America Education* (New York: Random House, 1970).

58. Kenneth Goodman, *What's Whole in Whole Language?* (Portsmouth, N.H.: Heinemann, 1986); Kenneth Goodman, *Phonics Phacts* (Portsmouth, N.H.: Heinemann, 1993); Constance Weaver, *Understanding Whole Language* (Portsmouth, N.H.: Heinemann, 1990); Constance Weaver, *Reading, Process and Practice: From Socio-Psycho Linguistics to Whole Language* (Portsmouth, N.H.: Heinemann, 1994).

59. Goodman, *What's Whole in Whole Language?* Diane Baker, classroom observation by authors, North Carolina.

60. Goodman, *What's Whole in Whole Language?* Mary Lane, classroom observation by authors, North Carolina.

61. Richard Woody, interview by authors, North Carolina.

62. Joel Spring, *The American School, 1642–1990: Varieties of Historical Interpretation of the Foundations and Development of American Education*, 2d ed. (New York: Longman, 1990).

63. Sidney P. Marland, "The Condition of Education in the Nation," *American Education* 7 (April 1971).

64. National Commission on Excellence in Education, *A Nation at Risk: The Imperative for Educational Reform* (Washington, D.C.: GPO, 1983).

65. U.S. Department of Education, *America 2000: An Education Strategy* (Washington, D.C.: U.S. Department of Education, 1991); New American Schools Development Corporation, *Designs for a New Generation of American Schools* (Arlington, Va.: NASDC, 1991); David Tyack and Larry Cuban, *Tinkering Toward Utopia: A Century of Public School Reform* (Cambridge, Mass.: Harvard University Press, 1995).

66. Jonathan Kozol, "Whittle and the Privateers," *The Nation*, September 21, 1992, 272–78; Tyack and Cuban, *Tinkering Toward Utopia.*

67. North Carolina Department of Public Instruction, *North Carolina Department of Public Instruction—Curriculum Guidelines* (Raleigh, N.C.: NCDPI, 1999); Steven A. Stahl, "Why Innovations Come and Go (and Mostly Go): The Case of Whole Language," *Educational Researcher* 28, no. 8 (November 1999): 13–22.

68. Ira Shor, *Culture Wars: School and Society in the Conservative Restoration, 1969–1984* (Boston: Routledge & Kegan Paul, 1986); Ruth Sheehan, "Saying No to Sex, Abstinence Education: Is It Working?" *News and Observer* (Raleigh, N.C.), April 2, 2000, Section A: 25–27.

69. For a discussion of the political environment that spawns these reforms of censorship see Shor, *Culture Wars;* For a list of "banned books" see the American Library Association website in appendix 2.

70. William H. Schubert, *Curriculum: Perspective, Paradigm, and Possibility* (New York: Macmillan, 1986).

Chapter 7: Moral Education

1. A recent Gallup Poll on public attitudes toward education demonstrates that from 1969 to 1985, student discipline consistently topped the list of the "biggest problems faced by the schools." Since then issues of drug use and finance have also concerned Americans, but discipline continues to be a major concern. This poll is also revealing about other aspects of public education in America. See Lowell C. Rose and Alec M. Gallup, "The 31st Annual Phi Delta Kappa/Gallup Poll of the Public's Attitudes Toward the Public Schools," *Phi Delta Kappan* 81, no. 1 (September 1999): 41–57.

2. Paul Leicester Ford, ed., *The New England Primer: A History of Its Origin and Development* (New York: Teachers College, 1962 [1727]).

3. Ibid.

4. David Nasaw, *Schooled to Order: A Social History of Public Schooling in the United States* (New York: Oxford University Press, 1979); *Harpers*, September 1856, 588.

5. Noah Webster, "On the Education of Youth in America," in *Essays on Education in the Early Republic*, ed. Frederick Rudolph, 1965 (Cambridge: Belknap Press of Harvard University Press, 1790); Samuel Harrison Smith, "Remarks on Education," in *Essays on Education in the Early Republic*, ed. Frederick Rudolph (Cambridge, Mass.: Harvard University Press, 1965 [1796]), 170.

6. Charles Northend, *The Teacher and the Parent: Treatise Upon Common School Education, Containing Practical Suggestions to Teachers and Parents* (Boston: Jenks, Hickling & Swan, 1853), 96; Alanzo Potter, *The School and the Schoolmaster: A Manual for the Use of Teachers, Employers, Trustees, Inspectors, Etc., of Common Schools*, pt. 1 (New York: Harpers and Brothers, 1842), 103.

7. William H. McGuffey, *The Eclectic Second Reader, for Young Children* (Milford, Mich.: Mott Media, 1982 [1936]).

8. Potter, *The School and the Schoolmaster*, 204–205; emphasis in the original. P. O.

Thacher, "Influence of Female Character," in *The North American Reader*, ed. Lyman Cobb (Zanesville, Ohio: J. R. and A. Lippett, 1836), 325–30; emphasis in the original.

9. Potter, *The School and the Schoolmaster,* 204–205.

10. Gannett, "Female Influence," in *The North American Reader*, ed. Lyman Cobb (Zanesville, Ohio: J. R. and A. Lippett, 1836), 26–28; Potter, *The School and the Schoolmaster,* 204–205.

11. Donald H. Parkerson, "How Mobile Were Nineteenth Century Americans?" *Historical Methods* 15 (summer 1982): 99–109; Marta Danylewycz, Beth Light and Alison Prentice, "The Evolution of the Sexual Division of Labor in Teaching: Nineteenth Century Ontario and Quebec Case Study," *Social History* (1983), 81–109.

12. Horace Mann, "Fourth Annual Report on Education–1840," in *The Republic and the School: Horace Mann on the Education of Free Man*, ed. Lawrence A. Cremin (New York: Teachers College Press, 1957), 44–52.

13. John Dewey, *Moral Principles in Education* (Boston: Houghton Mifflin, 1909).

14. National Education Association Department of Superintendence, *The Tenth Yearbook: Character Education* (Washington, D.C.: National Education Association, 1932), 11.

15. Dewey, *Moral Principles in Education.*

16. Ibid.

17. Colin A. Scott, *Social Education* (Boston, 1908); B. Edward McClellan, *Schools and the Shaping of Character: Moral Education in America, 1607–Present* (Bloomington, Ind.: ERIC, 1992). See also various issues of *Social Education*.

18. William Heard Kilpatrick, *The Project Method* (New York: Teachers College Press, 1918).

19. McClellan, *Schools and the Shaping of Character.*

20. Ibid., 58, 59. This tradition continues with the DARE program. Students are required to sign an oath promising never to take drugs.

21. National Education Association Commission on the Reorganization of Secondary Education, *Cardinal Principles of Secondary Education* (Washington, D.C.: Bureau of Education, 1918).

22. Ibid.

23. Ibid.

24. Educational Policies Commission of the National Education Association and the American Association of School Administrators, *Moral and Spiritual Values in the Public Schools* (Washington, D.C.: National Education Association, 1951).

25. McClellan, *Schools and the Shaping of Character,* 82–84.

26. Yonat Shimron, "Leaders Want Biblical Rules in Schools," *News and Observer* (Raleigh, N.C.), January 30, 2000, 1A.

27. Louis E. Raths, Merrill Harmin, and Sydney B. Simon, *Values and Teaching* (Columbus, Ohio: Charles E. Merrill, 1966), 5.

28. Sara Whitfield, interview by authors, North Carolina; Mildred Taylor, *Roll of Thunder: Hear My Cry* (St. Paul, Minn.: EMC/Paradigm, 1999).

29. William Casement, "Moral Education: Form Without Content?" *Educational Forum* 48 (winter 1984).

30. Lawrence Kohlberg, "Moral Education in the Schools: A Developmental View," *School Review* (spring 1966); Lawrence Kohlberg, "Moral Education for a Society in Moral Transition," *Educational Leadership* 33 (October 1975): 46–54.

31. William J. Bennett, *The Book of Virtues: A Treasury of Great Moral Stories* (New York: Simon & Schuster, 1993).

32. McClellan, *Schools and the Shaping of Character.*

33. Toni Marie Massaro, *Contitutional Literacy: A Core Curriculum for a Multicultural Nation* (Durham, N.C.: Duke University Press, 1993).

Chapter 8: Discipline

1. *The Holy Bible: Containing the Old and New Testaments, King James Version* (Nashville, Tenn.: National Publishing, 1978).

2. James Oliphant, ed., *The Educational Writings of Richard Mulcaster* (Glasgow, 1903); Bruce Curtis, "My Ladie Birchely Must Needs Rule": Punishment and the Materialization of Moral Character from Mulcaster to Lancaster," in *Discipline, Moral Regulation, and Schooling: A Social History*, ed. Kate Rousmaniere, Kari Dehli, and Ning deConinck-Smith (New York: Garland, 1997), 19–42.

3. James Axtell, *The School Upon a Hill: Education and Society in Colonial New England* (New Haven, Conn.: Yale University Press, 1974), 195, 196; Walter Herbert Small, *Early New England Schools* (New York: Arno Press & the *New York Times*, 1969), 386.

4. Axtell, *The School Upon a Hill*, 199.

5. Warren Burton, *The District School as It Was* (Boston: T. R. Marvin, 1852), 25.

6. Ibid., 30.

7. Ibid., 39.

8. Barbara Finkelstein, *Governing the Young: Teacher Behavior in Popular Primary Schools in Nineteenth-Century United States* (New York: Falmer Press, 1989), 155.

9. Burton, *The District School*, 40.

10. Finkelstein, *Governing the Young*, 170.

11. Burton, *The District School*, 119–20.

12. Ibid., 121.

13. Ibid., 122–24.

14. J. R. Dinwiddy, "The Nineteenth Century Campaign against Flogging in the Army," *English Historical Review* 97 (1982): 308–33; E. E. Steiner, "Separating the Soldier From the Citizen: Ideology and Criticism of Corporal Punishment in the British Armies, 1790–1815," *Social History* 8 (1983): 19–35; David Rothman, *The Discovery of the Asylum: Social Order and Disorder in the New Republic* (New York, 1971).

15. John Locke, *An Essay Concerning Human Understanding*, ed. Peter N. Nidditch (Oxford: Clarendon Press, 1979); Denis Diderot and Jean le Rond d'Alembert, *Encyclopedia*, trans. with an introduction and notes by Nelly S. Hoyt and Thomas Cassirer (Indianapolis: Bobbs-Merrill, 1965).

16. John Locke, "Some Thoughts Concerning Education," in *The Educational Writings of John Locke*, ed. James L. Axtell (Cambridge: Cambridge University Press, 1968 [1705]), 211.

17. Jean-Jacques Rousseau, *Emile*, trans. Barbara Foxley (London: Everyman's Library, 1974).

18. Donald H. Parkerson and Jo Ann Parkerson, *The Emergence of the Common School in the U.S. Countryside* (Lewiston, N.Y.: Edwin Mellen Press, 1998).

19. Michael Foucault, *Discipline and Punish* (New York: Pantheon, 1977), 176–77.

20. David Salmon, *Joseph Lancaster* (London: Longmans, Green, 1904).

21. Salmon, *Joseph Lancaster,* 9; Parkerson and Parkerson, *The Emergence of the Common School*; see chapter 1.

22. Parkerson and Parkerson, *The Emergence of the Common School*; see chapter 4.

23. Edwin C. Hewett, *A Treatise on Pedagogy for Young Teachers* (Cincinnati: Van Antwerp, Bragg, 1884), 218.

24. Charles Northend, *The Teacher and the Parent: Treatise Upon Common School Education, Containing Practical Suggestions to Teachers and Parents* (Boston: Jenks, Hickling and Swan, 1853), 150, 149, 151–52.

25. Hewett, *A Treatise on Pedagogy*, 67, 68.

26. Parkerson and Parkerson, *The Emergence of the Common School,* 87–89.

27. Benjamin F. Gue, *Diary of Benjamin F. Gue in Rural New York and Pioneer Iowa, 1847–1856,* ed. Earle D. Ross (Ames: Iowa State University Press, 1962), 93–94.

28. Lester Frank Ward, *Young Ward's Diary,* ed. Vernhard J. Stern (New York: G. P. Putnam's Son, 1935), December 24, 27; 1860, 26, 27.

29. Ward, *Young Ward's Diary,* January 5, 1861, 29; emphasis in the original.

30. Polly Welts Kaufman, *Women Teachers on the Frontier* (New Haven, Conn.: Yale University Press, 1984), 163.

31. Larry Cuban, *How Teachers Taught: Constancy and Change in American Classrooms, 1890–1980* (New York: Longman, 1984), chapter 12.

32. William Chandler Bagley, *Classroom Management* (New York, 1925).

33. Ibid.

34. Bagley, *Classroom Management.*

35. Bagley, *Classroom Management.*

36. E. W. Elmore, "Squads for Discipline," *American Physical Education Review* 28 (January 1923): 25–26.

37. B. F. Skinner, *Science and Human Behavior* (Boston: Houghton Mifflin, 1951), Introduction.

38. B. F. Skinner, "The Free and Happy Student," *Phi Delta Kappan* 55, no. 1 (1973): 13–16; B. F. Skinner, *Beyond Freedom and Dignity* (New York: Alfred A. Knopf, 1971).

39. B. F. Skinner, *Walden Two* (New York: Macmillan, 1974).

40. Fredric Jones, *Positive Classroom Discipline* (New York: McGraw-Hill, 1987); Lou Ann Ryan, classroom observation by authors, North Carolina.

41. Lee Canter and Marlene Canter, *Assertive Discipline* (Seal Beach, Calif.: Canter & Associates, 1976); Lee Canter and Marlene Canter, *Succeeding with Difficult Students* (Santa Monica, Calif.: Canter & Associates, 1993).

42. Barbara Taylor, classroom observation by authors, North Carolina.

43. Jean-Jacques Rousseau, *Emile,* trans. Barbara Foxley (London: Everyman's Library, 1974), 5, 178–79.

44. Lelia E. Partridge, "A Disciple of Francis W. Parker on the Distinguishing Features of the Quincy Schools," in *Education in the United States: A Documentary History,* vol. 3, ed. Sol Cohen (New York: Random House, 1885), 1814–15; also see Francis W. Parker, *Notes of Talks on Teaching, Given by Francis W. Parker, at the Martha's Vineyard Summer Institute, July 17 to August 19, 1882,* reported by Lelia E. Patridge (New York: E. L. Kellogg, 1883).

45. John Dewey and Evelyn Dewey, *Schools of To-Morrow* (New York: E. P. Dutton, 1915).

46. Dewey and Dewey, *Schools of To-Morrow.*

47. Rudolph Dreikers and P. Cassel, *Discipline without Tears* (New York: Hawthorn, 1972), 87.
48. Cathy Lee Gates, classroom observation and interview by authors, North Carolina.
49. Dreikers and Cassel, *Discipline without Tears.*
50. Jacob Kounin, *Discipline and Group Management in Classrooms* (New York: Holt, Rinehart & Winston, 1971).
51. Kounin, *Discipline and Group Management;* Cathy Lee Gates interview.
52. Kounin, *Discipline and Group Management.*
53. Haim Ginott, *Between Parent and Child* (New York: Avon, 1965); Haim Ginott, *Between Parent and Teenager* (New York: Macmillan, 1969); Haim Ginott, *Teacher and Child* (New York: Macmillan, 1971).
54. Amy Prescott, classroom observation by authors, North Carolina.
55. William Glasser, *Reality Therapy: A New Approach to Psychiatry* (New York: Harper & Row, 1965); William Glasser, *Schools without Failure* (New York: Harper & Row, 1969).
56. Glasser, *Reality Therapy*; Glasser, *Schools Without Failure.*
57. Glasser, "Ten Steps to Good Discipline," *Today's Education* 61 (1977): 23–24.
58. Ibid.
59. Justice Policy Institute, Report on Violence in Public Schools, April 2000.

Chapter 9: The Control of Teachers' Destinies

1. Laura Ingalls Wilder, *These Happy Golden Years* (New York: HarperTrophy, 1971 [1943]).
2. Ellwood P. Cubberley, *Public Education in the United States* (Boston: Houghton Mifflin, 1919).
3. Warren Burton, *The District School as It Was* (Boston: T. R. Marvin, 1852).
4. Cubberley, *Public Education in the United States*, 241.
5. Ibid., 185.
6. Samuel R. Hall, *Lectures on School Keeping* (Boston: Richardson, Lord, & Holbrook, 1829); David P. Page, *Theory and Practice of Teaching* (New York: American Book Company, 1867); Alanzo Potter, *The School and the Schoolmaster: A Manual for the Use of Teachers, Employers, Trustees, Inspectors, Etc., of Common Schools*, pt. 1 (New York: Harper and Brothers, 1842).
7. William B. Fowle, *The Teachers' Institute* (New York: A. S. Barnes, 1873).
8. Wilder, *These Happy Golden Years*, 99.
9. Benjamin F. Gue, *Diary of Benjamin F. Gue in Rural New York and Pioneer Iowa, 1847–1856*, ed. Earle D. Ross (Ames: Iowa State University Press, 1962), 59, 60, 61.
10. Ibid., 62–65.
11. Lester Frank Ward, *Young Ward's Diary*, ed. Vernhard J. Stern (New York: G. P. Putnam's Sons, 1935), 29–30.
12. Polly Welts Kaufman, *Women Teachers on the Frontier* (New Haven, Conn.: Yale University Press, 1984), 160.
13. Mrs. A. W. Fairbanks, *Emma Willard and Her Pupils: Or 50 Years of Troy Female Seminary, 1822–1872* (New York: Mrs. R. Sage, 1898), 155.
14. Anna Howard Shaw, *The Story of a Pioneer by Anna Howard Shaw* (New York: Harper, 1915), 44–46.
15. Ibid., 50–53.

16. Caroline Seabury, *The Diary of Caroline Seabury, 1854–1863*, ed. Suzanne L. Bunkers (Madison: University of Wisconsin Press, 1991).

17. Ibid., July 4, 1855, and January 10, 1857.

18. Kaufman, *Women Teachers on the Frontier,* 158.

19. Ibid.

20. Ibid.

21. Wilder, *These Happy Golden Years*, 22.

22. Ibid., 24.

23. Wayne J. Urban, *Why Teachers Organized* (Detroit: Wayne State University Press, 1982).

24. Marjorie Murphy, *Blackboard Unions: The AFT and the NEA, 1900–1980* (Ithaca, N.Y.: Cornell University Press, 1990); Wayne J. Urban, *Why Teachers Organized.*

25. National Education Association, "Report of the Sub-Committee on the Organization of City School Systems, 1895," *Journal of Addresses and Proceedings of the National Education Association* (1895); Murphy, *Blackboard Unions*; Urban, *Why Teachers Organized.*

26. Ibid.

27. National Education Association, "Report of the Sub-Committee on the Organization of City School Systems, 1895," 397.

28. Murphy, *Blackboard Unions.*

29. Ibid.

30. Ibid., 8–12.

31. Ibid.

32. Ibid.

33. Ibid., 8–12, 21–22.

34. Edgar Wesley, *NEA, The First One Hundred Years: The Building of the Teaching Profession* (New York: Harper, 1957).

35. Ibid.

36. Wesley, *NEA*; National Education Association, *National Education Association Proceedings* (1901), 174–81; Murphy, *Blackboard Unions*, 55; Margaret Haley, *Battleground: The Autobiography of Margaret Haley* (Chicago: University of Illinois Press, 1982), 134.

37. National Education Association, *National Education Association Proceedings* (1901); Haley, *Battleground*, 134–35.

38. Murphy, *Blackboard Unions*, 72–73; Associated Press, "Teacher: Dress Code Goes Too Far," *Daily Reflector* (Greenville, N.C.), Wednesday, March 22, 2000, Section B-6.

39. Murphy, *Blackboard Unions*, 72.

40. Joel Spring, *The American School, 1642–1990: Varieties of Historical Interpretation of the Foundations and Development of American Education*, 2d. ed. (New York: Longman, 1990).

41. Martin Lazerson, "Teachers Organize: What Margaret Haley Lost," *History of Education Quarterly* 21 (summer 1981): 261–70; Murphy, *Blackboard Unions.*

42. William Edward Eaton, *The American Federation of Teachers, 1916–1961* (Carbondale: Southern Illinois University Press, 1975).

43. Wesley, *NEA*; Murphy, *Blackboard Unions.*

44. Spring, *The American School*, 271–72.

45. Wesley, *NEA*; Urban, *Why Teachers Organized.*

46. Murphy, *Blackboard Unions*, 271.

47. Wesley, *NEA*. Also see various issues of the *NEA Research Bulletins*.

48. David Tyack, Robert Lowe, and Elisabeth Hansot, *Public Schools in Hard Times* (Cambridge: Harvard University Press, 1984).

49. Tyack, *Public Schools in Hard Times*; Wesley, *NEA*.

50. George S. Counts, *Dare the School Build a New Social Order?* (New York: John Day, 1932).

51. Committee on Social and Economic Goals for America, "Report from the Committee on Social and Economic Goals for America," in *National Education Association Proceedings* (1932).

52. Counts, *Dare the School Build a New Social Order?* See also various issues of the *Social Frontier*.

53. Eaton, *The American Federation of Teachers*.

54. Eaton, *The American Federation of Teachers*; Murphy, *Blackboard Unions*, 182–83.

55. Ibid.

56. Murphy, *Blackboard Unions*, 187.

57. Ibid., 192–93; Ellen Schrecker, *Many Are the Crimes: McCarthyism in America* (Boston: Little, Brown, 1998), ix.

58. Philip Taft, *United They Teach: The Story of the UFT* (Los Angeles: Nash, 1974); Spring, *The American School, 1642–1990*.

59. Arthur M. Schlesinger, Jr., *A Thousand Days: John F. Kennedy in the White House* (Boston: Houghton Mifflin, 1965); Gunnar Myrdal, *An American Dilemma: The Negro Problem and Modern Democracy* (New York: Harper & Row, 1944); Michael Harrington, *The Other America: Poverty in the United States* (New York: Macmillan, 1962); Walter Heller et al., "The Problem of Poverty in America," in *The Annual Report of the Council of Economic Advisors* (Washington, D.C.: U.S. Government Printing Office, 1964).

60. Stephen Bailey and Edith Mosher, "Elementary and Secondary Education Act of 1965, Public Law 89–10," in *ESEA: The Office of Education Administers a Law* (Syracuse, N.Y.: Syracuse University Press, 1968).

61. Julie Roy Jeffrey, *Education for Children of the Poor* (Columbus: Ohio State University Press, 1978); Spring, *The American School,* chapter 12.

62. Ira Shor, *Culture Wars: School and Society in the Conservative Restoration, 1969–1984* (Boston: Routledge & Kegan Paul, 1986); Joel Spring, *Political Agendas for Education: From the Christian Coalition to the Green Party* (Mahwah, N.J.: Lawrence Erlbaum, 1997), chapter 1.

63. National Council for Accreditation of Teacher Education, *Standards, Procedures, and Policies for the Accreditation of Professional Education Units* (Washington, D.C.: NCATE, 1997); Blake Rodman, "Alternate Route Said a Success," *Education Week*, February 24, 1988.

64. C. Emily Feistritzer and David T. Chester, *Alternative Teacher Certification: A State by State Analysis, 1996* (Washington, D.C.: National Center for Education Information, 1996).

65. Educational Testing Service, *Praxis—Tests at a Glance: (Various Disciplines)* (Princeton, N.J.: ETS, 1999); Educational Testing Service, *Praxis II—Subject Assessment: Study Guide* (Princeton, N.J.: ETS, 1999); Educational Testing Service, *Praxis II— Test Preparation Workshop* (Princeton, N.J.: ETS, 1999); Debbie Metcalf, "Electronic Portfolios: Using Multimedia to Assess Student Performance," paper presented to the Association for Supervision and Curriculum Development, San Diego, spring 2000.

66. National Board for Professional Teaching Standards, *Toward High and Rigorous*

Standards for the Teaching Profession: A Summary, Second Edition (Detroit: NBPTS, 1991); National Board for Professional Teaching Standards, *What Teachers Should Know and Be Able to Do* (Detroit: NBPTS, 1994).

67. National Board for Professional Teaching Standards, *Toward High and Rigorous Standards*.
68. Ibid.
69. "News in Brief," *Education Week*, February 5, 1992.
70. Gerald Grant and Christine E. Murray, *Teaching in America: The Slow Revolution* (Cambridge, Mass.: Harvard University Press, 1999).
71. Ibid.
72. Ibid.

Chapter 10: America's Third Educational Transition

1. John Higham, *Strangers in the Land, Patterns of American Nativism, 1860–1925*, 2d ed. (New Brunswick, N.J.: Rutgers University Press, 1988 [1970]).
2. For a general introduction to the 1920s see Frederick Lewis Allen, *Only Yesterday* (New York: John W. Wiley, 1997); Gary B. Nash et al., *The American People: Creating a Nation and a Society,* 4th ed. (New York: Longman, 1998); see chapter 23. For an embarrassing perspective on immigration written by one of the great educators of the early twentieth century, see Ellwood P. Cubberley, *Changing Conceptions of Education* (Boston: Houghton Mifflin, 1909).
3. Ronald Takaki, *A Different Mirror: A History of Multicultural America* (Boston: Little, Brown, 1993); Gary B. Nash et al., *The American People: Creating a Nation*; see chapter 29.
4. Ibid.
5. David E Lundstrom, *A Few Good Men from UNIVAC* (Bridgewater, N.J.: Replica Books, 1997); Nancy B. Stern, *From ENIAC to UNIVAC* (Bedford, Mass.: Digital Press, 1981).
6. Lundstrom, *A Few Good Men.*
7. T. R. Reid, *The Chip: How Two Americans Invented the Microchip and Launched a Revolution* (New York: Simon and Schuster, 1989).
8. Ibid.
9. Ibid.
10. Steven Lubar, *InfoCulture: The Smithsonian Book of Information Age Inventions* (Boston: Houghton Mifflin, 1993).
11. Ibid.
12. Harley Hahn and Rick Stout, *The Internet Complete Reference* (Berkeley: Osborne McGraw/Hill, 1997); Dennis Trinkle et al., *The History Highway: A Guide to Internet Resources* (Armonk, N.Y.: M. E. Sharpe, 1997).
13. Hahn and Stout, *The Internet Complete Reference.*
14. Ibid.
15. Ibid.
16. Ibid.
17. Nash et al., *The American People: Creating a Nation and a Society*; Appendix, "The Constitution of the United States of America."
18. Ibid.
19. John Maynard Keynes, *Treatise on Money* (New York: Harcourt Brace, 1930); John Maynard Keynes, *The General Theory of Employment, Interest and Money* (New York: Harcourt Brace, 1936).

20. Ibid.
21. Jeremy Atack and Peter Passell, *A New Economic View of American History from Colonial Times to 1940*, 2d ed. (New York: W. W. Norton, 1994); Richard Hofstadter, *The Age of Reform: From Bryan to F. D. R.* (New York: Harper & Row, 1955); Nash et al., *The American People: Creating a Nation and a Society*; appendix, "The Constitution of the United States of America."
22. William E. Leuchtenburg, *Franklin Delano Roosevelt and the New Deal* (New York: Harper & Row, 1963).
23. Roy Lubove, *The Struggle for Social Security* (Cambridge, Mass.: Harvard University Press, 1961).
24. Alanzo Hamby, *Beyond the New Deal: Harry S. Truman and American Liberalism* (New York: Columbia University Press, 1973).
25. Doris Kearns Goodwin, *Lyndon Johnson and the American Dream* (Norwalk, Conn.: Easton Press, 1987).
26. Ibid.
27. Joel Spring, *American Education, Eighth Edition* (Boston: McGraw-Hill, 1998).
28. Donald Warren, *To Enforce Education* (Detroit: Wayne State University Press, 1974).
29. Norman C. Thomas, *Education and National Politics* (New York: McKay, 1975); Hugh Davis Graham, *The Uncertain Triumph: Federal Education Policy in the Kennedy and Johnson Years* (Chapel Hill: University of North Carolina Press, 1984).
30. Graham, *The Uncertain Triumph;* Julie Roy Jeffrey, *Education for Children of the Poor* (Columbus: Ohio State University Press, 1978).
31. Maris Vinovskis, "Do Federal Compensatory Education Programs Really Work?" *American Journal of Education* 107, no. 3 (May 1999): 187–209.
32. Ibid.
33. Hofstadter, *The Age of Reform: From Bryan to F. D. R.*
34. Rachel Carson, *Silent Spring* (Boston: Houghton Mifflin, 1962).
35. Kilpatrick Sale, *The Green Revolution: The American Environmental Movement, 1962–1992* (New York: Hill and Wang, 1993).
36. Ibid.
37. National Commission on Excellence in Education, *A Nation at Risk: The Imperative for Educational Reform* (Washington, D.C.: GPO, 1983); also see Milton Goldberg and Anita Madan Renton, "A Nation at Risk: Ugly Duckling No More," in *Commissions, Reports, Reforms and Educational Policy*, ed. Rick Ginsberg and David N. Plank (Westport, Conn.: Praeger, 1995), 38.

Bibliography

120 Years of American Education: A Statistical Portrait. Edited by Thomas D. Snyder. Washington, D.C.: U.S. Department of Education, 1993.

Abbott, John S. L. "George Washington." *Harpers New Monthly Magazine* 12, no. 69 (February 1856): 291.

Abrams, Richard M., and Lawrence W. Levine, eds. *The Shaping of Twentieth-Century America: Interpretive Essays*. 2nd ed. Boston: Little, Brown, 1965, 1971.

Acuña, Rodolfo. *Occupied America: A History of Chicanos*. 3d ed. New York: Longman, 1988.

Aguirre, Benigno. "Differential Migration of Cuban Social Races." *Latin American Research Review* 11 (1976): 103–24.

Allen, Frederick Lewis. *Only Yesterday*. New York: Wiley, 1997.

Allen, Jim. *Without Sanctuary: Lynching Photography in America*. Santa Fe, N.M.: Twin Palms Press, 1999.

Anderson, James D. "Northern Foundations and the Shaping of Southern Black Rural Education, 1902–1935." In *The Social History of American Education*, edited by B. Edward McClellan and William J. Reese, 287–312. Urbana: University of Illinois Press, 1988.

Anderson, R. C., E. F. Hiebert, J. A. Scott, and A. G. Wilkinson. *Becoming a Nation of Readers: The Report of the Commission on Reading*. Washington, D.C.: National Institute of Education, 1985.

Anderson, Virginia D. *New England's Generation: The Great Migration and the Formation of Society and Culture in the Seventeenth Century*. Cambridge: Cambridge University Press, 1991.

Appleby, Joyce. "Republicanism and Ideology." *American Quarterly* 37 (Fall 1985): 461–73.

Aptheker, Herbert. *Nat Turner's Slave Rebellion*. New York: Humanities Press, 1966.

Aries, Philip. *Centuries of Childhood*. Harmondsworth, England: Penguin, 1973.

Associated Press. "Teacher: Dress Code Goes Too Far." *The Daily Reflector* (Greenville, N.C.), March 22, 2000, B6.

Atack, Jeremy, and Fred Bateman. *To Their Own Soil: Agriculture in the Antebellum North*. Ames: Iowa State University Press, 1987.

Atack, Jeremy, and Peter Passell. *A New Economic View of American History from Colonial Times to 1940*. 2d ed. New York: W. W. Norton, 1994.

Axtell, James. *The Invasion Within: The Contest of Cultures in Colonial North America*. New York: Oxford University Press, 1985.

———. *The School Upon a Hill: Education and Society in Colonial New England*. New Haven, Conn.: Yale University Press, 1974.

Bagley, William Chandler. *Classroom Management*. New York: Macmillan, 1925.

Bailey, Stephen, and Edith Mosher. "Elementary and Secondary Education Act of 1965, Public Law 89–10." In *ESEA: The Office of Education Administers a Law.* Syracuse, N.Y.: Syracuse University Press, 1968.

Bailyn, Bernard. *Education in the Forming of American Society: Needs and Opportunities for Study.* Chapel Hill: University of North Carolina Press, 1960.

———. *Ideological Origins of the American Revolution.* Cambridge, Mass.: Harvard University Press, 1967.

Becker, Gary. "An Economic Analysis of Fertility." In *Demographic and Economic Change in Developed Countries,* edited by the Committee for Economic Research, 209–31. Princeton, N.J.: Princeton University Press, 1960.

Beecher, Catherine. *A Treatise on Domestic Economy.* New York: Schocken Books, 1977.

Beecher, Lyman. *A Plea for the West.* 3d ed., n.p., 1835.

Bennett, William J. *The Book of Virtues: A Treasury of Great Moral Stories.* New York: Simon & Schuster, 1993.

Bernard, Richard M., and Maris Vinovskis. "Beyond Catherine Beecher: Female Education in the Antebellum Period." *Signs* 3 (summer 1978): 856–69.

Biddle, Nicholas. "Report on Education." *Journal of the Twenty First House of Representatives of the Commonwealth of Pennsylvania* (1810).

Bidwell, Percy Wells, and John I. Falconer. *History of Agriculture in the Northern United States, 1620–1860.* New York: Peter Smith, 1941.

Biklen, Sari Knopp. *School Work: Gender and the Cultural Construction of Teaching.* New York: Teacher College Press, 1995.

Billington, Ray Allen, ed. *The Journal of Charlotte L. Forten.* New York: W. W. Norton, 1953.

Blassingame, John. *The Slave Community.* Rev. ed. New York: Oxford University Press, 1979.

Blumin, Stuart. "The Hypothesis of Middle Class Formation in Nineteenth Century Society." *American Historical Review* 90 (April 1985): 299–338.

Bond, Horace Mann. *The Education of the Negro in the American Social Order.* New York: Octagon Books, 1966.

Bowles, Samuel, and Herbert Ginitis. *Schooling in Capitalist America.* New York: Basic Books, 1971.

Bronner, Edwin. *William Penn's "Holy Experiment."* New York: Temple University Publications (distributed by Columbia University Press), 1962.

Brooks, Charlotte. "In the Twilight Zone Between Black and White: Japanese American Resettlement and Community in Chicago, 1942–1945." *Journal of American History* 86, no. 4 (March 2000): 1655–87.

Brosio, Richard. *A Radical Critique of Capitalist Education.* New York: Peter Lang, 1991.

Brundage, W. Fitzhugh. *Lynching in the New South: Georgia and Virginia, 1880–1930.* Urbana: University of Illinois Press, 1993.

Buel, J. "On Education." *The Cultivator* 4, no. 7 (July 1837): 77.

Bullock, Henry A. *A History of Negro Education in the South: From 1619 to the Present.* Cambridge, Mass.: Harvard University Press, 1967.

Burgess, Randolph W. "Four Censuses of Teachers' Salaries." *American School Board Journal* 61 (September 1920): 27–28.

Burns, James A. *The Principles, Origin and Establishment of the Catholic School System in the United States.* New York: Arno Press & the *New York Times,* 1969.

Burt, Olive W. *Mary McLeod Bethune.* Indianapolis: Bobbs-Merrill, 1970.

Burton, Warren. *The District School as It Was.* Boston: T. R. Marvin, 1852.

Butler, Lindley S., and Alan D. Watson. *The North Carolina Experience: An Interpretive and Documentary History*. Chapel Hill: University of North Carolina Press, 1984.

Calhoun, Charles W., ed. *The Guilded Age: Essays on the Origins of Modern America*. Wilmington, Del.: Scholarly Resources, 1996.

Canter, Lee, and Marlene Canter. *Assertive Discipline*. Seal Beach, Calif.: Canter, 1976.

———. *Succeeding with Difficult Students*. Santa Monica, Calif.: Canter, 1993.

Carnegie Foundation for the Advancement of Teaching. *First Annual Report of the President and Treasurer*. New York: Carnegie Foundation for the Advancement of Teaching, 1906.

Carson, Rachel. *Silent Spring*. Boston: Houghton Mifflin, 1962.

Casement, William. "Moral Education: Form Without Content?" *Educational Forum* 48 (winter 1984): 177–90.

Cecelski, David. *Along Freedom Road: Hyde County, North Carolina and the Fate of Black Schools in the South*. Chapel Hill: University of North Carolina Press, 1994.

Cedoline, Anthony J. *Job Burnout in Public Education: Symptoms, Causes, and Survival Skills*. New York: Teachers College Press, 1982.

Chandler, Alfred. *The Visible Hand: The Managerial Revolution in American Business*. Cambridge, Mass.: Belknap Press of Harvard University Press, 1977.

Charles, C. M. *Building Classroom Discipline*. 6th ed. New York: Longman, 1999.

Child, Lydia. *Mother's Book*. Boston: Carter & Hendee/Arno Press, 1973 [1831].

Clifford, Geraldine Joncich. "Eve: Redeemed by Education and Teaching School." *History of Education Quarterly*, winter 1981, 479–91.

———. "Man/Woman/Teacher: Gender, Family, and Career in American Educational History." In *American Teachers: Histories of a Profession at Work*, edited by Donald Warren, 293–343. New York: Macmillan, 1989.

Clinton, DeWitt. "Address to the New York State Legislature, 1826." In *Public Education in the United States*, edited by Ellwood P. Cubberley, 112. Boston: Houghton Mifflin, 1919.

Cohen, Sheldon S. *A History of Colonial Education; 1607–1776*. New York: Wiley, 1974.

Cohen, Sol, ed. *Education in the United States: A Documentary History*. New York: Random House, 1974.

Commission on the Reorganization of Secondary Education, National Education Association. *Cardinal Principles of Secondary Education*. Washington, D.C.: Bureau of Education, 1918.

Committee on Labor and Public Welfare, U.S. Senate, 91st Congress. *Indian Education: A National Tragedy—A National Challenge, 1969 Report*. Washington, D.C.: U.S. Government Printing Office, 1969.

Committee on Social and Economic Goals for America. "Report from the Committee on Social and Economic Goals for America." In *National Education Association Proceedings*, Washington, D.C., National Education Association, 1932.

Commons, John, Ulrich Phillips, Eugene Gilmore, Helen Sumner, and John Andrews, eds., *Documentary History of American Industrial Society*. Cleveland: A. H. Clark, 1909–1911.

Conroy, Hilary. *The Japanese Frontier in Hawaii, 1868–1898*. New York: Arno Press, 1978.

Cordier, Mary Hurlbut. *Schoolwomen of the Prairies and Plains: Personal Narratives from Iowa, Kansas, Nebraska, 1860s–1920s*. Albuquerque: University of New Mexico Press, 1992.

Cotton, Calvin. *A Voice from America*. London, 1839.

Counts, George S. *Dare the School Build a New Social Order?* New York: John Day, 1932.

Craven, Wesley. *The Southern Colonies in the Seventeenth Century, 1607–1689.* Baton Rouge: Louisiana State University Press, 1949.

Cremin, Lawrence A. *American Education: The Colonial Experience, 1607–1783.* New York: Harper & Row, 1971.

———. *American Education: The National Experience, 1783–1876.* New York: Harper & Row, 1980.

———. *Traditions of American Education.* New York: Basic Books, 1976.

———. *The Transformation of the School: Progressivism in American Education.* New York: Vintage Books, 1961.

Cuban, Larry. *How Teachers Taught: Constancy and Change in American Classrooms, 1890–1980.* New York: Longman, 1984.

Cubberley, Ellwood P. *Changing Conceptions of Education.* Boston: Houghton Mifflin, 1909.

———. *Public Education in the United States.* Boston: Houghton Mifflin, 1919.

Cubberley, Ellwood P., and Edward C. Elliott. *State and County School Administration.* vol. 2, *A Source Book.* New York: Macmillan, 1927.

Cummins, Jim. *Bilingualism and Special Education: Issues in Assessment and Pedagogy.* San Diego: College-Hill Press, 1984.

Curran, Francis X. *The Churches and the Schools: American Protestantism and Popular Elementary Education.* Chicago: Loyola University Press, 1954.

Curtis, Bruce. "'My Ladie Birchely Must Needs Rule': Punishment and the Materialization of Moral Character from Mulcaster to Lancaster." In *Discipline, Moral Regulation, and Schooling: A Social History*, edited by Kate Rousmaniere, Kari Dehli, and Ning deConinck-Smith, 19–42. New York: Garland, 1997.

Daniels, Roger. *Coming to America: A History of Immigration and Ethnicity in American Life.* New York: HarperCollins, 1990.

———. *Politics of Prejudice.* Berkeley and Los Angeles: University of California Press, 1962.

Danylewycz, Marta, Beth Light, and Allison Prentice. "The Evolution of the Sexual Division of Labour in Teaching: Nineteenth-Century Ontario and Quebec Case Study." *Social History* 6, 31 (Spring 1983).

DeGarmo, Charles. *Herbart and the Herbartians.* New York: Scribner, 1895.

Dewey, John. *Democracy and Education: An Introduction to the Philosophy of Education.* New York: Macmillan, 1916.

———. *Experience and Education.* New York: Macmillan, 1938.

———. *Moral Principles in Education.* Boston: Houghton Mifflin, 1909.

———. *The School and Society.* Chicago: University of Chicago Press, 1965 [21st impression, originally published 1899].

Dewey, John, and Evelyn Dewey. *Schools of To-Morrow.* New York: E. P. Dutton & Co., 1915.

Diderot, Denis, and D'Alembert, Jean le Rond. *Encyclopedia.* Translated and with an introduction and notes by Nelly S. Hoyt and Thomas Cassirer. Indianapolis: Bobbs-Merrill, 1965.

Dillingham, George A. *The Foundation of the Peabody Tradition.* Lanham, Md.: University Press of America, 1989.

Dinwiddy, J. R. "The Nineteenth Century Campaign against Flogging in the Army." *English Historical Review* 97 (1982): 308–33.

Douglass, Frederick. *My Bondage and My Freedom.* New York: Miller, Orton & Mulligan, 1855.

———. *Narrative of the Life of Frederick Douglass.* Edited by Benjamin Quarles. Cambridge, Mass.: Belknap Press, 1960 [1845].

Dreikers, Rudolph, and P. Cassel. *Discipline without Tears.* New York: Hawthorn, 1972.

DuBois, W. E. B. *The College-Bred Negro American.* Atlanta: Atlanta University Press, 1900.

Dworkin, Anthony Gary. *Teacher Burnout in the Public Schools: Structural Causes and Consequences for Children.* Albany: State University of New York Press, 1987.

Dworkin, Martin S., ed. *Dewey on Education.* New York: Teachers College Press, 1959.

Eaton, William Edward. *The American Federation of Teachers, 1916–1961.* Carbondale: Southern Illinois University Press, 1975.

Educational Policies Commission of the National Education Association and the American Association of School Administrators. *Moral and Spiritual Values in the Public Schools.* Washington, D.C.: National Education Association, 1951.

Educational Testing Service. *Praxis—Tests at a Glance: Various Disciplines.* Princeton, N.J.: Educational Testing Service, 1999.

———. *Praxis II—Subject Assessment: Study Guide.* Princeton, N.J.: Educational Testing Service, 1999.

———. *Praxis II—Test Preparation Workshop.* Princeton, N.J.: Educational Testing Service, 1999.

Eggleston, Edward. *The Hoosier Schoolmaster.* Bloomington: Indiana University Press, 1984.

Ellis, David M., James A. Frost, Harold C. Syrett, and Harry J. Carman. *A Short History of New York State.* Ithaca, N.Y.: Cornell University Press, 1957.

Elmore, E. W. "Squads for Discipline." *American Physical Education Review* 28 (January 1923): 25–26.

Elson, Ruth Miller. *Guardians of Tradition.* Lincoln: University of Nebraska Press, 1964.

Eribon, Didier. *Michel Foucault.* Translated by Betsy Wing. Cambridge, Mass.: Harvard University Press, 1991.

Fairbanks, Mrs. A. W. *Emma Willard and Her Pupils: Or 50 Years of Troy Female Seminary, 1822–1872.* New York: Mrs. R. Sage, 1898.

Faler, Paul. "Cultural Aspects of the Industrial Revolution: Lynn, Massachusetts, Shoemakers and Industrial Morality, 1826–1868." *Labor History* 15 (1974): 367–94.

Feistritzer, C. Emily, and David T. Chester. *Alternative Teacher Certification: A State by State Analysis, 1996.* Washington, D.C.: National Center for Education Information, 1996.

Finkelstein, Barbara. *Governing the Young: Teacher Behavior in Popular Primary Schools in Nineteenth-Century United States.* New York: Falmer Press, 1989.

Foner, Eric. *Reconstruction: America's Unfinished Revolution, 1863–1877.* New York: Harper & Row, 1988.

Ford, Judith. "Innovative Methods in Elementary Education." Unpublished dissertation. School of Education, University of Oklahoma, 1977.

Ford, Paul Leicester, ed. *The New England Primer: A History of Its Origin and Development.* New York: Teachers College Press, 1962, reprint.

Foster, Sarah Jane. *Teacher of the Freedmen: A Diary and Letters.* Edited by Wayne E. Reilly. Charlottesville: University Press of Virginia, 1990.

Foucault, Michel. *Discipline and Punish.* New York: Pantheon, 1977.

Fowle, William B. *The Teachers' Institute.* New York: A. S. Barnes, 1873.

Foy, Rena, ed. *The World of Education: Selected Readings*. New York: Macmillan, 1968.

Franklin, Benjamin. *The Autobiography of Benjamin Franklin*. Edited by Leonard W. Labaree. New Haven, Conn.: Yale University Press, 1964.

Fuller, Edmund. *Prudence Crandall*. Middletown, Conn.: Wesleyan University Press, 1971.

Fuller, Wayne E. *One Room Schools of the Midwest*. Lawrence: University Press of Kansas, 1994.

Galenson, David W. "Determinants of the School Attendance of Boys in Early Chicago." *History of Education Quarterly* 35 (winter 1995): 371–400.

Gannett. "Female Influence." In *The North American Reader*, edited by Lyman Cobb, 26–28. Zanesville, Ohio: J. R. and A. Lippett, 1836.

Garraty, John. *The New Commonwealth: 1877–1890*. New York: Harper & Row, 1968.

Gartner, Lloyd P., ed. *Jewish Education in the United States: A Documentary History*. New York: Teachers College Press, 1970.

Gidney, R. D., and W. P. J. Milar. "From Voluntarism to State Schooling: The Creation of the Public School System in Ontario." *Canadian Historical Review* 66, no. 4 (December 1985): 443–73.

Ginott, Haim. *Between Parent and Child*. New York: Avon, 1965.

———. *Between Parent and Teenager*. New York: Macmillan, 1969.

———. *Teacher and Child*. New York: Macmillan, 1971.

Glaab, Charles N., and A. Theodore Brown. *A History of Urban America*. 3d ed. New York: Macmillan, 1983.

Glasser, William. *Reality Therapy: A New Approach to Psychiatry*. New York: Harper & Row, 1965.

———. *Schools without Failure*. New York: Harper & Row, 1969.

———. "Ten Steps to Good Discipline." *Today's Education* 61 (1977): 23–24.

Goldberg, Milton, and Anita Madan Renton. "A Nation at Risk: Ugly Duckling No More." In *Commissions, Reports, Reforms and Educational Policy*, edited by Rick Ginsberg and David N. Plank, 1–10. Westport, Conn.: Praeger, 1995.

Goodman, Kenneth. *Phonics Phacts*. Portsmouth, N.H.: Heinemann, 1993.

———. *What's Whole in Whole Language?* Portsmouth, N.H.: Heinemann, 1986.

Goodwin, Doris Kearns. *Lyndon Johnson and the American Dream*. Norwalk, Conn.: Easton Press, 1987.

Graff, Harvey. *The Literacy Myth: Literacy and Social Structure in the Nineteenth-Century City*. New York: Academic Press, 1979.

Graham, Hugh Davis. *The Uncertain Triumph: Federal Education Policy in the Kennedy and Johnson Years*. Chapel Hill: University of North Carolina Press, 1984.

Grant, Gerald, and Christine E. Murray. *Teaching in America: The Slow Revolution*. Cambridge, Mass.: Harvard University Press, 1999.

Gray, William S., and Marion Monroe. *The New Fun with Dick and Jane*. Glenview, Ill.: Scott Foresman, 1951.

———. *The New We Come and Go*. Glenview, Ill.: Scott Foresman, 1951.

Gray, William S., et al. *The New We Look and See*. Glenview, Ill.: Scott Foresman, 1951.

Gue, Benjamin F. *Diary of Benjamin F. Gue in Rural New York and Pioneer Iowa, 1847–1856*. Edited by Earle D. Ross. Ames: Iowa State University Press, 1962.

Guest, Avery, and Stuart Tolney. "Children's Roles and Fertility." *Social Science History* 7, no. 4 (1983): 355–80.

Hackley, Delos. *Diary of Delos Hackley*. Batavia, N.Y.: n.p., 1850–1870.

Hahn, Harley, and Rick Stout. *The Internet Complete Reference*. Berkeley: Osborne McGraw Hill, 1997.

Hainstock, Elizabeth. *The Essential Montessori*. New York: Plume, Penguin Group, 1986.

Haley, Margaret. *Battleground: The Autobiography of Margaret Haley*. Edited by Robert L. Reid. Urbana: University of Illinois Press, 1982.

Hall, G. Stanley. "Introduction to Leonard and Gertrude." In *Readings in the Methods of Education*, edited by Frank L. Steeves. New York: Odyssey Press, 1964 [1885].

Hall, Samuel R. *Lectures on School Keeping*. Boston: Richardson, Lord, & Holbrook, 1829.

Hamby, Alanzo. *Beyond the New Deal: Harry S. Truman and American Liberalism*. New York: Columbia University Press, 1973.

Harlan, Louis R. *Separate and Unequal: Public School Campaigns and Racism in the Southern Seaboard States, 1901–1915*. Chapel Hill: University of North Carolina Press, 1958.

Harpers New Monthly Magazine, September 1856.

Harrington, Michael. *The Other America: Poverty in the United States*. New York: Macmillan, 1962.

Haygood, Atticus G. *A Report to the Board of Trustees of the Stater Fund (1885)*. In *Education in the United States: A Documentary History*, Vol. 3, edited by Sol Cohen, 1680–81. New York: Random House, 1974.

Heatwole, Cornelius J. *A History of Education in Virginia*. New York: Macmillan, 1916.

Heilbroner, Robert. *Visions of the Future*. New York: Oxford University Press, 1995.

Heller, Walter. "The Problem of Poverty in America." In *The Annual Report of the Council of Economic Advisors*. Washington, D.C.: U.S. Government Printing Office, 1964.

Henretta, James. *The Evolution of American Society, 1700–1815: An Interdisciplinary Analysis*. Lexington, Mass.: D. C. Heath, 1973.

Herrnstein, Richard, and Charles Murray. *The Bell Curve: Intelligence and Class Structure in American Life*. New York: Free Press, 1994.

Hewett, Edwin C. *A Treatise on Pedagogy for Young Teachers*. Cincinnati: Van Antwerp, 1884.

Hickman, Larry A. "Dewey, John (1959–1952)." In *Philosophy of Education: An Encyclopedia*, edited by J. J. Chambliss, 146–53. New York: Garland, 1996.

Higham, John. *Strangers in the Land, Patterns of American Nativism, 1860–1925*. New Brunswick, N.J.: Rutgers University Press, 1988 [1963].

Higley, Mrs. Mary C. J. *One Hundred Year Biographical Directory of Mount Holyoke College, 1837–1937*. South Hadley, Mass.: Alumnae Association of Mount Holyoke College, 1937.

Hoffman, Nancy. *Woman's "True" Profession: Voices from the History of Teaching*. New York: Feminist Press & McGraw-Hill, 1981.

Hofstadter, Richard. *The Age of Reform: From Bryan to FDR*. New York: Harper & Row, 1955.

Hogan, David. "The Market Revolution and Disciplinary Power: Joseph Lancaster and the Psychology of the Early Classroom System." *History of Education Quarterly* 29, no. 3 (1989): 381–417.

Holmes, Madelyn, and Beverly J. Weiss. *Lives of Women Public Schoolteachers: Scenes from American Educational History*. New York: Garland Publishing, Inc., 1995.

Hoskin, Keith. "Foucault Under Examination." In *Foucault and Education*, edited by Stephen J. Ball, 29–53. London: Routledge, 1990.

Huggins, Nathan. *Harlem Renaissance*. New York: Oxford University Press, 1971.

James, William. *Principles of Psychology*. New York: Dover, 1950 [1890].

Jefferson, Thomas. "Comprehensive Education Bill, 1817." In *Popular Education and Democratic Thought in America*, edited by Rush Welter, 82–83. New York: Columbia University Press, 1962.

Jefferson, Thomas. "For the More General Diffusion of Knowledge." In *American Education*, edited by Tyrus Hillway, 21–27. Boston: Houghton Mifflin, 1964 [1779].

———. "Letter to Joseph Cabell, 1816." In *American Writings on Popular Education: The Nineteenth Century*, edited by Rush Welter, 9–13. New York: Bobbs-Merrill, 1971.

———. "Notes on the State of Virginia." In *Crusade Against Ignorance*, edited by Gordon C. Lee, 96–97. New York: Teachers College Press, 1961.

Jeffrey, Julie Roy. *Education for Children of the Poor*. Columbus: Ohio State University Press, 1978.

Jewel, Frederick. *School Government: A Practical Treatise*. New York: n.p., 1866.

Jones, Fredric. *Positive Classroom Discipline*. New York: McGraw-Hill, 1987.

Jones, Jacqueline. *Labor of Love, Labor of Sorrow: Black Women, Work, and the Family from Slavery to the Present*. New York: Basic Books, 1985.

Journal of the Twenty First House of Representatives of the Commonwealth of Pennsylvania. Lancaster, Penn., 1810.

Kaestle, Carl. *Pillars of the Republic: Common Schools and American Society, 1780–1860*. New York: Hill and Wang, 1983.

———. "Social Change, Discipline, and the Common School in Early Nineteenth-Century America." *Journal of Interdisciplinary History* 9 (summer 1978): 1–17.

———, ed. *Joseph Lancaster and the Monitorial School Movement: A Documentary History*. New York: Teachers College Press, 1973.

Kaestle, Carl, and Maris Vinovskis. "From Fireside to Factory: School Entry and School Leaving in Nineteenth-Century Massachusetts." In *Transitions: The Family and the Life Course in Historical Perspective*, edited by Tamara K. Hareven, 136–37. New York: Academic Press, 1978.

———. *Education and Social Change in Nineteenth-Century Massachusetts*. Cambridge: Cambridge University Press, 1980.

Kandel, Isaac Leon. *The New Era in Education: A Comparative Study*. Cambridge, Mass.: Riverside Press, 1955.

Katz, Michael. *Class Bureaucracy and Schools: The Illusion of Educational Change in America*. New York: Praeger, 1975.

———. *The Irony of Early School Reform: Educational Innovation in Mid Nineteenth-Century Massachusetts*. Cambridge, Mass.: Harvard University Press, 1969.

———. "The Origins of Public Education." In *The Social History of American Education*, edited by Edward McClellan and William J. Reese, 91–117. Urbana: University of Illinois Press, 1988.

———. "Who Went to School." *History of Education* 12 (fall 1972): 432–54.

Kaufman, Polly Welts. *Women Teachers on the Frontier*. New Haven, Conn.: Yale University Press, 1984.

Kemple, Ann. "The Myth of Agrarianism in Rural Educational Reform." *History of Education Quarterly* 2 (June 1962): 100–11.

Kennedy, David M. *Over Here: The First World War in American Society*. New York: Oxford University Press, 1980.

Kessner, Thomas. *The Golden Door: Italian and Jewish Immigrant Mobility in New York City, 1880–1915*. New York: Oxford University Press, 1977.

Keynes, John Maynard. *The General Theory of Employment, Interest and Money.* New York: Harcourt Brace, 1936.

———. *Treatise on Money.* New York: Harcourt Brace, 1930.

Kilpatrick, William H. *The Project Method.* New York: Teachers College Press, 1918.

———., ed. *The Educational Frontier.* New York: D. Appleton-Century Company, 1933.

Kirkham, Samuel. *English Grammar in Familiar Lectures.* New London, Conn.: Bolles & Williams, 1847.

Kliebard, Herbert M. *The Struggle for the American Curriculum, 1893–1958.* New York: Routledge, 1995.

Kluger, Richard. *Simple Justice: The History of Brown v. Board of Education and Black America's Struggle for Equality.* New York: Knopf, 1975.

Knight, Edgar W. *Education in the South.* Chapel Hill: University of North Carolina Press, 1924.

———. *The Influence of Reconstruction on Education in the South.* New York: Teachers College Press, 1913.

———, ed. *A Documentary History of Education in the South Before 1860.* Chapel Hill: University of North Carolina Press, 1949.

———. *Reports on European Education.* New York: McGraw Hill, 1930.

Knox, Samuel. "An Essay on the Best System of Liberal Education." In *Essays on Education in the Early Republic*, edited by Frederick Rudolph, 306. Cambridge, Mass.: Harvard University Press, 1965 [1799].

Kohl, Herbert. *36 Children.* New York: New American Library, 1967.

Kohlberg, Lawrence. "Moral Education for a Society in Moral Transition." *Educational Leadership* 33 (October 1975): 46–54.

———. "Moral Education in the Schools: A Developmental View." *School Review* 74 (spring 1966).

Kounin, Jacob. *Discipline and Group Management in Classrooms.* New York: Holt, Rinehart & Winston, 1971.

Kozol, Jonathan. "Whittle and the Privateers." *The Nation*, September 21, 1992, 272–78.

Kramer, Rita. *Maria Montessori.* New York: G.P. Putnam's Sons, 1976.

Kuhn, Thomas. *The Structure of Scientific Revolutions.* Chicago: University of Chicago Press, 1962.

Lazerson, Martin. "Teachers Organize: What Margaret Haley Lost." *History of Education Quarterly* 21 (summer 1981): 261–70.

Lemke, L. C. "Attracting and Retaining Special Educators in Rural and Small Schools: Issues and Solutions." *Rural and Special Education Quarterly* 14, no. 20 (1995): 25–30.

Lerner, Gerda, ed. *The Female Experience: An American Documentary.* New York: Oxford University Press, 1977, 1992.

Leuchtenburg, William E. *Franklin Delano Roosevelt and the New Deal.* New York: Harper & Row, 1963.

Lind, Andrew W. *Hawaii's Japanese.* Princeton, N.J.: Princeton University Press, 1946.

Locke, John. *An Essay Concerning Human Understanding.* Edited by Peter N. Nidditch. Oxford: Clarendon Press, 1979.

———. "Some Thoughts Concerning Education." In *The Educational Writings of John Locke*, edited by James Axtell. Cambridge: Cambridge University Press, 1968 [1705].

Lockridge, Kenneth. *Literacy in Colonial New England*. New York: Norton, 1974.

Lofton, John. *Denmark Vesey's Plot: The Slave Plot That Lit a Fuse to Fort Sumter*. Kent, Ohio: Kent State University Press, 1983.

Lubar, Steven. *InfoCulture: The Smithsonian Book of Information Age Inventions*. Boston: Houghton Mifflin, 1993.

Lubove, Roy. *The Struggle for Social Security*. Cambridge, Mass.: Harvard University Press, 1961.

Lundstrom, David E. *A Few Good Men from UNIVAC*. Bridgewater, N.J.: Replica Books, 1997.

Luther, Seth. *An Address to the Workingmen of New England on the State of Education*. Boston: self-published, 1836.

MacMullen, Edith Nye. *In the Cause of True Education: Henry Barnard and Nineteenth-Century School Reform*. New Haven, Conn.: Yale University Press, 1991.

Mann, Horace. "Boston Grammar and Writing Schools." *Common School Journal* 7, no. 19 (October 1, 1845): 289–304.

———. "Fifth Annual Report—1841." In *The Republic and The School: Horace Mann on the Education of Free Man*, edited by Lawrence A. Cremin, 53. New York: Teachers College Press, 1957.

———. "Fourth Annual Report—1840." In *The Republic and The School: Horace Mann on the Education on Free Man*, edited by Lawrence A. Cremin, 44–52. New York: Teachers College Press, 1957.

———. *Report of the Educational Tour in Germany*. London: n.p., 1846.

———. "Tenth Annual Report—1846." In *The Republic and The School: Horace Mann on the Education on Free Man*, edited by Lawrence A. Cremin, 59–77. New York: Teachers College Press, 1957.

———. "Twelfth Annual Report on Education—1848." In *The Republic and the School: Horace Mann on the Education of Free Man*, edited by Lawrence A. Cremin, 79–112. New York: Teachers College Press, 1957.

Manning, Diane. *Hill Country Teacher: Oral Histories from the One-Room School and Beyond*. Boston: Twayne, 1990.

Marland, Sidney P. "The Condition of Education in the Nation." *American Education* 7 (April 1971): 3–5.

Massaro, Toni Marie. *Constitutional Literacy: A Core Curriculum for a Multicultural Nation*. Durham, N.C.: Duke University Press, 1993.

Maurer, Charles L. *Early Lutheran Education in Pennsylvania*. Philadelphia: Dorrance, 1932.

McCarty, Joan, and John Carrera Willshire. *New Voices: Immigrant Students in U.S. Public Schools*. Boston: National Coalition of Advocates for Students, 1988.

McClellan, B. Edward. *Schools and the Shaping of Character: Moral Education in America, 1607-Present*. Bloomington, Ind.: Educational Resources Information Clearinghouse, 1992.

McCluskey, Neil G., ed. *Catholic Education in America: A Documentary History*. New York: Bureau of Publications, Teachers College Press, 1964.

McGuffey, William H. *The Eclectic First Reader, for Young Children*. Milford, Mich.: Mott Media, 1982 [1936].

———. *The Eclectic Fourth Reader*. Milford, Mich.: Mott Media, 1982 [1838].

———. *The Eclectic Second Reader, for Young Children*. Milford, Mich.: Mott Media, 1982 [1936].

———. *The Eclectic Third Reader*. Milford, Mich.: Mott Media, 1982 [1837].

————. *McGuffey's Fifth Eclectic Reader.* New York: New American Library, 1962 [1879].

McMillen, Neil. *Dark Journey: Black Mississippians in the Age of Jim Crow.* Urbana: University of Illinois Press, 1989.

Meier, August, and Elliott Rudwick, eds. *The Making of Black America: Essays in Negro Life and History,* vol. 2: *The Black Community in Modern America.* New York: Atheneum, 1969.

Metcalf, Debbie. "Electronic Portfolios: Using Multimedia to Assess Student Performance." Paper presented to the Association for Supervision and Curriculum Development, San Diego, spring 2000.

Miller, George Frederick. *The Academy System of the State of New York.* New York: Arno Press & the *New York Times,* 1969.

Miller, Zane L. *The Urbanization of Modern America.* New York: Harcourt Brace Jovanovich, 1973.

Monroe, Paul. *Source Book of the History of Education.* New York: Macmillan, 1901.

Montessori, Maria. *The Montessori Method.* New York: Schocken Books, 1964.

Montgomery, William E. *Under Their Own Vine and Fig Tree: The African-American Church in the South, 1865–1900.* Baton Rouge: Louisiana State University Press, 1993.

Morain, Thomas. "The Departure of Males from the Teaching Profession in Nineteenth-Century Iowa." *Civil War History* 26, no. 2 (June 1980): 161–70.

Morgan, Harry. *Historical Perspectives on the Education of Black Children.* Westport, Conn.: Praeger, 1995.

Mosier, Richard. *Making of the American Mind: Social and Moral Ideas in the McGuffey Readers.* New York: Kings Crown Press, 1947.

Moskos, Charles C. Jr. "Racial Integration in the Armed Forces." *American Journal of Sociology* 72 (September 1966): 132–48.

Mr. Payson. "Address to the Essex Agricultural Society." *The Cultivator,* January 1848.

Mrs. A. X. "Educate the Daughter." *The Mothers Journal and Family Visitant,* 23 (1858).

Murphy, Marjorie. *Blackboard Unions: The AFT and the NEA, 1900–1980.* Ithaca, N.Y.: Cornell University Press, 1990.

Myrdal, Gunnar. *An American Dilemma: The Negro Problem and Modern Democracy.* New York: Harper & Row, 1944.

Nasaw, David. *Schooled to Order: A Social History of Public Schooling in the United States.* New York: Oxford University Press, 1979.

Nash, Gary B. *Quakers and Politics: Pennsylvania, 1681–1726.* Princeton, N.J.: Princeton University Press, 1968.

Nash, Gary B., Julie Ray Jeffrey, John R. Howe, Peter J. Frederick, Allen F. Davis, and Allen M. Winkler. *The American People: Creating a Nation and a Society.* 4th ed. New York: Longman, 1998.

National Board for Professional Teaching Standards. *Toward High and Rigorous Standards for the Teaching Profession: A Summary.* 2d ed. Detroit, Mich.: National Board for Professional Teaching Standards, 1991.

————. *What Teachers Should Know and Be Able to Do.* Detroit, Mich.: National Board for Professional Teaching Standards, 1994.

National Commission on Excellence in Education. *A Nation at Risk: The Imperative for Educational Reform.* Washington, D.C.: U.S. Government Printing Office, 1983.

National Council for Accreditation of Teacher Education. *Standards, Procedures, and Poli-*

cies for the Accreditation of Professional Education Units. Washington, D.C.: National Council for Accreditation of Teacher Education, 1997.

National Education Association. "Report of the Sub-Committee on the Organization of City School Systems, 1895." *Proceedings and Journal of Addresses of the National Education Association*, Washington, D.C., National Education Association, 1895.

National Education Association Department of Superintendence. *The Tenth Yearbook: Character Education*. Washington, D.C.: National Education Association, 1932.

New American Schools Development Corporation. *Designs for a New Generation of American Schools*. Arlington, Va.: New American Schools Development Corporation, 1991.

Newman, Joseph W. *America's Teachers: An Introduction to Education*. 3d ed. New York: Longman, 1998.

"News in Brief." *Education Week*, February 5, 1992, 2–3.

Nieves, Victor. "Citizen Strangers: Puerto Ricans in New York City." Unpublished M.A. Thesis. Greenville, N.C.: East Carolina University, 1996.

Nightengale, Carl Husemoller. *On the Edge: A History of Poor Black Children and Their American Dreams*. New York: Basic Books, 1993.

Noble, Stuart. *A History of Education*. New York: Rinehart & Co., 1955.

North Carolina Department of Public Instruction. *North Carolina Department of Public Instruction—Curriculum Guidelines*. Raleigh: North Carolina Department of Public Instruction, 1999.

Northend, Charles. *The Teacher and the Parent: Treatise Upon Common School Education, Containing Practical Suggestions to Teachers and Parents*. Boston: Jenks, Hickling & Swan, 1853.

Norton, M. Scott. "Teacher Retention: Reducing Costly Teacher Turnover." *Contemporary Education* 70, no. 3 (spring 1999): 52–55.

"The Old Deluder Law of 1647." In *American Education*, edited by Tyrus Hillway. Boston: Houghton Mifflin, 1964.

Oliphant, James, ed. *The Educational Writings of Richard Mulcaster*. Glasgow: n.p., 1903.

Page, David P. *Theory and Practice of Teaching*. New York: American Book Company, 1867.

Paine, Thomas. *Common Sense*. Edited by Bruce Kuklick. New York: Cambridge University Press, 1989.

Parker, Francis W. *Notes of Talks on Teaching, Given by Francis W. Parker, at the Martha's Vineyard Summer Institute, July 17 to August 19, 1882*. Translated and reported by Lelia E. Patridge. New York: E. L. Kellogg, 1883.

Parkerson, Donald H. *The Agricultural Transition in New York State: Markets and Migration in Mid-Nineteenth Century America*. Ames: Iowa State University Press, 1995.

———. "How Mobile Were Nineteenth-Century Americans?" *Historical Methods* 15 (summer 1982): 99–109.

Parkerson, Donald H., and Jo Ann Parkerson. *The Emergence of the Common School in the U.S. Countryside*. Lewiston, N.Y.: Edwin Mellen Press, 1998.

———. "Fewer Children of Greater Spiritual Quality: Religion and the Decline of Fertility in Nineteenth-Century America." *Social Science History* 12 (spring 1989): 49–70.

Patridge, Lelia E. "A Disciple of Francis W. Parker on the Distinguishing Features of the Quincy Schools." In *Education in the United States: A Documentary History*. Vol. 3, edited by Sol Cohen, 1814–15. New York: Random House, 1885.

Perkins, Linda M. *Fanny Jackson Coppin and the Institute for Colored Youth, 1865–1902*. New York: Garland Publishing, 1987.

———. "The History of Blacks in Teaching: Growth and Decline Within the Profession." In *American Teachers: Histories of a Profession at Work*, edited by Donald Warren, 344–69. New York: Macmillan, 1989.

Perkinson, Henry J. *The Imperfect Panacea: American Faith in Education, 1865–1990*. New York: McGraw-Hill, 1991.

Perman, Michael. *Reunion Without Compromise: The South and Reconstruction, 1865–1868*. Cambridge: Cambridge University Press, 1973.

———. *The Road to Redemption: Southern Politics, 1869–1879*. Chapel Hill: University of North Carolina Press, 1984.

Pestalozzi, Johann Heinrich. *How Gertrude Teaches Her Children*. Edited by Ebenezer Cooke, translated by Lucy E. Holland and Francis C. Turner. London, 1894.

———. *Leonard and Gertrude*. Edited and translated by Eva Channing. Lexington, Mass.: D. C. Heath, 1901 [1781].

Pleck, Elizabeth Hafkin. *Black Migration and Poverty; Boston 1865–1900*. New York: Academic Press, 1979.

Porter, Jessica. "School Violence Down, Reports says, But Worry High." *Education Week* 19, 31 (April 12, 2000): 3.

Ponessa, J. "High Teacher Attrition Grabs Attention in North Carolina." *Education Week* 15, no. 39 (June 1996): 3.

Portes, Alejandro, and Ruben G. Rumbaut. *Immigrant America: A Portrait*. 2d ed. Berkeley and Los Angeles: University of California Press, 1996.

Potter, Alonzo. *The School and the Schoolmaster: A Manual for the Use of Teachers, Employers, Trustees, Inspectors, Etc., of Common Schools*. Pt. 1. New York: Harper & Brothers, 1842.

Potter, J. "The Growth of Population in America, 1700–1860." In *Population in History: Essays in Historical Demography*, edited by D. V. Glass and D. E. C. Eversley, Chicago: Aldine, 631–688, 1965.

Prentice, Alison, and Marjorie R. Theobald, eds. *Women Who Taught*. Toronto: University of Toronto Press, 1991.

Pulliam, John D., and James VanPatten. *History of Education in America*. 6th ed. Englewood Cliffs, N.J.: Merrill, Prentice-Hall, 1995.

Randall, S. S. *History of the Common School System of the State of New York*. Chicago: Ivison, Blakeman, Taylor, 1871.

Raths, Louis E., Merrill Harmin, and Sydney B. Simon. *Values and Teaching*. Columbus, Ohio: Charles E. Merrill, 1966.

Rawick, George. *From Sundown to Sunup: The Making of a Black Community*. Westport, Conn.: Greenwood, 1972.

Reeder, Rudolph R. *The Historical Development of School Readers and of Method in Teaching Reading*. Columbia University Contributions to Philosophy, Psychology, and Education, vol. 8, no. 2. New York: Macmillan, 1900.

Reese, William J. *The Origins of the American High School*. New Haven, Conn.: Yale University Press, 1995.

Reese, William J., ed. *Hoosier Schools: Past and Present*. Bloomington: Indiana University Press, 1998.

Reid, T. R. *The Chip: How Two Americans Invented the Microchip and Launched a Revolution*. New York: Simon & Schuster, 1989.

Reinier, Jacqueline. "The Republican Child: Attitudes and Practices in Post-Revolutionary Philadelphia." *William & Mary Quarterly* 39, no. 3 (1982): 150–63.

Rhees, J. L. *A Pocket Manual of the Lancasterian System of Education in Its Most Improved State, as Practiced in the Model School.* Philadelphia, n.p., 1827.

Rippa, S. Alexander. *Education in a Free Society: An American History.* 8th ed. New York: Longman, 1997.

Roberts, Isaac Phillips. *Autobiography of a Farm Boy.* Ithaca, N.Y.: Cornell University Press, 1946 [1916].

Rodman, Blake. "Alternate Route Said a Success." *Education Week*, February 24, 1988, 7.

Rogg, Eleanor Meyer. *The Assimilation of Cuban Exiles: The Role of Community and Class.* New York: Aberdeen Press, 1974.

Rose, Lowell C., and Alec M. Gallup. "The 31st Annual Phi Delta Kappa/Gallup Poll of the Public's Attitudes Toward the Public Schools." *Phi Delta Kappan* 81, no. 1 (September 1999): 41–57.

Rothman, David. *The Discovery of the Asylum: Social Order and Disorder in the New Republic.* Boston: Little, Brown, 1971.

Rousmaniere, Kate. *City Teachers: Teaching and School Reform in Historical Perspective.* New York: Teachers College Press, 1997.

Rousmaniere, Kate, Kari Dehli, and Ning deConinck-Smith, eds. *Discipline, Moral Regulation, and Schooling: A Social History.* New York: Garland, 1997.

Rousseau, Jean-Jacques. *Emile.* Translated by Barbara Foxley. London: Everyman's Library, 1974.

Rudwick, Elliott. "The Niagara Movement." *Journal of Negro History* 42, no. 3 (July 1957): 177–200.

———. *Race Riot at East St. Louis, July 2, 1917.* Carbondale: Southern Illinois University Press, 1964.

Rugg, Harold, and William Withers. *Social Foundations of Education.* Englewood Cliffs, N.J.: Prentice-Hall, 1955.

Rush, Benjamin. "A Plan for the Establishment of Public Schools and the Diffusion of Knowledge in Philadelphia, Pennsylvania, 1786." In *Essays on Education in the Early Republic*, edited by Frederick Rudolph, 1–24. Cambridge, Mass.: Belknap Press of Harvard University Press, 1965.

———. "Thoughts Upon Female Education." In *Essays on Education in the Early Republic*, edited by Frederick Rudolph, 25–40. Cambridge, Mass: Belknap Press of Harvard University Press, 1965.

Saint-Pierre, Abbe de. *Observations on the Continuous Progress of Universal Reason.* London, 1737.

Sale, Kilpatrick. *The Green Revolution: The American Environmental Movement, 1962–1992.* New York: Hill & Wang, 1993.

Salmon, David. *Joseph Lancaster.* London: Longmans, Green, 1904.

Schlesinger, Arthur M. *The Rise of the City, 1878–1898.* Chicago: Quadrangle Books, 1971 [1933].

Schlesinger, Arthur M. Jr. *A Thousand Days: John F. Kennedy in the White House.* Boston: Houghton Mifflin, 1965.

Schrecker, Ellen. *Many Are the Crimes: McCarthyism in America.* Boston: Little, Brown, 1998.

Schubert, William H. *Curriculum: Perspective, Paradigm, and Possibility.* New York: Macmillian, 1986.

Schwartz, Sally. *A Mixed Multitude: The Struggle for Toleration in Colonial Pennsylvania*. New York: New York University Press, 1987.

Scott, Anne Firor. "The Ever Widening Circle: The Diffusion of Feminist Values from the Troy Female Seminary." *History of Education Quarterly*, spring 1979, 3–25.

Scott, Colin A. *Social Education*. Boston: n.p., 1908.

Seabury, Caroline. *The Diary of Caroline Seabury, 1854–1863*. Edited by Suzanne L. Bunkers. Madison: University of Wisconsin Press, 1991.

Seller, Maxine, and Lois Weis. *Beyond Black and White: New Faces and Voices in U.S. Schools*. Albany: State University of New York Press, 1997.

Sellers, Charles. *The Market Revolution*. Oxford: Oxford University Press, 1991.

Shaw, Anna Howard. *The Story of a Pioneer by Anna Howard Shaw*. New York: Harper, 1915.

Sheehan, Ruth. "Saying No to Sex, Abstinence Education: Is It Working?" *News & Observer* (Raleigh, N.C.), April 2, 2000, 25–27A.

Shimron, Yonat. "Leaders Want Biblical Rules in Schools." *News & Observer* (Raleigh, N.C.), January 30, 2000, 1A.

Shor, Ira. *Culture Wars: School and Society in the Conservative Restoration, 1969–1984*. Boston: Routledge & Kegan Paul, 1986.

Silber, Kate. *Pestalozzi: The Man and His Work*. London: Routledge & Kegan Paul, 1960.

Silberman, Charles E. *Crisis in the Classroom: The Remaking of America Education*. New York: Random House, 1970.

Simpson, Stephen. "A Manual for Workingmen." In *Public Education in the United States*, edited by Ellwood P. Cubberley. Boston: Houghton Mifflin, 1919.

Sitkoff, Harvard. *The Struggle for Black Equality, 1954–1992*. Rev. ed. New York: Hill & Wang, 1993.

Skerry, Peter. *Mexican Americans: The Ambivalent Minority*. New York: Free Press, 1993.

Skinner, B. F. *Beyond Freedom and Dignity*. New York: Alfred A. Knopf, 1971.

———. "The Free and Happy Student." *Phi Delta Kappan* 55, no. 1 (1973): 13–16.

———. *Science and Human Behavior*. Boston: Houghton Mifflin, 1951.

———. *Walden Two*. New York: Macmillan, 1974.

Slosson, Edwin E. *The American Spirit in Education: A Chronicle of Great Teachers*. New Haven, Conn.: Yale University Press, 1921.

Small, Walter Herbert. *Early New England Schools*. New York: Arno Press & the *New York Times*, 1969.

Smith, Adam. *An Inquiry Into the Wealth of Nations*. Vol. 2. Edited by R. H. Campbell and A. S. Skinner. Oxford: Oxford University Press, 1976.

———. *The Theory of Moral Sentiments*. Edited by D. D. Raphael and A. L. Macfie. Oxford: Oxford University Press, 1976.

Smith, Samuel Harrison. "Remarks on Education." In *Essays on Education in the Early Republic*, edited by Frederick Rudolph. Cambridge, Mass.: Harvard University Press, 1965.

Soltow, Lee, and Edward Stevens. "Economic Aspects of School Participation in Mid-Nineteenth-Century United States." *Journal of Interdisciplinary History* 8, no. 2 (autumn 1977): 221–43.

———. *The Rise of Literacy and the Common School in the United States*. Chicago: University of Chicago Press, 1981.

Spear, Allan H. *Black Chicago: The Making of a Negro Ghetto, 1890–1920*. Chicago: University of Chicago Press.

Spengler, J. *Population Change, Modernization and Welfare.* Englewood Cliffs, N.J.: Prentice Hall, 1974.

Spring, Joel. *American Education.* 8th ed. Boston: McGraw-Hill, 1998.

———. *The American School, 1642–1990: Varieties of Historical Interpretation of the Foundations and Development of American Education.* 2d ed. New York: Longman, 1990.

———. *Conflict of Interests: The Politics of American Education.* 2d ed. New York: Longman, 1993.

———. *The Cultural Transformation of a Native American Family and Its Tribe, 1763–1995: A Basket of Apples.* Mahwah, N.J.: Lawrence Erlbaum, 1996.

———. *Education and the Rise of the Corporate State.* Boston: Beacon Press, 1972.

———. *Political Agendas for Education: From the Christian Coalition to the Green Party.* Mahwah, N.J.: Lawrence Erlbaum, 1997.

Stahl, Steven A. "Why Innovations Come and Go (and Mostly Go): The Case of Whole Language." *Educational Researcher* 28, no. 8 (November 1999): 13–22.

Steinberg, Stephen. *The Ethnic Myth: Race, Ethnicity, and Class in America.* Boston: Beacon Press, 1981.

Steiner, E. E. "Separating the Soldier From the Citizen: Ideology and Criticism of Corporal Punishment in the British Armies, 1790–1815." *Social History* 8 (1983): 19–35.

Stennette, Janet. "Teaching for the Freedmen's Bureau: Lynchburg, Virginia, 1865–1871." Unpublished Ph.D. dissertation. Charlottesville: University of Virginia, 1995.

Stern, Nancy B. *From ENIAC to UNIVAC.* Bedford, Mass.: Digital Press, 1981.

Stickney, Benjamin D., and Laurence R. Marcus. *The Great Education Debate: Washington and the Schools.* Springfield, Ill.: Charles C Thomas, 1984.

Stowe, Sarah D. Locke. *History of Mount Holyoke Seminary, South Hadley, Massachusetts, During the First Half-Century.* South Hadley, Mass.: n.p., 1887.

Strachan, Grace C. *Equal Pay for Equal Work.* New York: n.p., 1910.

Strober, Myra H., and David Tyack. "Why Do Women Teach and Men Manage?: A Report on Research on Schools." *Signs* 5, no. 3 (spring 1980), 494–503.

Strober, Myra, and Audri Gordon Langford. "The Feminization of Teaching: A Cross-Sectional Analysis." *Signs* 11, no. 2 (1986), 212–35.

Taft, Philip. *United They Teach: The Story of the UFT.* Los Angeles: Nash, 1974.

Takaki, Ronald. *A Different Mirror: A History of Multicultural America.* Boston: Little, Brown, 1993.

Taylor, J. Orville. *The District School.* New York: Harper & Brothers, 1834.

Taylor, Marvin J. *Religious and Moral Education.* New York: Center for Applied Research in Education, 1965.

Taylor, Mildred. *Roll of Thunder: Hear My Cry.* St. Paul: EMC/Paradigm, 1999.

Teaford, Jon. "The Transformation of Massachusetts Education, 1670–1780." In *The Social History of American Education*, edited by B. Edward McClellan and William J. Reese, 23–38. Urbana: University of Illinois Press, 1988.

"Texas Schools May Lose Accreditation." *Education Week*, May 24, 1989, 4.

Thacher, P.O. "Influence of Female Character." In *The North American Reader*, edited by Lyman Cobb, 325–30. Zanesville, Ohio: J. R. and A. Lippett, 1836.

Theobald, Paul. *Call School.* Carbondale: Southern Illinois University Press, 1995.

Thomas, Norman C. *Education and National Politics.* New York: McKay, 1975.

Thompson, E. P. "Time, Work, Discipline and the Industrial Capitalism." *Past and Present* 38 (December 1967): 56–97.

Thornbrough, Emma Lou. "Segregation in Indiana During the Klan Era of the 1920s." *Mississippi Valley Historical Review* 47 (March 1961): 594–618.

Thorndike, Edward. *Educational Psychology*. New York: Teachers College Press, 1913.

Tocqueville, Alexis de. *Democracy in America*. New York: Vintage Books, 1945.

Toppin, E. A. *A Biographical History of Blacks and America Since 1528*. New York: David McKay, 1971.

Trelease, Allen. *White Terror: The Ku Klux Klan Conspiracy and Southern Reconstruction: War, Radicalism, and Race in Louisiana, 1862–1877*. New York: Harper & Row, 1971.

Trinkle, Dennis, Dorothy Auchter, Scott Merriman, and Todd Larson. *The History Highway: A Guide to Internet Resources*. Armonk, N.Y.: M. E. Sharpe, 1997.

Tucker, Luther. *The Cultivator* 8, no. 12 (December 1851).

Tuttle, William M. Jr. *Race Riot: Chicago in the Red Summer of 1919*. New York: Atheneum, 1980.

Tyack, David. "Forming the National Character: Paradox in the Educational Thought in the Revolutionary Generation." *Harvard Educational Review* 36 (1966): 29–41.

———. *The One Best System: A History of American Urban Education*. Cambridge, Mass.: Harvard University Press, 1974.

Tyack, David, and Larry Cuban. *Tinkering Toward Utopia: A Century of Public School Reform*. Cambridge, Mass.: Harvard University Press, 1995.

Tyack, David, and Elizabeth Hansot. *Managers of Virtue: Public School Leadership in America, 1820–1980*. New York: Basic Books, 1984.

Tyack, David, Robert Lowe, and Elisabeth Hansot. *Public Schools in Hard Times*. Cambridge, Mass.: Harvard University Press, 1984.

U.S. Department of Education. *America 2000: An Education Strategy*. Washington, D.C.: U. S. Department of Education, 1991.

Ueda, Reed. *Postwar Immigrant America: A Social History*. Boston: Bedford Books of St. Martin's Press, 1994.

Ulich, Robert. *History of Educational Thought*. New York: American Book Company, 1950.

Urban, Wayne J. *Why Teachers Organized*. Detroit: Wayne State University Press, 1982.

Vinovskis, Maris. "Do Federal Compensatory Education Programs Really Work?" *American Journal of Education* 107, no. 3 (May 1999): 187–209.

———. *Education, Society, and Economic Opportunity*. New Haven, Conn.: Yale University Press, 1995.

Voltaire. *Philosophical Dictionary*. Edited and with an introduction and glossary by Peter Gay. New York: Harcourt, Brace, & World, 1962.

Ward, Lester Frank. *Young Ward's Diary*. Edited by Vernhard J. Stern. New York: G. P. Putnam's Sons, 1935.

Warren, Donald. *To Enforce Education*. Detroit: Wayne State University Press, 1974.

Warren, Donald, ed. *American Teachers: Histories of a Profession at Work*. New York: Macmillan, 1989.

Washington, Booker T. "Atlanta Exposition Address." In *Education in the United States: A Documentary History*. Vol. 3, edited by Sol Cohen, 1672–75. New York: Random House, 1974.

———. "Up From Slavery." In *Three Negro Classics*, edited by John Hope Franklin. New York: Avon Books, 1965.

Wasley, Patricia A. *Stirring the Chalkdust: Tales of Teachers Changing Classroom Practice*. New York: Teachers College Press, 1994.

Watson, John B. *Behaviorism*. New York: W. W. Norton, 1924.

Weaver, Constance. *Reading, Process and Practice: From Socio-Psycho Linguistics to Whole Language*. Portsmouth, N.H.: Heinemann, 1994.

————. *Understanding Whole Language*. Portsmouth, N.H.: Heinemann, 1990.

Weaver, Robert. *The Negro Ghetto*. New York: Russell & Russell, 1967 [1948].

Webber, Thomas L. *Deep Like Rivers: Education in the Slave Quarters, 1831–1865*. New York: W. W. Norton, 1978.

Webster, Noah. "On the Education of Youth in America." In *Essays on Education in the Early Republic*, edited by Frederick Rudolph, 65. 1965. Cambridge, Mass.: Belknap Press of Harvard University Press [1790].

Weglyn, Michi. *Years of Infamy: The Untold Story of America's Concentration Camps*. Seattle: University of Washington Press, 1996.

Wesley, Edgar. *NEA, The First One Hundred Years: The Building of the Teaching Profession*. New York: Harper, 1957.

Westheimer, Joel. *Among School Teachers: Community Autonomy and Ideology in Teachers' Work*. New York: Teachers College Press, 1998.

White, Patricia. *Civic Virtues and Public Schooling: Educating Citizens for a Democratic Society*. New York: Teachers College Press, 1996.

Wilder, Laura Ingalls. *These Happy Golden Years*. New York: Harper Trophy, 1971 [1943].

Wilentz, Sean. *Chantz Democratic: New York City and the Rise of the American Working Class, 1788–1850*. New York: Oxford University Press, 1994.

Wood, Gordon. *The Creation of the American Republic, 1776–1787*. New York: W. W. Norton, 1972.

Woodson, Carter G. *The African Background Outlined: Or Handbook for the Study of the Negro*. New York: Negro Universities Press, 1968.

————. *The Education of the Negro Prior to 1861*. New York: Arno Press & the *New York Times*, [1919].

Woodward, C. Vann. *Origins of the New South, 1877–1913*. Baton Rouge: Louisiana State University Press, 1951.

————. *The Strange Career of Jim Crow*. 3d rev. ed. New York: Oxford University Press, 1974.

Woody, Thomas. *Early Quaker Education in Pennsylvania*. New York: Arno Press and the *New York Times*, 1969.

————. *A History of Women's Education in the United States*. Vol. 1. New York: The Science Press, 1929.

Zuniga-Hill, Carmen, and Carol Barnes. "Effective Teacher Preparation for Diverse Student Populations: What Works Best?" In *Class, Culture, and Race in American Schools*, edited by Stanley William Rothstein, 163–97. Westport, Conn.: Greenwood, 1995.

Index